SOVIET
TANK UNITS
1939–45

THE ESSENTIAL
VEHICLE IDENTIFICATION GUIDE

SOVIET
TANK UNITS
1939–45

DAVID PORTER

amber
BOOKS

This edition published in 2009 by
Amber Books Ltd
Bradley's Close
74–77 White Lion Street
London N1 9PF
www.amberbooks.co.uk

A catalogue record for this book is available from the British Library.

ISBN: 978-1-906626-21-1

Project Editor: Michael Spilling
Design: Hawes Design
Picture Research: Terry Forshaw

Printed in Thailand

PHOTOGRAPH AND ILLUSTRATION CREDITS
Art-Tech/Aerospace: 13 top
Courtesy of the Central Museum of the Armed Forces Moscow: 6, 148
Cody Images: 43, 59 top, 89 top, 129 top, 138
Corbis: 15 top (Bettmann)
Nik Cornish @ STAVKA: 80, 93 top, 110 top
Public Domain: 124
From the fonds of the RGAKFD at Krasnogorsk: 10, 104
Topfoto: 30 (RIA Novosti), 126 (Ullstein Bild)
Ukrainian State Archive: 8, 9, 22, 32, 50 top, 52, 56, 64, 74 top, 77 top, 78, 79 top,
    82 top, 87 top, 89 bottom, 98, 101 top, 108 top, 114 top, 116 top, 118 bottom,
    131 top, 133 bottom, 136, 140 top, 145 top, 147 top, 163-164 all, 173, 184

All artworks are courtesy of **Oliver Missing (www.o5m6.de)** apart from the following:

Alcaniz Fresno's S.A.: 23, 28, 29 bottom, 54, 55 both, 70 bottom, 73 top & centre,
    132, 133 top, 153 both
Art-Tech/Aerospace: 16, 17 both, 29 centre, 35 top, 37 bottom, 38, 75, 77 bottom,
    84 bottom, 86 top, 106, 117, 142 top, 146, 156 top

Contents

Introduction

In 1941 the Red Army was little more than a collection of raw conscripts whose officers' authority was undermined by fanatical but militarily incompetent political commissars. Despite this, it survived the German invasion and four years of bloody combat to become one of the world's most formidable armies by 1945. This book provides an introduction to the key vehicles that made that transformation possible, setting the scene with a summary of the pre-war Red Army's equipment. There is detailed coverage of the war years, including the little-known 'August Storm' Offensive against the Japanese forces in Manchuria in 1945. Whilst the emphasis is on the Soviet and Lend-Lease armoured fighting vehicles (AFVs) of the period, there is also coverage of their essential support vehicles, including 'Katyusha' rocket launchers, artillery tractors and transport.

◀ **Tank attack**
'Tank riders' (*tankodesantniki*) cluster on an SU-76 self-propelled gun as they advance through northern Europe, late 1944. Even in 1945, most Soviet assault infantry were still carried on tanks, where they formed a concentrated target for MG and artillery fire.

T HE RED ARMY OF WORLD WAR II might well be described in Churchill's phrase about Russia itself: 'It is a riddle, wrapped in a mystery, inside an enigma…'

While the riddle has become slightly less puzzling with the release of vast amounts of previously classified or censored material since the collapse of the former Soviet Union, there are still many problems. An astonishing number of sources disagree about key dates and statistics, and all too few Soviet documents are available in translation to resolve the discrepancies. It would take a far longer book than this volume to treat exhaustively such a huge subject as the tanks and vehicles of the wartime Red Army, but hopefully this introduction to the subject will encourage readers to delve more deeply into this fascinating topic.

From its foundation in 1918 until the early 1930s, the Red Army was little more than a vast conscript force of infantry, cavalry and artillery, with few motor vehicles and even fewer Armoured Fighting Vehicles (AFVs). The handful of tanks and armoured cars in

service were largely ageing vehicles captured from the White Russian armies during the Civil War.

Reorganization

The situation was to undergo a dramatic change from 1931, when Marshal Tukhachevsky effectively took charge of the army's training and equipment. Within a few years, the commitment of massive resources was creating an ultra-modern, well-equipped armoured force far more powerful than that of any other nation. All this progress was swept away by Stalin's paranoia, when in 1937 he turned on the leadership of the Red Army, fearing that it might stage a military coup.

The self-inflicted wound of the purges was very nearly fatal for the Red Army and the Soviet Union itself. The fiasco of the Winter War against Finland in 1939–40 gave warning of just how bad the situation was, and reforms began to restore combat capability, but the process was slow and much remained to be done by the time of the German invasion.

Operation *Barbarossa* came terrifyingly close to success – the mere survival of the Red Army was a

▲ **Winter offensive**
Whitewashed T-34/76 Model 1943 tanks of the 1st Ukrainian Front wait by the roadside near Kiev, December 1943. The wide tracks of the T-34 made them ideal for operations in the snow and mud of a Russian winter.

▲ **Capture of Berlin**
Soviet infantry ride on the back of an SU-100 self-propelled gun following the
capture of Berlin, May 1945.

victory in itself. This victory allowed it to exploit its
inherent resilience and adaptability, raising small
armoured units to give largely untrained officers the
chance to learn essential command skills. The powers
of the political commissars were gradually reduced so
that front-line officers were not constantly in fear of
denunciation by fanatical but militarily incompetent
'Party hacks'.

Although command skills dramatically improved
as the war went on, the level of unit effectiveness
remained low. This was largely because the most able
officers were rapidly promoted, leaving a mixture of
inept 'old hands' and new recruits at unit level. (The
situation was worsened by the lack of a professional
cadre of NCOs to handle basic training.)

Leadership problems were a major factor
contributing to the horrendous Soviet casualties
sustained throughout the war. The Red Army is
estimated to have lost 10,000,000 dead: its victory in
1945 was truly hard-won.

KEY TO TACTICAL SYMBOLS USED IN ORGANIZATION CHARTS

▷	Symbol for division or larger	*Sig*	Signals
■	Symbol for regiment or brigade-sized formation	*Pio*	Pioneer unit
		Sup	Support unit
▷	Symbol for battalion	*Inf*	Infantry unit
HQ	HQ units	*Bat*	Battery
Lt	Light tank unit (battalion or company)	*Mn*	Maintenance unit
Med	Medium tank unit	*Flm*	Flamethrower unit
Hv	Heavy tank unit	*Btn*	Battalion
AC	Armoured car unit	*Br*	Bridge-building unit
MC	Motorcycle unit	*AA*	Anti-aircraft unit

Chapter 1

The Pre-war Years

In the 15 years following its victory in the Russian Civil War, the Red Army developed equipment and operational concepts that were as advanced as any in the world. It created the world's largest armoured force and the doctrine of 'deep operations', which was formally adopted in 1936. Stalin's paranoid fear of a military *coup d'etat* drove him to launch the murderous purges of the late 1930s, which destroyed much of this sophisticated military structure. Possibly 50 per cent of the Soviet officer corps was executed or imprisoned and innovative military thought was brutally suppressed. The effects of the purges were still all too evident in 1941 and were instrumental in bringing the Red Army to the very brink of total defeat.

◀ **Propaganda weapons**
A unit of British-made Mark V 'male' tanks captured from the White forces during the Russian Civil War in 1920–21 parades across Red Square on May Day 1930. The number '3' denotes the battalion and the encircled numbers the company and the number of the individual tank.

Pre-war development
1914–39

The Imperial Russian Army began developing armoured forces from the beginning of World War I, but the first foreign supplied tanks went into action only in the Russian Civil War (1918–21).

IN THE 10 YEARS leading up to the outbreak of World War I, the Imperial Russian army began an ambitious modernization programme. The first Russian AFVs were eight French-designed Nakashidze-Charron armoured cars, which entered service in 1908 and underwent prolonged troop trials. By 1913, the results were so promising that even the conservative Imperial Artillery Commission was forced to authorize orders for a variety of armoured cars from Russian and foreign sources.

Automobile Corps
Deliveries had only just started at the beginning of the war, but the first unit of the newly formed Automobile Corps – 15 machine-gun (MG) armed Russo-Balt light armoured cars and three Putilov-Garford armoured lorries with 76mm (3in) guns – was in action against Austro-Hungarian forces as early as October 1914. Its effectiveness prompted increased orders for AFVs and throughout 1915 and 1916 new units were formed as fast as vehicles could be obtained. These were:
- Detachments – each with two MG-armed light armoured cars and a single gun-equipped heavy.

- Companies – each with 12 lights and three heavies.

Development of tanks was much slower and only a single example of the tiny *Vezdekhod* light tank was built. A prototype of the gigantic Tsar 'tank' was also completed in 1915; this was a 36-tonne (40-ton) wheeled vehicle with two main wheels 10m (32ft 10in) in diameter and triple trail wheels perhaps a fifth of that size. Each main wheel was powered by a 186kW (250hp) Sunbeam engine and it was planned to fit turret and sponson-mounted MGs.

Trials rapidly showed just how impractical the machine was, and future efforts were concentrated on obtaining British and French tanks, but none had arrived by the time of the collapse of the Tsarist regime in 1917.

First actions
The first 'Russian' tanks to go into action were small numbers of Medium Mark Vs, Whippets and Renault FTs supplied to the anti-Bolshevik White forces during the Russian Civil War of 1918–21. Many of these were taken over by the Red Army after the war and formed virtually its entire tank strength

Specifications

Crew: 1 driver (plus 15 troops)	Height: 1.97m (6ft 6in)
Weight: 1.55 tonnes (1.5 tons)	Engine: 29.8kW (40hp) 4-cylinder SV petrol
Length: 5.33m (17ft 6in)	Speed: 70km/h (43.5mph)
Width: 2.1m (7ft)	

▲ **GAZ-AA 4x2 1½-ton truck**
The GAZ-AA 4x2 1½-ton truck was the workhorse of the pre-war Red Army. A licence-built copy of the Ford AA-Model 1929, it provided essential logistic support for Soviet experiments in armoured warfare during the 1930s. Over 150,000 vehicles were delivered by 1941.

▶ **Comrades-in-arms**

Lenin and Stalin, 1922. By 1945, Stalin's ruthlessness had transformed Lenin's ragged Red Army into one of the world's most powerful armoured forces.

until 1929, when Soviet tank production reached levels that allowed large-scale experiments with armoured units. An experimental Mechanized Brigade was formed during the summer of 1929 comprising a tank regiment, a motor rifle regiment, an artillery battalion and support units. By 1931, the lessons learned were being applied in the formation of a new tank 'regiment' that included:

■ A Scout Group of two tankette battalions, an armoured car detachment, a lorried MG battalion and an artillery battery.

■ An Attack Group with two tank battalions and two batteries of SU-12 76mm (3in) lorry-mounted self-propelled (SP) guns.

■ A Support Group based on a motor rifle battalion.

■ An Artillery Group with three batteries (76mm/3in and 122mm/4.8in guns) plus an anti-aircraft (AA) battery.

▶ **D-8 armoured car**

The D-8 armoured car was produced in small numbers from 1932 until 1934. Late production versions such as the vehicle seen here were fully enclosed and armed with two side-mounted 7.62mm (0.3in) MGs.

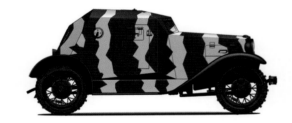

Specifications	
Crew: 2	Engine: 31.3kW (42hp) GAZ-A 4-cylinder petrol
Weight: 1.58 tonnes (1.55 tons)	Speed: 85km/h (53mph)
Length: 2.63m (8ft 7in)	Range: 225km (140 miles)
Width: 1.7m (5ft 6in)	Armament: 2 x 7.62mm (0.3in) DT MGs
Height: 1.8m (5ft 10in)	

▶ **T-26A Model 1931 light tank**

The twin-turreted T-26 Model 1931, fitted with a single 7.62mm (0.3in) DT MG in each turret.

Specifications	
Crew: 3	Engine: 68kW (91hp) GAZ T-26 8-cylinder
Weight: 9.3 tonnes (9.2 tons)	petrol
Length: 4.8m (15ft 8in)	Speed: 28km/h (17mph)
Width: 2.39m (7ft 10in)	Range: 200km (124 miles)
Height: 2.33m (7ft 8in)	Radio: N/A
	Armament: 2 x 7.62mm (0.3in) DT MGs

▶ **T-26TU Model 1931 command tank**

The T-26TU Model 1931 command tank, with prominent 'clothes line' radio aerial.
These vehicles were armed with a 37mm (1.5in) gun in the right hand turret and
a 7.62mm (0.3in) DT MG in the left.

Specifications

Crew: 3	Speed: 28km/h (17mph)
Weight: 9.3 tonnes (9.2 tons)	Range: 200km (124 miles)
Length: 4.8m (15ft 8in)	Radio: RSMK
Width: 2.39m (7ft 10in)	Armament: 1 x 45mm (1.8in) tank gun Model
Height: 2.33m (7ft 8in)	1932, 1 x coaxial 7.62mm (0.3in) DT MG
Engine: 68kW (91hp) GAZ T-26 8-cylinder petrol	

Development and expansion

**During the 1930s, Soviet tank designers began producing faster and more powerful combat
vehicles, despite the depradations of Stalin's purges.**

OVER THE NEXT few years, annual tank production
figures soared, which allowed the creation of two
larger armoured units in the form of mechanized
corps. Each included two mechanized brigades
totalling 430 tanks and 215 armoured cars, plus a
lorried infantry brigade and support units.

This expansion was matched by a flood of written
theories of armoured warfare and ever-larger annual
manoeuvres, which culminated in the huge 1935
exercises held in the Kiev Military District. Western
observers at these manoeuvres were staggered to see
the hundreds of AFVs deployed and would have been
even more amazed had it been known that the Soviets
had more tank units (and indeed more AFVs) than

the rest of the world's armies combined. Many of
these AFVs were highly advanced – the T-26 Model
1933 light tank had a high-velocity 45mm (1.8in)
gun in contrast to the MG armament of its Western
counterparts, while the BT-5 fast tank's 298kW
(400hp) engine and Christie suspension gave it a top
speed of 72km/h (45mph).

A new generation of commanders provided the
driving force for such developments, and of these
generals the most influential was Mikhail
Tukhachevsky, a former lieutenant in the Tsarist army
who had made his name during the Russian Civil
War commanding Red Army units opposing the
forces of Admiral Kolchak. Ironically, it was

◀ **T-26 Model 1933 light tank**

The small twin turrets of the T-26 Model 1931 severely limited attempts at up-
gunning the design. The much larger single turret of the Model 1933 allowed the
installation of the powerful new 45mm (1.8in) tank gun Model 1932.

Specifications

Crew: 3	Speed: 28km/h (17mph)
Weight: 10.4 tonnes (10.3 tons)	Range: 200km (124 miles)
Length: 4.8m (15ft 8in)	Radio: N/A
Width: 2.39m (7ft 10in)	Armament: 1 x 45mm (1.8in) AT gun;
Height: 2.33m (7ft 8in)	1 x 7.62mm (0.3in) DT MG
Engine: 68kW (91hp) GAZ T-26 8-cylinder petrol	

▶ **Mikhail Nikolayevich Tukhachevsky (1893–1937)**

Marshal Tukhachevsky was the driving force of Red Army modernization in the 1930s. Tried for espionage, he became one of the most prominent victims of Stalin's purges and was executed in 1937.

Tukhachevsky's very ability that was to prove fatal, as Stalin came to see him as a threat to his power, a view that may have been influenced by information planted by German intelligence. Stalin began a series of bloody purges of the Communist Party in 1936 and turned his attention to the Red Army in the following year.

Show trials

On 9 June 1937, Tukhachevsky and his most prominent supporters were suddenly arrested on treason charges, tried by a special military court on 11 June and shot at dawn the next day. Over the next year or so, the total of those executed or imprisoned rose to three of the five Marshals of the Soviet Union plus 14 of the 16 army commanders, 60 of 67 corps commanders, 136 of 199 divisional commanders and 221 of 397 brigade commanders.

Thousands of more junior officers were also shot or imprisoned and the wave of terror spread out to include the heads of the defence industries and even weapons design teams. Their successors were appointed more because they were politically 'safe' than for their military abilities and were, in any case, understandably terrified of Stalin's secret police, the NKVD.

The result of this terror was the stagnation of Soviet military thought – at one stage, armoured warfare was officially condemned as 'bourgeois, reactionary and unworthy of Marxist society'.

▶ **T-37 Model 1934 amphibious light tank**

The T-37 Model 1934 amphibious light tank equipped many reconnaissance units during the Winter War against Finland and was still in service at the time of the German invasion. An estimated 1200 vehicles were produced between 1933 and 1936.

Specifications

Crew: 2	Engine: 30kW (40hp) GAZ-AA petrol
Weight: 3.2 tonnes (3 tons)	Speed: 35km/h (22mph)
Length: 3.75m (12ft 4in)	Range: 185km (115 miles)
Width: 2.10m (6ft 10in)	Radio: N/A
Height: 1.82m (6ft)	Armament: 1 x 7.62mm (0.3in) DT MG

Specifications

Crew: 11	Speed: 30km/h (18.5mph)
Weight: 45 tonnes (44.3 tons)	Range: 150km (93miles)
Length: 9.72m (31ft 10in)	Radio: RSMK
Width: 3.20m (10ft 6in)	Armament: 1 x 76mm (3in) gun Model
Height: 3.43m (11ft 4in)	27/32 (main gun); 2 x 37mm (1.5in) guns
Engine: 370kW (500hp) Mikulin M-17M	(secondary turrents); 5 or 6 x 7.62mm
12-cylinder petrol	(0.3in) DT MGs

▲ **T-35 Model 1932**

5th Independent Heavy Tank Brigade, Moscow 1935

The T-35 Model 1932 was the first of a family of 'land battleships' all bearing the T-35 designation. It was armed with a 76mm (3in) howitzer in the main turret, flanked by four sub-turrets, two with 37mm (1.5in) guns and the other two with 7.62mm (0.3in) machine-guns. Only 10 examples of the Model 1932 were completed before production switched to the Model 1935, in which the 37mm (1.5in) guns were replaced with the more potent 45mm (1.8in) weapons.

Khalkhyn Gol
1939

By the late 1930s, Japan had established control of Manchuria (renamed Manchukuo) in northern China. This move brought it into conflict with the neigbouring Soviet satellite state of Mongolia.

THE JAPANESE CLAIMED that the Khalkhyn Gol (Khalkha River) formed the border between Manchukuo and Mongolia, while the Mongolians and Soviets maintained that it ran 16km (10 miles) east of the river, just east of Nomonhan village.

The Kwantung Army formed the main Japanese force in Manchukuo, and it included some of the best Japanese units. However, the western region of Manchukuo was garrisoned by the newly raised 23rd Division at Hailar, together with various Manchukuoan army and border guard units. On the other side of the frontier, the Red Army's LVII Special Corps, deployed from the Trans-Baikal Military District, was responsible for the defence of the border between Siberia and Manchuria.

Small border skirmishes in May 1939 gradually escalated, leading to the destruction of a regiment of the Kwantung Army's 64th Division at the end of the

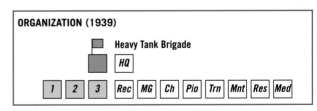

ORGANIZATION (1939)

Heavy Tank Brigade

HQ

| 1 | 2 | 3 | Rec | MG | Ch | Pio | Trn | Mnt | Res | Med |

month. Large-scale Japanese air attacks the following month raised the tension still further as the Kwantung Army prepared an offensive to 'expel the invaders'.

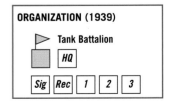

ORGANIZATION (1939)

Tank Battalion

HQ

| Sig | Rec | 1 | 2 | 3 |

This was to be a pincer movement by elements of the 23rd Division and the Yashuoka Detachment to encircle and destroy Soviet and Mongolian forces along the Khalkhyn Gol. (The Yasuoka Detachment was one of the few sizeable Japanese armoured formations, with almost 100 AFVs.)

While preparations for the offensive were under way, Georgi Zhukov, the most promising general to survive Stalin's purges, was appointed to command the Soviet forces. He quickly recognized the need for massive transport resources to support the powerful armoured force needed to inflict a decisive defeat on Japanese – initially 1000 fuel tankers and over 1600 cargo trucks were deployed over the 750km (466-mile) route from his supply bases to the front-line, later supplemented by a further 1625 vehicles from European Russia. This logistic support allowed him to assemble a striking force of as many as 550 tanks (mainly T-26s and BT-7s), plus 450 armoured cars.

The Japanese offensive opened on 2 July, in which the Yasuoka Detachment lost more than half its tanks

to Soviet anti-tank (AT) guns, while perhaps 120 Soviet AFVs were destroyed. Despite these losses, Zhukov still had overwhelming armoured strength totalling nearly 500 tanks and 350 armoured cars to spearhead a devastating counter-offensive, launched on 20 August. Within five days, this achieved a classic double envelopment of the Japanese 23rd Division, which was effectively destroyed by 31 August.

Zhukov had proved himself a capable commander of armoured forces, and his decisive actions had effectively ended the power of the 'Strike North' group within the Japanese High Command, which sought to expand into Soviet Central Asia and Siberia. After almost two years of uneasy peace, the Soviet-Japanese Neutrality Pact of April 1941 finally removed the lingering threat to Stalin's eastern frontiers.

▶ **BA-20 armoured car**

The command version of the BA-20, which was the standard light armoured car of Soviet reconnaissance units at the time of the invasion of Poland.

Specifications	
Crew: 3	Engine: 37kW (50hp) GAZ-M1 petrol
Weight: 2.5 tonnes (2.46 tons)	Speed: 85km/h (53mph)
Length: 4.31m (14ft 2in)	Range: 450km (280 miles)
Width: 1.75m (5ft 8in)	Radio: RSMK
Height: 2.13m (7ft)	Armament: 1 x 7.62mm (0.3in) DT MG

Specifications	
Crew: 6	Speed (road): 37km/h (23mph)
Weight: 28 tonnes (27.4 tons)	Range: 220km (137 miles)
Length: 7.44m (24ft 5in)	Radio: N/A
Width: 2.87m (9ft 5in)	Armament: 1 x 76mm (3in) L-10 L/26 gun; 4 x
Height: 2.82m (9ft 3in)	7.62mm (0.3in) DT MGs
Engine: 373kW (500hp) Mikulin M-17	

▲ **T-28 Model 1938 medium tank**

The 76mm (3in) L/16.5 Model 1927/32 gun of the T-28 Model 1934 was a low-velocity weapon, optimized for firing high-explosive (HE) in the infantry support role. In the Model 1938, it was replaced by the higher-velocity 76mm (3in) L-10 L/26 gun, which had markedly better armour-piercing performance.

▲ **BT-2 fast tank**

A 1932 vintage BT-2 in markings typical of those used during the opening phases of *Barbarossa*, summer 1941.

Specifications

Crew: 3

Weight: 10.2 tonnes (9.8 tons)

Length: 5.58m (18ft 3in)

Width: 2.23m (7ft 3in)

Height: 2.20m (7ft 2in)

Engine: 298kW (400hp) Liberty

Speed: 100km/h (62mph)

Range: 300km (186 miles)

Radio: N/A

Armament: 1 x 37mm (1.5in) Model 1931 gun;
1 x 7.62mm (0.3in) coaxial DT MG

Heavy Tank Brigade (1939)	BA-20	BTs	T-28
Brigade HQ	–	–	2
HQ Company	5	–	–
Reconnaissance Company	10	6	–
Signal Platoon	5	3	–
Reconnaissance Platoon	3	–	–
Heavy Tank Company x 3	5	3	10

▼ Heavy Tank Company (1939)

Three of these companies formed the main strike force of each heavy tank battalion. (Each heavy tank brigade had three such battalions.) Even by the standards of 1939, the T-28 was inadequately armoured for its role and proved to be vulnerable to Finnish 37mm (1.5in) anti-tank guns during the Winter War. A number of vehicles were rebuilt, with frontal armour increased from 30mm to 80mm (1.2in to 3.1in), but the extra weight impaired speed, range and agility.

Heavy Tank Company (10 x T-28s) and signals platoon (5 x BA-20s, 3 x BTs)

▶ **T-26TU Model 1936 command tank**
The T-26TU Model 1936 command tank, fitted with a distinctive turret-mounted
'horse shoe' radio aerial.

Specifications	
Crew: 3	Speed: 28km/h (17mph)
Weight: 10.4 tonnes (10.3 tons)	Range: 200km (124 miles)
Length: 4.8m (15ft 8in)	Radio: RSMK
Width: 2.39m (7ft 10in)	Armament: 1 x 45mm (1.8in) AT gun;
Height: 2.33m (7ft 8in)	1 x 7.62mm (0.3in) DT MG; additional
Engine: 68kW (91hp) GAZ T-26	7.62mm (0.3in) DT MG ball-mounted into
8-cylinder petrol	turret rear

Spanish Civil War
1936–39

Stalin's reign of terror also contributed to the wrong lessons being drawn from the Spanish Civil War, in which General Pavlov commanded a sizeable Soviet armoured contingent in support of the Republicans. This force included 300 T-26s and 50 BT-5s.

WHILE THERE WERE no large-scale tank battles, a number of actions proved that these machines were technically far superior to the Panzer Is and Italian tankettes fielded by the Nationalist forces.

The first such action took place on 29 October 1936 in and around the small town of Sesena about 40km (25 miles) south of Madrid. Sesena had just been taken by Nationalist cavalry spearheading a force of eight infantry brigades supported by 23 artillery batteries and a single Italian tank company with CV 33/35s – a 15,000-strong force that posed a clear threat to the capital.

Although the first Soviet-equipped Republican tank units were still forming, the situation was so serious that ad hoc combat teams were rushed to the front, including one with 15 T-26s commanded by an able Russian tank officer, Major Paul Arman, who was serving under the code-name 'Greisser'. His force led a counterattack by two Republican infantry brigades to recapture Sesena, but almost immediately three tanks were disabled by mines and the remainder lost contact with their infantry. The Nationalist cavalry holding the town were supported by two Italian 65mm (2.5in) howitzer batteries that now opened fire, destroying one T-26 and immobilizing

another (it continued to return fire for 40 minutes before it was knocked out by a newly arrived Spanish 75mm/2.9in field gun). Arman's 10 surviving tanks pushed on into Sesena, shooting up targets of opportunity, but their lack of infantry meant that they could not hold the positions they had overrun. This situation made them vulnerable to attack by the determined Nationalist troopers, who destroyed another T-26 with improvised petrol bombs, soon to become famous as 'Molotov Cocktails'. The rest of the unit broke out of the town and headed east in a raid on the Nationalist rear areas.

They destroyed a field gun battery, then encountered three CV 33/35s. Two tankettes were knocked out and the T-26s went on to destroy nearby military stores and 20–30 lorries before returning to the Republican lines. By November

Soviet Tanks Delivered to Spain		
Date of arrival	T-26	BT-5
12 Oct 36	50	–
25 Nov 36	37	–
30 Nov 36	19	–
6 Mar 37	60	–
8 Mar 37	40	–
7 May 37	50	–
10 Aug 37	–	50
13 Mar 38	25	–

1936, Nationalist forces were closing in on Madrid and had begun to receive German tanks and AT guns. The Panzer Is were hopelessly out-gunned by the T-26s, although the Soviet tanks' thin armour was vulnerable to armour-piercing MG rounds at ranges up to 100m (328ft). In practice, this wasn't much help as the T-26s' 45mm (1.8in) guns could wreck the little Panzer I or the CV 33/35 at ranges of more than 1000m (3280ft), which forced the Nationalists to attach up to five 37mm (1.5in) or 47mm (1.9in) AT guns per tank company to provide additional protection. Other measures included fitting a few Panzer Is with 20mm (0.79in) gun, the first experimental use of the Condor Legion's 88mm (3.5in) Flak guns in the AT role and even the offer of cash rewards for every T-26 captured in running order. These moves, coupled with increasingly effective Nationalist air attacks, helped the situation, but the Republican tanks kept their technical edge throughout the war.

In early 1937, the Nationalists attempted a further attack on Madrid, this time from the north-east. The first stage was an offensive by four Italian divisions aimed at Guadalajara and Alcala, and it opened in foul weather on 8 March. Heavy snow reduced visibility to a few metres and prevented the planned massive Nationalist air support, while Republican aircraft could operate freely thanks to good weather over their bases. At times, over 100 Soviet-supplied fighters were committed to ground-attack missions in which their MG and cannon fire destroyed many of the Italian supply vehicles and even knocked out a few of the CV 33/35s. (The single battalion of these tankettes allocated to spearhead the attack was no match for the 60 T-26s deployed by General Pavlov to stiffen the Republican defences.) After two days, the Italian advance was halted and the Republicans were able to counterattack. On the 13th, T-26s destroyed five CV 33/35s and damaged two more without loss to themselves, and five days later, they

▶ **T-26 Model 1936 light tank**

A former Republican T-26 Model 1936 pressed into Nationalist service sports a non-standard camouflage finish. This vehicle carries additional armament comprising a 7.62mm (0.3in) DT MG in the turret rear and a similar weapon or P-40 AA mounting.

Specifications	
Crew: 3	Speed: 28km/h (17mph)
Weight: 10.4 tonnes (10.3 tons)	Range: 200km (124 miles)
Length: 4.8m (15ft 8in)	Armament: 1 x 45mm (1.8in) tank gun
Width: 2.39m (7ft 10in)	Model 1932; 1 x coaxial 7.62mm (0.3in)
Height: 2.33m (7ft 8in)	DT MG; 2 x additional 7.62mm (0.3in) DT
Engine: 68kW (91hp) GAZ T-26	MGs, one ball-mounted in turret rear and
8-cylinder petrol	one on P-40 AA mount

▶ **T-26 Model 1935 light tank**

A captured Republican T-26 Model 1935 in Spanish Nationalist service. The prominent red/yellow/red recognition markings were applied in an attempt to minimize the risk from 'friendly fire'.

Specifications	
Crew: 3	Speed: 28km/h (17mph)
Weight: 10.4 tonnes (10.3 tons)	Range: 200km (124 miles)
Length: 4.8m (15ft 8in)	Radio: N/A
Width: 2.39m (7ft 10in)	Armament: 1 x 45mm (1.8in) AT gun;
Height: 2.33m (7ft 8in)	1 x 7.62mm (0.3in) DT MG; additional
Engine: 68kW (91hp) GAZ T-26 8-cylinder	7.62mm (0.3in) DT MG ball-mounted into
petrol	turret rear

led a further counterattack that routed several Italian units and secured the approaches to Guadalajara. By this time, breakdowns, artillery and AT guns had reduced Pavlov's force to only nine operational tanks, ruling out any chance of a decisive victory.

Fuentes de Ebro was the only major action fought by the Republican International Tank Regiment, which was equipped with 48 of the BT-5s shipped to Spain in August 1937. Besides a cadre of Soviet 'volunteers', their crews included Spaniards and International Brigade personnel who had trained at

the Red Army's Gorkiy Tank School. On 13 October 1937, the formation was committed to a hastily planned attack on the town of Fuentes de Ebro, an attack intended to open the road to Saragossa. In fact, it would be fairer to say that the operation was improvised rather than planned – it was scheduled for noon on the 13th, but the tank crews received their orders only at 2300 hours the previous day and then had a 50km (31-mile) road march to the assembly area. Barely two hours before the attack was due to start, the formation was told that it would be carrying

▲ **BT-5 fast tank**
A Republican BT-5 captured by Nationalist forces on the Ebro Front, 1938.

Specifications

Crew: 3	Speed: 72km/h (44mph)
Weight: 11.5 tonnes (11 tons)	Range: 200km (124 miles)
Length: 5.58m (18ft 3in)	Radio: N/A
Width: 2.23m (7ft 3in)	Armament: 1 x 45mm (1.8in) Model 1932 gun;
Height: 2.25m (7ft 5in)	1 x 7.62mm (0.3in) coaxial DT MG
Engine: 298kW (400hp) Model M-5	

▲ **BT-5 fast tank**
A captured BT-5 in full Nationalist markings. (In this case, the recognition stripes run right around the turret.)

Specifications

Crew: 3	Speed: 72km/h (44mph)
Weight: 11.5 tonnes (11 tons)	Range: 200km (124 miles)
Length: 5.58m (18ft 3in)	Radio: N/A
Width: 2.23m (7ft 3in)	Armament: 1 x 45mm (1.8in) Model 1932 gun;
Height: 2.25m (7ft 5in)	1 x 7.62mm (0.3in) coaxial DT MG
Engine: 298kW (400hp) Model M-5	

infantry from the 15th International Brigade into action on its tanks, despite the fact that neither unit had any training for this role. The harassed crews were then told that there was no time to carry out any battlefield reconnaissance and that the Republican commanders could not give any information about the terrain or enemy AT defences, which they regarded as trivial matters.

In the circumstances, it was hardly surprising that things went wrong from the beginning of the operation – the BTs fired a single salvo before racing off with the infantry clinging to their sides. Many fell off as the tanks bucked and bounced across country, while others became casualties when startled front-line Republican infantry (who had not been warned of the attack), opened fire as the BTs came roaring over their positions. After clearing this unexpected hazard, the attackers found that the plain in front of the Nationalist defences consisted mainly of sugar cane fields, criss-crossed with irrigation ditches. As the tanks attempted to force their way through, they came under increasingly effective fire from enemy artillery and AT guns hidden in farm buildings. The

handful of infantry who remained with the tanks were too few to neutralize the Nationalist guns or hold the ground that had been gained, and the operation was finally abandoned with the loss of 19 tanks plus several more damaged.

Limited impact

Despite the technological superiority of Soviet tanks, their operations were crippled by poor communications and a lack of properly integrated infantry and artillery. Even if these problems could have been solved, it is hardly likely that the limited Soviet armoured force committed to Spain could have prevented the ultimate Nationalist victory in March 1939. It seems likely that Pavlov and his staff appreciated that these problems affected the Red Army as much as the Spanish Republican forces, but this was the era of Stalin's most savage purges and no-one was safe from the NKVD. In the circumstances, it is hardly surprising that official reports tended to play down serious problems, blaming them on poorly trained Spanish troops rather than failings in Soviet doctrine or equipment.

▲ **Training exercise**
A BT-7 advances with infantry – the lack of any camouflage or extra kit stowed on the tank and the remarkably evenly spaced shell bursts would suggest that this is a pre-war exercise rather than a true combat photograph.

Poland
SEPTEMBER 1939

On 17 September 1939, Soviet forces invaded Poland, which had been desperately fighting against the German invasion for over two weeks.

THE RED ARMY deployed over 3000 AFVs against Polish forces, but took unnecessary losses in a number of actions through over-confidence and tactical ineptitude. At Grodno on 20 September, the XV Tank Corps attempted a frontal assault on the city with minimal infantry support, and was beaten off with the loss of 19 tanks and four armoured cars. On 28 September, a scratch Polish force comprising elements of the Border Defence Corps and the Independent Operational Group *Polesie* ambushed the 52nd Rifle Division and its supporting T-26 brigade near Szack, inflicting roughly 2000 casualties and destroying or capturing 40 tanks.

These setbacks were no more than pin-pricks, as Soviet forces were deployed in overwhelming strength, but the warning signs were ignored by Stalin and his cronies. In November 1939, the four Tank Corps (which had replaced the former Mechanized Corps barely a year earlier) were broken up to form motorized divisions. These had roughly 275 tanks apiece and were intended to operate in conjunction with horsed cavalry. Independent tank brigades were to be more closely integrated with infantry and cavalry, while it was planned to increase the armoured component of rifle divisions from a tank battalion to a tank brigade.

Belarus (9/1939)	T-37	T-26	BT	T-28	Arm Car
XV Tank Corps	–	–	461	–	122
6th Tank Bde	–	–	248	–	–
21st Tank Bde	–	–	29	105	19
22nd Tank Bde	–	219	–	–	3
25th Tank Bde	–	251	–	–	27
29th Tank Bde	–	188	–	–	3
32nd Tank Bde	–	220	–	–	5

Ukraine (9/1939)	T-37	T-26	BT	T-28	Arm Car
XXV Tank Corps	–	27	435	–	74
10th Tank Bde	–	10	30	98	19
23rd Tank Bde	–	8	209	–	5
24th Tank Bde	–	8	205	–	28
26th Tank Bde	–	228	–	–	22
36th Tank Bde	–	301	–	–	24
38th Tank Bde	4	141	–	–	4

▲ **BT-5 fast tank**

Byelorussian Front / XV Tank Corps / 27th Light Tank Brigade

A BT-5 of the Soviet Belorussian Front during the invasion of Poland, 1939.

Specifications

Crew: 3

Weight: 11.5 tonnes (11 tons)

Length: 5.58m (18ft 3in)

Width: 2.23m (7ft 3in)

Height: 2.25m (7ft 5in)

Engine: 298kW (400hp) Model M-5

Speed: 72km/h (44mph)

Range: 200km (124 miles)

Armament: 1 x 45mm (1.8in) Model 1932 gun;
1 x 7.62mm (0.3in) coaxal DT MG

Specifications

Crew: 3

Weight: 14.5 tonnes (13.8 tons)

Length: 5.66m (18ft 6in)

Width: 2.29m (7ft 6in)

Height: 2.52m (8ft 1in)

Engine: 373kW (500hp) Model M-17T

Speed: 86km/h (53mph)

Range: 250km (155 miles)

Radio: N/A

Armament: 1 x 76mm (3in) KT-28 Model
1927/32 howitzer; 3 x 7.62mm (0.3in) DT MGs
(coaxial, rear turret, hatch)

▲ BT-7A 'artillery tank'

Byelorussian Front / XV Tank Corps / 27th Light Tank Brigade

A BT-7A 'artillery tank', armed with a 76mm (3in) howitzer for the close support role. The 76mm (3in) HE shell was far more effective against AT guns or field defences than the rounds fired by the 45mm (1.8in) guns of the standard BT tanks.

▾ Heavy Tank Brigade, Reconnaissance Company (September 1939, Poland)

As befitted its role, the reconnaissance company was a fast-moving unit, hampered only by the differing mobility of its BTs and armoured cars. While the latter could outpace the tanks on roads, they had very limited off-road capability and were apt to become bogged down when attempting cross-country moves.

6 x BTs plus 10 x BA-20s

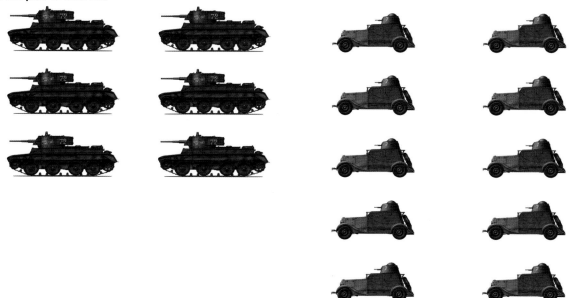

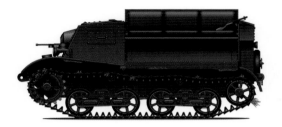

◀ *Komsomolyets* **artillery transporter**

Over 4000 of these partially armoured artillery tractors were produced between 1937 and 1941. They were mainly used as prime movers for the 45mm (1.8in) anti-tank gun.

Specifications

Crew: 2 (plus 6 seats for gun crew)	Engine: 37kW (50hp) GAZ-M 4-cylinder petrol
Weight: 3.5 tonnes (3.44 tons)	Speed: 50km/h (31mph)
Length: 3.45m (11ft 4in)	Range: 250km (155miles)
Width: 1.86m (6ft 1in)	Armament: 1 x 7.62mm (0.3in) DT MG
Height: 1.58m (5ft 1in)	

Humiliation in Finland
NOVEMBER 1939 – MARCH 1940

The extent of the self-inflicted damage to the combat capability of the Red Army was shown in the bloody fiasco of Russia's Winter War against Finland, which began on 30 November 1939.

IN KARELIA, THE INITIAL Soviet assaults by the Seventh Army against the fortifications of the Mannerheim Line were repulsed with heavy losses, despite the support of the three tank brigades of X Tank Corps and four artillery regiments. At least 180,000 troops, 900 guns and 1400 AFVs were committed against roughly 133,000 Finnish defenders who were woefully short of artillery and armour – the most critical shortage being AT guns, only 67 of which were available.

Before being overwhelmed, the Finns graphically demonstrated the shortcomings of contemporary Soviet armoured warfare practice. The Red Army's

Armoured Units (Finland 1939)	Battalions
Seventh Army (Karelian Isthmus)	
10th Tank Bde	1st, 4th, 6th, 8th, 9th, 15th, 19th
20th Tank Bde	90th, 91st, 95th
35th Tank Bde	105th, 108th, 112th
40th Tank Bde	155th, 157th, 160th, 161st
Eighth Army (Ladoga)	
34th Tank Div	76th, 82nd, 83rd
Ninth Army (mid Finland)	97th, 100th, 312th, 365th
Fourteenth Army (Northern Lapland)	349th, 411th

▶ **T-26 Model 1938 light tank**

Seventh Army / 10th Tank Brigade / 15th Tank Battalion

The T-26 Model 1938 was fitted with a new turret that used sloped armour to improve protection. Despite this, it proved vulnerable to even light AT weapons during the Winter War against Finland.

Specifications

Crew: 3	Speed: 28km/h (17mph)
Weight: 10.4 tonnes (10.3 tons)	Range: 200km (124 miles)
Length: 4.8m (15ft 8in)	Armament: 1 x 45mm (1.8in) tank gun
Width: 2.39m (7ft 10in)	Model 1932; 1 x coaxial 7.62mm (0.3in)
Height: 2.33m (7ft 8in)	DT MG; 2 x additional 7.62mm (0.3in) DT
Engine: 68kW (91hp) GAZ T-26	MGs, one ball-mounted in turret rear and
8-cylinder petrol	one on P-40 AA mount

tanks were frequently committed to assaults without adequate reconnaissance and with abysmal levels of artillery and infantry support. These failings made them horribly vulnerable to well-camouflaged Finnish AT guns, and infantry AT teams that scored numerous kills with Molotov Cocktail incendiaries and demolition charges. While most AT guns opened fire at ranges of 400–600m (1312–1968ft), an unofficial record was set by a 37mm (1.5in) Bofors gun of the 7th Anti-Tank Detachment, which destroyed a T-37 on the ice of Lake Ladoga at a range of 1700m (5577ft).

It seems likely that as many as 6000 Soviet AFVs were deployed against Finland during the three-and-a-half months of the war and that losses from all causes may have exceeded 3500 vehicles. Finnish forces captured or destroyed roughly 1600 of these, besides inflicting an estimated 250,000 casualties, highlighting the inadequacies of the Red Army.

Light Tank Brigade (1940)	Arm Car	T-37	T-26
Signal Company	5	–	–
Armoured Car Company	16	–	–
Light Tank Company	–	16	–
Battalion HQ	–	–	3
Reconnaissance Platoon x 3	1	1	–
Tank Company x 3	–	–	17
Reserve Tank Company	–	–	8

▼ Light Tank Brigade, Tank Battalion (January 1940, Karelian Front)

By the standards of 1939/1940, these tank battalions were powerful units, but their potential was never fully realized due to poor training, coupled with abysmal command and control.

Battalion HQ (3 x T-26s)

Tank Company x 3 (17 x T-26s)

Reconnaissance Platoon (1 x T-37 plus 1 x AC)

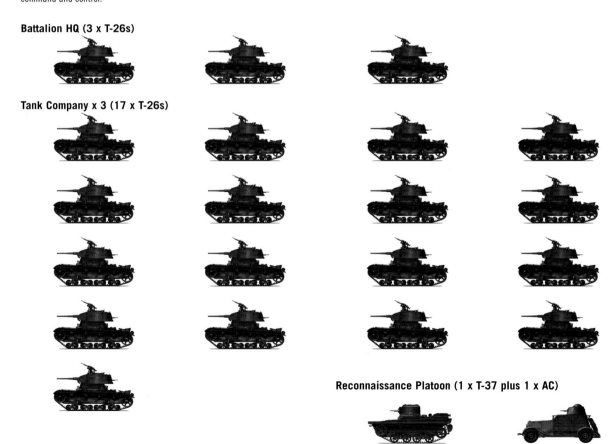

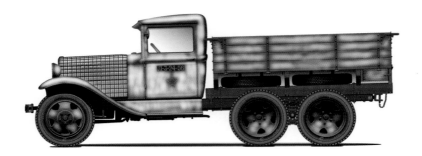

Specifications

Crew: 1 driver

Weight: 3.52 tonnes (3.46 tons)

Length: 5.34m (17ft 6in)

Width: 2.36m (7ft 9in)

Height: 2.1m (6ft 11in)

Engine: 37kW (50hp) GAZ-M 4-cylinder

Speed: 35km/h (21.75mph)

▲ GAZ-AAA 6x4 truck

The GAZ-AAA was the first Soviet 6x4 truck and was a familiar sight in Red Army supply columns from the mid-1930s until 1945. Total production ran to roughly 37,000 vehicles.

▲ GAZ-60 cargo halftrack

A GAZ-60 cargo halftrack, as used in Finland during the Winter War of 1939–40. Almost 900 vehicles were delivered to the Red Army in 1939–40, based on the GAZ-AAA truck and the French Citroën-Kegresse halftrack suspension.

Specifications

Crew: 1 driver

Weight: 3.52 tonnes (3.46 tons)

Length: 5.34m (17ft 6in)

Width: 2.36m (7ft 9in)

Height: 2.1m (6ft 11in)

Engine: 37kW (50hp) GAZ-M 4-cylinder

Speed: 35km/h (21.75mph)

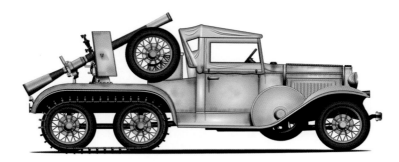

Specifications

Crew: 2

Weight: 1.5 tonnes (1.47 tons)

Length: 4.4m (14ft 5in)

Width: 1.7m (5ft 7in)

Height: 1.6m (5ft 3in)

Engine: 31.3Kw (42hp) GAZ-A 4-cylinder petrol

Speed: 63km/h (39.15mph)

Armament: 1 x 76mm (3in) recoilless gun

▲ GAZ-TK 76mm recoilless gun

A total of 23 experimental GAZ-TK 76mm self-propelled recoilless guns were produced in the mid-1930s. Two of these were lost undergoing combat trials during the Winter War and it seems likely that the remainder succumbed to mechanical failure during the first weeks of Operation *Barbarossa*.

Calm before the storm
JANUARY–MAY 1941

Even Stalin was finally forced to face reality in the aftermath of the German victory in France, and the mechanized corps underwent reform from June 1940 onwards. By the time of the German invasion in June 1941, no less than 30 corps had been raised.

ALTHOUGH FRANTIC EFFORTS were made, these corps were far from being effective combat units when they were thrown into action a year later, despite the massive numbers of AFVs then available (see table opposite).

Even these holdings were inadequate to meet the needs of so many massive formations – over 6000 more tanks were required. The situation was even worse than the totals would suggest, as there were far too few modern vehicles – 3000 more KVs and almost 11,000 more T-34s should have been available.

Equally seriously, the emphasis on producing new tanks rather than spare parts led to appalling serviceability – it seems likely that only 27 per cent of Soviet tanks were fully operational at the time of the German invasion.

▼ KV-1 Model 1940 heavy tank
Special Western Military District / Tenth Army / VI Mechanized Corps

The KV-1 was the outcome of a 1938 requirement for a heavy tank to replace the obsolescent T-35. Initial designs were the very similar twin-turreted SMK and T-100, both of which underwent combat trials in the Winter War, together with a single-turreted version of the SMK, designated the KV (*Klimenti Voroshilov*). These trials indicated the clear superiority of the KV, which entered production as the KV-1 in early 1940.

Mechanized Equipment, RKKA (May 1941)	Strength
Tanks:	
T-27	400
T-37	2400
T-38	1200
T-40	222
T-18M	400
T-26	11,000
BT	6000
T-28	500
T-34	967
T-35	40
KV	508
Armoured cars:	4819
Tractors:	
STZ-3	3658
STZ-5	7170
Komsomolyets	4041
Komintern	1017
Voroshilovyets	228
Kommunar	504
Other motor vehicles (trucks/cars/etc):	272,600

Specifications
Crew: 5
Weight: 45 tonnes (44.3 tons)
Length: 6.75m (22ft 2in)
Width: 3.32m (10ft 10in)
Height: 2.71m (8ft 9in)
Engine: 450kW (600hp) 12-cylinder diesel Model V-2
Speed: 35km/h (22mph)
Range: 335km (208 miles)
Radio: N/A
Armament: 1 x 76mm (3in) F-32 gun; 3 x 7.62mm (0.3in) DT MGs

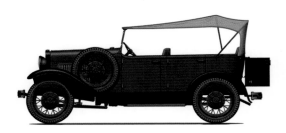

◀ GAZ-A staff car

Special Western Military District / Third Army / XI Mechanized Corps

The GAZ-A was developed from a licence-built copy of the 1927 Ford Model A - approximately 42,000 vehicles were produced between 1932 and 1936. Its simplicity and ability to withstand harsh operating conditions ensured that surviving examples remained in service throughout the war.

Specifications

Crew: 1 driver	Height: 1.8m (5ft 10in)
Weight: 1.08 tonnes (1.06 tons)	Engine: 31.3kW (42hp) GAZ-A 4-cylinder petrol
Length: 3.87m (12ft 7in)	Speed: 90km/h (60mph) on paved road
Width: 1.7m (5ft 6in)	

▶ BA-10 armoured car

Odessa Military District / Twelfth Army / XV Mechanized Corps

It seems likely that as many as 1200 BA-10 heavy armoured cars were produced between 1938 and 1940. Large numbers were captured in the opening stages of *Barbarossa* and were subsequently taken into German service for anti-partisan duties as the *Panzerspahwagen* BAF 203(r).

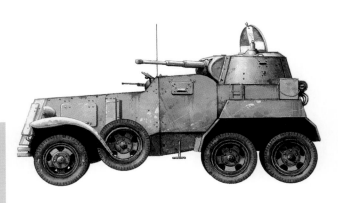

Specifications

Crew: 4	Engine: 37kW (50hp) GAZ-MM
Weight: 5.14 tonnes (5.05 tons)	Speed: 53km/h (33mph)
Length: 4.65m (15ft 3in)	Range: 300km (186miles)
Width: 2m (6ft 6in)	Armament: 45mm (1.8in) gun 20-K plus
Height: 2.20m (7ft 2in)	2 x 7.62 (0.3in) DT MGs

Specifications

Crew: 5	Speed: 26km/h (17mph)
Weight: 52 tonnes (51.1 tons)	Range: 140km (87 miles)
Length: 6.79m (22ft 3in)	Radio: N/A
Width: 3.32m (10ft 10in)	Armament: 1 x M-10 152mm (5.9in) howitzer;
Height: 3.65m (12ft)	1 x 7.62mm (0.3in) DT MG
Engine: 410kW (550hp) Model V-2	
12-cylinder diesel	

▲ KV-2 heavy tank

The horrendous Soviet casualties incurred in assaulting Finnish defences during the Winter War led to demands for a heavy tank with a large-calibre 'bunker-busting' weapon. The hull of the KV-1 was fitted with a massive slab-sided turret mounting a 152mm (5.9in) howitzer, which proved highly effective in trials against captured Finnish bunkers. However, the design was totally unsuitable for the fast-moving armoured warfare of 1941 and most of the 334 examples completed were lost in the opening stages of *Barbarossa*.

Chapter 2

Defending the Motherland

**The Soviet-German Non-Aggression Pact of
August 1939 shocked governments across the world.
They could not have imagined such fierce enemies making a
lasting treaty. Yet from the beginning, both Stalin and Hitler
were trying to twist its provisions for their own advantage.
In less than a year, Stalin seized a great arc of territory to
protect his western frontiers, including eastern Poland,
eastern Finland, the Rumanian provinces of
northern Bukhovina and Bessarabia, Lithuania, Latvia and
Estonia. Hitler had temporarily removed any threat of a war
on two fronts and was able to concentrate his forces for the
campaigns in Norway and France. Significantly, it was in
July 1940 that Hitler ordered the first studies for the
invasion that finally evolved into Operation *Barbarossa*,
which was intended to be launched by a total of
152 divisions on 15 May 1941.**

◀ **Raising the banner**
A Soviet tank crewman raises a regimental flag on his KV-1 heavy tank during the defence of Moscow,
31 December 1941.

Operation *Barbarossa*
22 June 1941

The overall objective of *Barbarossa* was to trap and destroy the bulk of the Red Army in a series of encirclements in western Russia before finally securing a line from Archangel to Astrakhan.

THREE MAIN ARMY GROUPS would be used in the invasion. Army Group North was to advance from East Prussia through the Baltic states and join with the Finns to take Leningrad. Army Group Centre's initial operations from its concentration areas around Warsaw were intended to clear the invasion route to Moscow as far as Smolensk before swinging north to help the attack on Leningrad. After the city was taken, the advance on Moscow would be resumed. Army Group South, including Rumanian and Hungarian divisions, was tasked with taking the rich agricultural lands of the Ukraine. The invasion's chances of success depended on the 19 Panzer divisions concentrated in four *Panzergruppen*, which

also incorporated the 14 motorized divisions. These had the daunting task of cutting through the massive forces that the Red Army could deploy in European Russia, which totalled perhaps 170 divisions, including up to 60 tank divisions and at least 13 motorized divisions.

The bulk of the Soviet units were deployed close to the frontier, and for almost 50 years the accepted explanation for this was Stalin's obsession with securing his newly conquered territories. German wartime claims that they invaded to pre-empt a Soviet attack have almost always been dismissed as crude propaganda, but this traditional view has been challenged in recent years as new material has

▲ **T-34 company**

A column of T-34 Model 1941 tanks in an assembly area, southern Ukraine, autumn 1941. By this time, the *Luftwaffe* had complete air superiority and such formations were prime targets for devastating dive-bomber attacks.

emerged from Soviet archives. One of the most significant of these documents is the plan formulated by Zhukov in May 1941 on his appointment as Chief of the Soviet General Staff. The introduction to the draft plan stated: 'In view of the fact that Germany at present keeps its army fully mobilized with its rear services deployed, it has the capacity of deploying ahead of us and striking a sudden blow. To prevent this I consider it important not to leave the operational initiative to the German command in any circumstances, but to anticipate the enemy and attack the German army at the moment when it is in the process of deploying...'

This plan proposed a pre-emptive strike by 152 Red Army divisions (including 76 tank divisions and 44 mechanized divisions) against the Axis forces assembling in German-occupied Poland. While this may have been no more than a contingency plan, it is at least possible that Stalin really was intending to make just such an attack.

The attack begins

The German offensive achieved almost complete surprise when it opened on 22 June 1941. The *Panzergruppen* quickly broke through the Soviet lines; General Hoepner's *Panzergruppe* IV played a key role in the destruction of the Soviet III and XII Mechanized Corps before driving through the Baltic states as the spearhead of Army Group North's advance on Leningrad, which was besieged by 8 September. *Panzergruppen* II (Guderian) and III

(Hoth) leading Army Group Centre's advance pulled off a spectacular encirclement east of Minsk, which trapped about 30 Soviet divisions (including six mechanized corps) barely a week after the invasion began. These units were destroyed by the following German infantry divisions over the next three weeks whilst Guderian and Hoth raced on to trap a further 21 Red Army divisions around Smolensk in mid-July.

Kleist's *Panzergruppe* I, forming the main armoured strength of Army Group South, had thrust deep into Ukraine, advancing to within 20km (12.4 miles) of Kiev by 11 July after decimating desperate counterattacks launched by the five mechanized corps of the Kiev Special Military District.

AFV Strength (22 June 1941)	Required	Actual
KV heavy tanks	3528	508
T-34 medium tanks	11,760	967
T-28 tanks (obsolete)	–	500
BT light tanks	7840	6000
T-26 light tanks	5880	11,000
T-37/38/40 scout tanks	476	4222
Total Tanks	29,484	23,197
Armoured cars	7448	4819

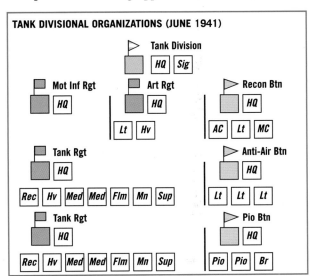

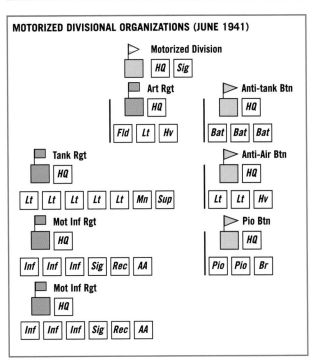

Facing Army Group Centre

By mid-July 1941, Soviet losses were staggering, totalling perhaps 5700 AFVs, 4500 guns and 610,000 prisoners, while the Soviet Air Force had been virtually wiped out, losing almost 6000 aircraft.

COMPLETE GERMAN AIR superiority allowed the *Luftwaffe* to mount unopposed reconnaissance and bombing sorties that disrupted many Soviet counterattacks before they got under way. Those that were delivered were usually badly mishandled, often being made by armour without any proper infantry or artillery support. Soviet armour was generally decimated by German AT units screening the flanks of the advance before the Panzers mopped up the remnants.

On the technical level, the majority of Soviet AFVs were far outclassed by their German counterparts – very few Red Army vehicles had radios, a fact that reinforced their crews' tendency to stick rigidly to detailed orders regardless of rapidly changing battlefield conditions. By contrast, the radio-controlled Panzers could concentrate quickly to defeat the clumsy counterattacks. (The hapless Red Army tank crews soon found that the signal flags on which they were supposed to rely were almost

▶ **T-40 Model 1940 amphibious light tank**

XI Mechanized Corps / 29th Tank Division

The T-40 was the last Soviet amphibious light tank to enter service before the German invasion. Probably no more than 230 were delivered during 1940/41 before wartime priorities forced production to switch a simpler version, the non-amphibious T-60.

Specifications

Crew: 3

Weight: 5.6 tonnes (5.5 tons)

Length: 4.43m (13ft 6in)

Width: 2.51m (8ft 3in)

Height: 2.12m (6ft 11in)

Engine: 70kW (52hp) GAZ-202 petrol

Speed: 45km/h (28mph)

Range: 350km (215 miles)

Radio: 71-TK-3 (when fitted)

Armament: 1 x 12.7mm (0.5in) DShK HMG plus
1 x coaxal 7.62mm (0.3in) DT MG

SPECIAL WESTERN MILITARY DISTRICT					
	Tank Div	Mot Div	Commander (Maj-Gen)	Staging Area	Strength
6 MK	4, 7 TD	29 MD	MG Khatskilevich	Bialystok	1000
11 MK	29, 33 TD	204 MD	DK Mostovenko	Grodno	204
13 MK	27, 31 TD	4 MD	PN Akhlyustan	Belsk	300
14 MK	22, 30 TD	205 MD	SI Oborin	Brest	508
17 MK	25, 54 TD	103 MD	MA Petrov	Baranovichi	300
20 MK	26,38 TD	210 MD	N Vedeneyev	Minsk	300

MOSCOW MILITARY DISTRICT					
	Tank Div	Mot Div	Commander (Maj-Gen)	Staging Area	Strength
7 MK	14, 18 TD	1 MD	VI Vinogradov	Vitebsk-Kaluga	1000
21 MK	42, 46 TD	185 MD	DD Lelyushenko	Opochka	98

▾ Reconnaissance Battalion (June 1941)

In common with all Red Army armoured units of the time, the reconnaissance battalion's effectiveness was troubled by the very limited number of radio-equipped AFVs. It was also handicapped by the differing levels of mobility of its three companies – the light tanks had difficulty keeping up with the armoured cars and motorcycles during road moves, but had far better cross-country performance.

Armoured Car Company (15 x BA-10s)

Light Tank Company (17 x T-40s)

Motorcycle Company (12 x motorcycles with 3 mortars)

impossible to read accurately under combat conditions.) The thinly armoured BTs and T-26s that formed a high proportion of the total Red Army tank strength at the beginning of the campaign were vulnerable to almost all German tank and AT guns at normal battle ranges. In contrast, the Soviet 45mm (1.8in) could penetrate the up-armoured Panzer IIIH/J and Panzer IVE/F only at point-blank range. Moreover, the three-man turrets of the Panzer III and IV allowed the commander to concentrate on command duties, which gave them a distinct edge in tank-versus-tank actions against most Red Army AFVs – in his two-man turret, the Soviet commander was distracted by having also to act as gunner or loader.

The run of German victories provoked drastic action from Stalin, who had General Pavlov, the commander of the Western Front facing Army Group Centre, arrested and shot on 22 July, together with his Chief of Staff and chief signals officer. This warning was reinforced by the 'dual command' principle, under which a political commissar shared authority with each CO. All too often, the effect was simply to saddle hard-pressed COs with political officers whose fanaticism was matched only by their military incompetence. Corps Commissar Vashugin, for example, while commanding a counterattack by a reinforced tank division from IV Mechanized Corps, actually directed it into a swamp, losing the entire formation in the fiasco.

▶ **T-26 Model 1938 light tank**

XXII Mechanized Corps / 41st Tank Division

The T-26 formed the bulk of the Soviet tank fleet in June 1941, with an estimated 11,000 vehicles in service. Huge numbers were lost during the early stages of Barbarossa and in the winter battles of 1941/42.

Specifications

Crew: 3	Speed: 28km/h (17mph)
Weight: 10.4 tonnes (10.3 tons)	Range: 200km (124 miles)
Length: 4.8m (15ft 8in)	Radio: N/A
Width: 2.39m (7ft 10in)	Armament: 1 x 45mm (1.8in) AT gun;
Height: 2.33m (7ft 8in)	3 x 7.62mm (0.3in) DT MG (coaxial, rear
Engine: 68kW (91hp) GAZ T-26 8-cylinder	turret, turent hatch)
petrol	

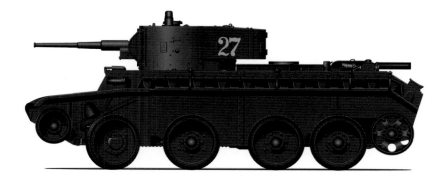

▲ **BT-5 Model 1935 fast tank**

IV Mechanized Corps / 32nd Tank Division

This BT-5 is operating in the wheeled mode with the tracks stowed. Almost all the BT series had this capability, but removing and refitting tracks was a lengthy business and was avoided whenever possible.

Specifications

Crew: 3	Speed: 72km/h (44mph)
Weight: 11.5 tonnes (11 tons)	Range: 200km (124 miles)
Length: 5.58m (18ft 3in)	Radio: N/A
Width: 2.23m (7ft 3in)	Armament: 1 x 45mm (1.8in) Model 1932 gun;
Height: 2.25m (7ft 5in)	1 x 7.62mm (0.3in) coaxal DT MG
Engine: 298 kW (400hp) Model M-5	

▶ **T-60 Model 1941 light tank**

I Guards Special Rifle Corps / 4th Tank Brigade

The T-60 Model 1941 was about to enter service at the time of the German invasion. Over 6000 vehicles, including the up-armoured T-60 Model 1942, were produced before the design was superseded by the T-70 in September 1942.

Specifications

Crew: 2	Speed: 45km/h (28mph)
Weight: 5.8 tonnes (5.7 tons)	Range: 450km (280 miles)
Length: 4.1m (13ft 5in)	Radio: N/A
Width: 2.46m (8ft 1in)	Armament: 1 x 20mm (0.79in) TNSh gun;
Height: 1.89m (6ft 2in)	1 x 7.62mm (0.3in) coaxial DT MG
Engine: 2 x GAZ-202 52+52kW (70+70hp)	

Defence of the North

The general picture of Panzer superiority was marred only by the relatively few encounters with T-34s and KVs, both of which were formidable opponents.

APART FROM THE FEW Panzer IIIs armed with the 50mm (2in) L/60 gun, the T-34's sloped armour was almost invulnerable to all German AFV weapons except at point-blank range, whilst the KVs were only effectively countered by 88mm (3.5in) Flak guns or medium artillery.

The KVs had the greatest psychological impact as even single vehicles could impose significant delays on the German advance. On 23/24 June, a single KV-2 of III Mechanized Corps cut the supply route to 6th Panzer Division's bridgeheads across the Dubissa River in Lithuania for over 24 hours. It

▲ **KV-1 Model 1940 heavy tank**

I Mechanized Corps / 1st Tank Division

Lieutenant Kolobanov's tank, one of five KV-1s that mauled the 8th Panzer Division on 14 August 1941 during its advance on Leningrad. The KV-1 was fitted with a 71-TK-2 radio (although even by 1945, not all Soviet AFVs had radios).

Specifications

Crew: 5	Speed: 35km/h (22mph)
Weight: 45 tonnes (44.3 tons)	Range: 335km (208 miles)
Length: 6.75m (22ft 2in)	Radio: 71-TK-2
Width: 3.32m (10ft 10in)	Armament: 1 x coaxial 7.62mm (0.3in) DT MG;
Height: 2.71m (8ft 9in)	2 x additional 7.62mm (0.3in) DT MGs, 1
Engine: 450kW (600hp) model V-2	ball-mounted in turret rear and 1 ball-
12-cylinder diesel	mounted in hull front

LENINGRAD MILITARY DISTRICT					
	Tank Div	Mot Div	Commander (Maj-Gen)	Staging Area	Strength
1 MK	1, 3 TD	163 MD	ML Chernyavskiy	Pskov	163
10 MK	21, 24 TD	198 MD	Lavrionovich	N of Leningrad	–

SPECIAL BALTIC MILITARY DISTRICT					
	Tank Div	Mot Div	Commander (Maj-Gen)	Staging Area	Strength
3 MK	2, 5 TD	84 MD	AV Kurkin	Vilno	460
12 MK	23, 28 TD	202 MD	NM Shestpalov	Shauliya	690

▼ Heavy Tank Battalion (1941)

When fully up to strength, the heavy tank battalions were the world's most powerful armoured units of their size in 1941. However, only a small number of these battalions were fully operational at the time of the German invasion, as the Red Army had only 508 of the 3528 KVs it required to equip all its units.

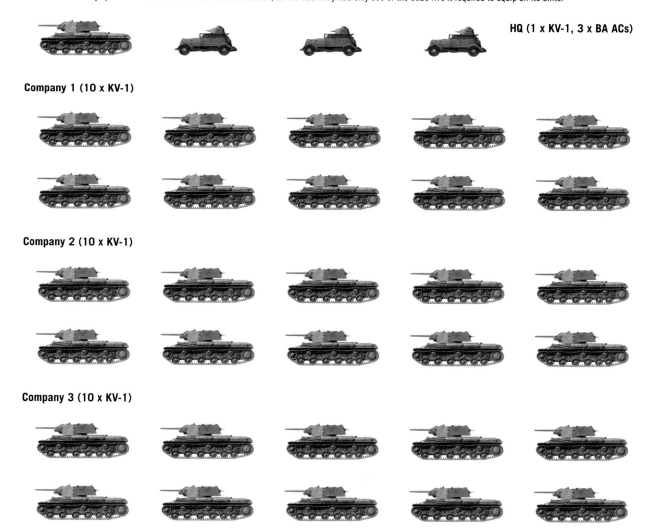

HQ (1 x KV-1, 3 x BA ACs)

Company 1 (10 x KV-1)

Company 2 (10 x KV-1)

Company 3 (10 x KV-1)

proved invulnerable to fire from German tanks and was only destroyed by an '88' brought up to close range while a Panzer platoon acted as a decoy.

In another incident, the leading elements of the 8th Panzer Division were badly mauled on 14 August by five well-camouflaged KV-1s dug in at Krasnogvardeysk near Leningrad. The Soviet commander, Lieutenant Zinoviy Kolobanov, had carefully selected the position to cover the region's only road at the point where it crossed a swamp. Each KV-1 was loaded with some extra ammunition and Kolobanov issued his instructions that the other tanks should hold fire until ordered, to conceal the strength of the detachment.

KV defence

As the 8th Panzer Division's vanguard approached, Kolobanov's KV knocked out the lead tank with its first shot. The Germans assumed that an AT mine was responsible and halted the column, giving Kolobanov the opportunity to destroy the second tank. Only then did the Germans realize that they were under attack. At this point, Kolobanov knocked out the rear German tank, trapping the entire column, which began firing blindly.

Kolobanov's tank was subjected to heavy fire, but German tanks moving off the road bogged down in the swampy ground and became easy targets. A total of 22 German tanks and two towed artillery pieces fell victim to Kolobanov's KV before it ran out of ammunition. He then called up another KV-1, and 21 more German tanks were destroyed before the half-hour battle ended. After the battle, Kolobanov's crew counted a total of 135 hits on their tank, none of which had penetrated the armour.

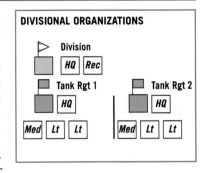

DIVISIONAL ORGANIZATIONS

The short L/30.5 76mm (3in) gun of the early T-34s and KV-Is was soon replaced by a 76mm (3in) L/41.2 with a significantly improved armour-piercing performance. Fortunately for the Germans, many T-34s and KVs had been destroyed in air raids or captured on their rail transporters while moving up to the front and others had been abandoned after breakdowns or had run out of fuel.

Soviet AFV camouflage was generally very simple, with most vehicles finished in dark green (top). A small number of tanks were finished in a variety of disruptive patterns, using random brown or black bands or patches over the standard dark-green finish (lower). Given the devastating effects of the *Luftwaffe's* air superiority, tank crews soon came to appreciate the benefits of using natural foliage to conceal their vehicles whenever possible.

▲ **Improvised Tank Destroyer**

Leningrad Garrison, autumn 1941

Shortly after the '900-day siege' of Leningrad began in September 1941, the city's factories began production of a bewildering variety of improvised AFVs. The vehicle illustrated is a tank destroyer based on a partially armoured ZiS-5 lorry armed with a 45mm (1.8in) Model 1937 AT gun and a 7.62mm (0.3in) MG.

Specifications

Crew: 4/5

Weight: (Estimated) 6.1tonnes (6 tons)

Length: 6.06m (19ft 10in)

Width: 2.24m (7ft 4in)

Height: (Estimated) 2.76m (9ft 1in)

Engine: carburettor liquid-cooled 73hp/2300rpm (from I 1944 - 76hp/2400rpme

Radio: N/A

Armament: 1 x 45mm (1.8in) Model 1937 antitank gun; 1 x 7.62mm (0.3in) DT MG

▶ T-30B light tank

I Mechanized Corps / 3rd Tank Division

The T-30B light tank was designed as a simpler, non-amphibious version of the T-40, with thicker armour and an improved armament of a 20mm (0.79in) ShVAK gun and a coaxial MG. Only a small number of vehicles were completed before production switched to the improved T-60 in mid 1941.

Specifications

Crew: 2	Speed: 45km/h (28mph)
Weight: 5.8 tonnes (5.7 tons)	Range: 450km (280 miles)
Length: 4.1m (13ft 5in)	Radio: 71-TK-3 (when fitted)
Width: 2.46m (8ft 1in)	Armament: 1 x 20mm (0.79in) gun;
Height: 1.89m (6ft 2in)	1 x 7.62mm (0.3in) coaxial DT MG
Engine: 2 x GAZ-202 52+52 kW (70+70 hp)	

Retreat from Byelorussia

Theoretically, General Pavlov's Western Front was a match for Army Group Centre since it had 700,000 men, over 2000 tanks (including 383 T-34s and KVs) plus 1900 aircraft, but events were to turn out very differently.

ARMY GROUP CENTRE'S initial offensive into Byelorussia achieved almost complete surprise. Its progress was greatly assisted by *Luftflotte* II's thousand or so aircraft, which effectively destroyed the VVS (Red Air Force) units assigned to the Western Front within a matter of days. Elements of the garrison of the border fortress of Brest-Litovsk, which included

fanatical NKVD units, held out for almost a month, but most of the Western Front's formations were swept away by the speed of the German advance.

Pavlov's initial reaction was to order an immediate counterattack by the Tenth Army, which was concentrated around Bialystok – this predictably failed and simply ensured that the Tenth Army would

Specifications

Crew: 3	Speed: 86km/h (53mph)
Weight: 14 tonnes (13.2 tons)	Range: 250km (155 miles)
Length: 5.66m (18ft 6in)	Radio: N/A
Width: 2.29m (7ft 6in)	Armament: 1 x 45mm (1.8in) Model 1932 gun;
Height: 2.42m (7ft 10in)	1 x 7.62mm (0.3in) coaxial DT MG
Engine: 373kW (500hp) Model M-17T	

▲ BT-7 Model 1937 fast tank

XIV Mechanized Corps / 205th Motorized Division

A BT-7 Model 1937 in markings typical of the opening stages of Operation Barbarossa. BTs and T-26s formed the bulk of the Red Army's tank strength during the first few months of the campaign.

be the first major Soviet formation to be encircled and destroyed when the German Third and Fourth Armies sealed off the Bialystok pocket on 25 June. A further counterattack by VI and XI Mechanized Corps, plus VI Cavalry Corps, was ordered against the flank of *Panzergruppe* III, which was making rapid progress towards Vilnius. The operation was harried by constant air attacks and finally collapsed when the Soviet forces hit a strong German AT screen supported by infantry.

On 28 June, *Panzergruppen* II and III linked up east of Minsk, the Byelorussian capital, which was captured 24 hours later. In six days, they had advanced over 320km (199 miles), covering a third of the distance to Moscow. It was undoubtedly a spectacular achievement – when the remnants of the Soviet Third, Fourth, Tenth and Thirteenth Armies finally surrendered, the Red Army had lost roughly 420,000 men (including 290,000 prisoners) plus 2500 tanks and 1500 guns. However, the Panzers had far out-run their supporting infantry divisions, which were essential for effectively sealing the pocket, and a large number of Soviet troops (possibly as many as 250,000) were able to break out after abandoning their heavy equipment. Nonetheless, it seemed as though the road to Moscow was open.

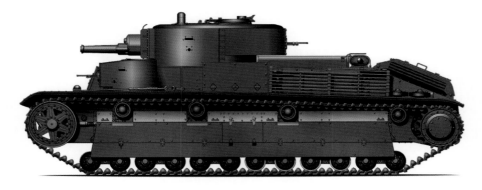

▲ T-28 Model 1938 medium tank
XIII Mechanized Corps / 27th Tank Division

One of the 500 T-28s in service during the summer of 1941. By the end of the year, the Soviet armies may well have lost as many as 20,000 of the 22,500 tanks which they held just before the war.

Specifications

Crew: 6	Speed (road): 37km/h (23mph)
Weight: 28 tonnes (27.4 tons)	Range: 220km (137 miles)
Length: 7.44m (24ft 5in)	Radio: N/A
Width: 2.87m (9ft 5in)	Armament: 1 x 76mm (3in) L-10 L/26 gun;
Height: 2.82m (9ft 3in)	4 x 7.62mm (0.3in) DT MGs
Engine: 373kW (500hp) Mikulin M-17 12-cylinder	

▲ SU-12 76mm (3in) self-propelled gun
XX Mechanized Corps / 26th Tank Division

The SU-12 was the first Soviet SP gun to enter service in the 1930s. It was a simple conversion of the 6x4 GAZ-AAA truck mounting the 76mm (3in) Model 1927 regimental gun, which remained in service until 1945.

Specifications

Note: for Gaz-AAA chassis	Width: 2.36m (7ft 9in)
Crew: 1 driver	Height: 2.1m (6ft 11in)
Weight: 3.52 tonnes (3.46 tons)	Engine: 37kW (50hp) GAZ-M 4-cylinder
Length: 5.34m (17ft 6in)	Speed: 35km/h (21.75mph)

RVGK (HIGH COMMAND RESERVE)					
	Tank Div	Mot Div	Commander (Maj-Gen)	Staging Area	Strength
5 MK	13, 17 TD	109 MD	IP Alekseyenko	Vinista	700
23 MK	44, 48 TD	220 MD	–	–	–
25 MK	50, 55 TD	219 MD	SM Krivoshein	Kharkov	–

Specifications

Crew: 1 driver, plus 2/3 gun crew

Weight: 3.52 tonnes (3.46 tons)

Length: 5.34m (17ft 6in)

Width: 2.36m (7ft 9in)

Height: 2.1m (6ft 11in)

Engine: 37kW (50hp) GAZ-M 4 cylinder,

Speed: 35km/h (21.75mph)

Armament: quadruple 7.62mm (0.3in) MGs on
  a pedestal AA mounting

▲ GAZ-AAA 6x4 truck

XIII Mechanized Corps / 4th Motorized Division

The 6x4 GAZ-AAA was produced in vast numbers – over 37,000 vehicles were delivered between 1934 and 1943. One of its many roles was that of air defence when armed with the 4M system, which consisted of quadruple 7.62mm (0.3in) MGs on a pedestal AA mounting.

▲ ZiS-6 BM-13-16 'Katyusha' salvo rocket launcher

NKVD Independent Artillery Battery

The ZiS-6 6x4 truck was the first vehicle to mount the 132mm (5.2in) 'Katyusha' salvo rocket launcher. The operational debut of the first seven vehicle batteries was a bombardment of the key Orsha rail junction in July 1941.

Specifications

Crew: 1 (rocket crew in separate vehicle)

Weight: 4.23 tonnes (4.66 tons)

Length: 4.44m (14.57ft)

Width: 0m (0ft)

Height: 2.16m (8.5ft)

Engine: 54kW (73hp) 6-cylinder

Speed: 55km/h (34mph)

Rocket Range: 8.5km (5.28 miles)

Armament: 16 x 132mm (5.2in) M-13 rockets

TRANSBAIKAL MILITARY DISTRICT					
	Tank Div	Mot Div	Commander (Maj-Gen)	Staging Area	Strength
30 MK	58, 60 TD	239 MD	–	–	–

FAR EASTERN FORCE					
	Tank Div	Mot Div	Commander (Maj-Gen)	Staging Area	Strength
26 MK	–	12 MD	–	–	–
27 MK	–	–	–	–	–
29 MK	–	–	–	–	–

▲ **Multi-turreted monster**

A knocked-out T-35 Model 1935, autumn 1941. The vehicle appears to have suffered internal explosions that have blown off both the front MG sub-turret and the rear 45mm (1.8in) sub-turret.

Disaster in the Ukraine

German Army Group South had the largest area of operations in the opening phases of *Barbarossa*, but spearheaded by Kliest's *Panzegruppe* I, were able to cover vast tracts of territory.

THESE SAME VICTORIES led to Hitler's increasing interference in all aspects of operations, with devastating consequences for Germany's chances of victory. Despite Army Group South's success at Uman in early August, where 20 Red Army divisions were surrounded and destroyed, he ordered the suspension of the advance on Moscow so that

Guderian's *Panzergruppe* II was freed to turn south to help complete the conquest of the Ukraine.

Kliest's *Panzergruppe* I was ordered to strike northeastwards to link up with Guderian and encircle Kiev. These moves caught the Soviets entirely by surprise and their frantic efforts to reinforce Kiev only increased the losses when the city's defenders were finally surrounded on 16 September. Over the next two weeks, they were subjected to constant air and ground attacks before the final collapse.

As a result of this victory, Army Group South was able to complete the occupation of the Black Sea coast as far east as the Crimea and the Sea of Azov, although the heavily fortified naval base of Sevastopol was to hold out until the summer of 1942.

Saving the Soviet tank industry

The Axis advance rapidly threatened the tank factories that were concentrated around Kharkov and Leningrad. Fortunately for the Red Army, pre-war industrialization of the Urals and central Asia had provided a measure of reserve capacity well beyond the reach of the invading German forces.

The trains that brought troops to the front were used to evacuate key factories to safe areas such as the Urals, Siberia and Kazakhstan far from the front-lines. Such evacuations often had to carried out at breakneck speed – the Zaporozhstal steelworks in the Ukraine was stripped bare in 19 days (19 August–5 September), during which time 16,000 railway wagons were loaded with vital machinery, including the especially valuable rolling-mill equipment.

Between July and November 1941, no fewer than 1523 industrial enterprises, including 1360 large war production, plants had been moved to the east. The equipment evacuated amounted to a one and a half million railway wagon-loads. The massive evacuation programme put 300 armament factories temporarily out of production, but draconian measures quickly

Tank Divisional Strength (Autumn 1941)	Strength
Reconnaissance battalion:	
T-40	10
Armoured cars	26
Motorcycle company	12
Tank regiments x 2:	
Armoured cars	3
Quad anti-aircraft machine guns	3
KV	10
T-34	20
T-26	60

restored output. Beria, the head of the NKVD state security apparatus, was appointed to the State Defence Committee (GKO) with responsibility for armament production, and ruthlessly used the millions of prisoners in the Gulag as slave labour.

In addition to running the Gulag, the NKVD played a key role in 'supporting' Soviet scientific research and arms development. Many researchers and engineers who had been convicted for political crimes were held in privileged prisons colloquially known as *sharashkas* (which were much more comfortable than the Gulag), where they continued their work under extremely close NKVD supervision. After their release, some went on to become world leaders in science and technology, notably the aircraft designer Andrei Tupolev, who would produce numerous post-war civil and military aircraft types.

▶ **NI Tank**

Odessa Garrison, September 1941

The huge losses of Soviet tanks suffered in the initial stages of Operation *Barbarossa* led to a plethora of improvised AFVs reminiscent of those produced by the Home Guard in 1940. Workshops in the besieged port of Odessa built 68 of these NI Tanks (*Na Ispug:* Terror Tanks) in August/September 1941 based on the hulls of STZ-5 tractors, which were fitted with boiler plate 'armour' and MG turrets from T-26 Model 1931 tanks.

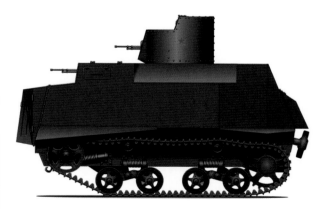

Specifications

Crew: 3

Length: 4.15m (13ft 6in)

Width: 1.86m (6ft 1in)

Height: 0m (0ft)

Engine: 39kW (52hp) 4-cylinder petrol-kerosene

Armament: 2 x 1 x 7.62mm (0.3in) DT MGs, one turret mouted, one in hull

ODESSA MILITARY DISTRICT					
	Tank Div	Mot Div	Commander (Maj-Gen)	Staging Area	Strength
2 MK	11, 16 TD	15 MD	YuV Novoselskiy	Lipkany	350
18 MK	36, 47 TD	209 MD	–	–	350

▶ T-26 M1938 light tank

South-Western Front / Fifth Army / IX Mechanized Corps / 20th Tank Division

At the time of the German invasion, IX Mechanized Corps was entirely equipped with older vehicles such as this T-26.

Specifications

Crew: 3	Speed: 28km/h (17mph)
Weight: 10.4 tonnes (10.3 tons)	Range: 200km (124 miles)
Length: 4.8m (15ft 8in)	Radio: N/A
Width: 2.39m (7ft 10in)	Armament: 1 x 45mm (1.8in) AT gun;
Height: 2.33m (7ft 8in)	1 x 7.62mm (0.3in) DT MG; additional
Engine: 68kW (91hp) GAZ T-26 8-cylinder	7.62mm (0.3in) DT MG ball-mounted into
petrol engine	turret rear

▶ STZ-3 artillery tractor

47th Tank Division / 47th Motorized Artillery Regiment

The STZ-3 artillery tractor entered production in 1937 and was a standard prime mover for medium and heavy artillery throughout the war.

Specifications

Crew: 1	Engine: 52hp/1250rpm, straight 4-cylinder
Weight: 5.1 tonnes (5.02tons)	petrol start kerosene working OHV, 7461c
Length: 3.70m (12 1½in)	Speed: 8km/h (4.97mph)
Width: 1.86m (6 1 ½in)	60km (37.28 miles)
Height: 2.21m (7 3in)	

▶ KhTZ tank destroyer

Kharkov Garrison, October 1941

Following the German invasion, the Kharkov Tractor Works produced roughly 60 KhTZ tank destroyers based on the STZ-3 hull and armed with a 45mm (1.8in) gun and coaxial MG in a limited traverse mounting.

Specifications

Crew: 2	Engine: (52hp) 4-cylinder petrol
Weight (estimated): 7 tonnes (6.89 tons)	Speed: 8km/h (4.97mph)
Length: 3.70m (12ft 1½in)	Range: 50km (31.07 miles)
Width: 1.86m (6ft 1 ½in)	Armament: 1 x 45mm (1.8in) tank gun Model
Height: 2.21m (7ft 3in)	1932; 1 x coaxial 7.62mm (0.3in) DT MG

▼ Light Tank Battalion (June 1941)

Five of these battalions were intended to form the tank regiment of each motorized division. By the standards of 1941, such regiments would have been powerful and highly mobile forces, well suited for exploiting breakthroughs made by the more heavily armoured AFVs of the tank divisions. Very few were at full strength in the summer of 1941 and all lacked the training to carry out heir roles effectively.

HQ (3 x BT-5)

Company 1 (17 x BT-5)

Company 2 (17 x BT-5)

Company 3 (17 x BT-5)

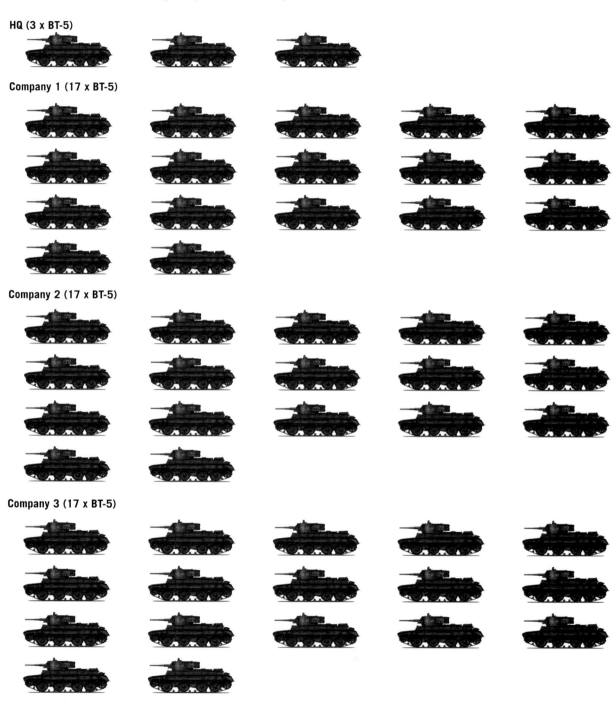

Fall of Kiev
SEPTEMBER 1941

Operation *Barbarossa*'s most demanding tasks were assigned to Field Marshal von Rundstedt's Army Group South. He had only Kleist's *Panzergruppe* I to provide the armoured punch for a motley collection of forces, including ill-equipped Rumanian, Hungarian and Italian formations.

THESE FACED GENERAL KIRPONOS' South-Western Front, the best-equipped Soviet Front (see table right for units and numbers). The initial Soviet response to the invasion was to activate the Zhukov pre-emptive strike plan. All eight mechanized corps were to destroy *Panzergruppe* I before launching an offensive across the frontier into German-occupied Poland to seize Lublin. Unfortunately for Kirponos, some of his forces had to cover 400km (248.5 miles) to intercept Kleist, a recipe for disaster given *Luftwaffe* air superiority.

Untrained and underequipped

Even worse, most of the mechanized corps were far from being fully trained and equipped formations. At the time, the future Marshal Rokossovsky commanded IX Mechanized Corps, and in his memoirs, he recalled: 'Up to the beginning of the war our corps was up to half of its establishment for personnel, but had not received basic equipment: tanks and motor transport. Here, the stocks were no more than 30 percent of the authorized strength.... Put simply, the corps was unready for military operations as a mechanized unit in any form. There was no way that the Kiev Special Military District (KOVO) headquarters and the General Staff did not know this.'

The five-pointed red star of the Soviet Union was used as a national identification symbol throughout the war on both AFVs and support vehicles. Usually, it would be placed on the turret, hull or glacis plate.

South-Western Front (June 1941)	AFVs (total)	T-34s/KVs
IV Mechanized Corps	979	460
VIII Mechanized Corps	899	170
IX Mechanized Corps	316	–
XV Mechanized Corps	749	133
XVI Mechanized Corps	478	–
XIX Mechanized Corps	453	2
XXII Mechanized Corps	712	31
XXIV Mechanized Corps	222	–

Kirponos initially planned to halt (and hopefully destroy) *Panzergruppe* I with flank attacks by six mechanized corps – a total of 3700 tanks. The concentration of the corps was chaotic – air attacks and mechanical breakdowns took a steady toll of tanks and support vehicles long before they encountered Kleist's Panzers. The Soviet formations were committed to action piecemeal and suffered accordingly. On 26 June, the counterattack was finally made in the Brody-Dubno area. Elements of

SPECIAL KIEV MILITARY DISTRICT					
	Tank Div	Mot Div	Commander (Maj-Gen)	Staging Area	Strength
4 MK	8, 32 TD	81 MD	AA Vlasov	Lvov	860
8 MK	12, 34 TD	7 MD	DI Ryabyshev	Dubno	600
9 MK	20, 35 TD	131 MD	KK Rokossovskiy	Zytomierz	700
15 MK	10, 37 TD	212 MD	II Karpezo	Zytomierz	915
16 MK	15, 39 TD	240 MD	AD Sokolov	Ksmenets-Podolskiy	–
19 MK	40, 43 TD	213 MD	NV Feklenko	Zytomierz	160
22 MK	19, 41 TD	215 MD	SM Kondrusev	Rovno-Dubno	–
24 MK	45, 49 TD	216 MD	VI Christyakov	Proskurov	–

VII, IX, XV and XIX Mechanized Corps were sent against Kleist's flanks, with the aim of cutting the *Panzergruppe* in two. Although the 16th Panzer Division took significant casualties and the *Panzergruppe*'s advance was delayed for several days, by the beginning of July all four mechanized corps had been comprehensively defeated. South-Western Front had sustained over 173,000 casualties,

▶ **GAZ M-1 command car**

XXII Mechanized Corps / 19th Tank Division / HQ

The GAZ M-1 was based on the 1933 US Ford V8-40 and no less than 63,000 vehicles were produced from 1936 until 1941. It was the principal staff car in the early war years and was widely used by Red Army commanders, but its 4x2 configuration was a major drawback under operational conditions.

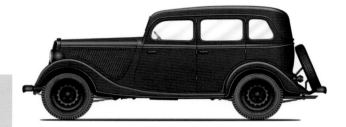

Specifications	
Crew: 1	Height: 1.78m (5ft 10in)
Weight: 1.37 tonnes (1.35 tons)	Engine: 37kW (50hp) 4-cylinder
Length: 4.62m (15ft 2in)	Speed: 100km/h (62.1mph)
Width: 1.77m (5ft 10in)	

▶ **GAZ-61-40 staff car**

XXII Mechanized Corps / 41st Tank Division / HQ

The GAZ-61-40 was the first Soviet 4x4 staff car to enter service, proving far more versatile than earlier 4x2 vehicles.

Specifications	
Crew: 1	Height: 1.9m (6ft 3in)
Weight: 1.54 tonnes (1.52 tons)	Engine: 63kW (85hp) 6-cylinder
Length: 4.67m (15ft 3in)	Speed: 100km/h (62.1mph)
Width: 1.75m (5ft 9in)	

Specifications	
Crew: 1	Height: 1.97m (6ft 6in)
Weight: 3.46 tonnes (3.41 tons)	Engine: 37kW (50hp) 4-cylinder
Length: 5.33m (17ft 6in)	Speed: 70km/h (43.5mph)
Width: 2.04m (6ft 8in)	

▲ **GAZ-MM 1½-ton truck**

XIX Mechanized Corps / 43rd Tank Division / Transport Battalion

The GAZ-MM was essentially a simplified version of the GAZ-AA, with a more powerful engine and modified cargo platform.

terrifying numbers compounded by the loss of an estimated 4381 tanks and 1218 aircraft.

As Army Group Centre's advance approached Smolensk in mid-July, Hitler became concerned at the potential threat to its southern flank posed by the still substantial Soviet forces in the Ukraine. By late August, he was convinced that Army Group South needed reinforcement to eliminate this threat and ordered Guderian's *Panzergruppe* II into the Ukraine. Guderian made rapid progress, linking up with Kleist on 16 September and trapping the South-Western Front in the vast Kiev pocket, which surrendered 10 days later, with the loss of approximately 665,000 men, 880 tanks and 3700 guns.

▲ GAZ-55 Ambulance
XX Mechanized Corps / 41st Tank Division / Medical Battalion
The GAZ-55 equipped the medical battalions of most tank divisions in 1941.

Specifications	
Crew: 2 (10 capacity)	Height: 2.34m (7ft 8in)
Weight: 2.37 tonnes (2.33 tons)	Engine: 4 cylinder, carb., 4-stroke, sv;
Lengt: 5.43m (17ft 1in)	50hp @ 2800 rpm
Width: 2.04m (6ft 8in)	Speed: 70km/h (43.5mph)

▲ ZiS-6 Parm 1b 6x4 mobile workshop
XX Mechanised Corps / 41st Tank Division / Maintenance Battalion
Many Soviet tank losses were due to breakdowns caused by inadequate holdings of spare parts and poor maintenance. The situation was worsened by the destruction of many support vehicles in the opening stages of *Barbarossa*.

Specifications	
Crew: 1	Height: (Estimated) 2.74m (9ft)
Weight: (Estimated) 6.73 tonnes (6.62 tons)	Engine: ZiS-5, 6 cylinder, 54Kw (73hp)
Length: 6.06m (19ft 11in)	Speed: 55km/h (34mph)
Width: 2.24m (7ft 4in)	

Defence of Moscow

SEPTEMBER–DECEMBER 1941

As it became clear that the Kiev pocket was doomed, Hitler ordered that Leningrad was not to be stormed, but blockaded and starved into surrender in order to free resources for a renewed attack on Moscow.

TO GIVE THE NEW OFFENSIVE a reasonable chance of success before it became bogged down by the autumn rains, both Army Group North and Army Group South had to be stripped of most of their Panzer units. Guderian's command was re-designated Second Panzer Army and launched the drive on Moscow (code-named Operation *Typhoon*) on 30 September while the other two *Panzergruppen* began their attacks two days later.

Both sides were now feeling the effects of three months of fierce combat – the Red Army's massive losses had forced the disbandment of the Mechanized Corps as early as mid-July and in August most of the surviving armour was concentrated in tank brigades with a nominal strength of 93 tanks in a single tank regiment plus a motor rifle battalion. The tank

▶ **Mobile repairs**
AFV maintenance in the depths of a Russian winter posed major problems for both sides. Here the turret is lifted from a BT-5 in a field workshop during the winter of 1941/42.

Specifications

Crew: 1/2, plus gun crew of 4/5	Height: 1.97m (6ft 6in)
Weight: 2.54 tonnes (2.5 tonnes)	Armament: ZiS 57mm (2.2in) AT gun; 1 x
Length: 5.33m (17ft 6in)	7.62mm (0.3in) DT MG
Width: 2.1m (7ft)	

▲ **ZiS-41 tank destroyer**
Trials Unit, Moscow

The ZiS-2 57mm (2.2in) AT gun was mounted on an armoured ZiS-22M halftrack to produce the experimental ZiS-41 tank destroyer. Although the vehicle underwent trials in November 1941, it did not get beyond the prototype stage.

Tank Regiment – Personnel Strength (November 1941)	Officers	NCOs	Other
Headquarters	14	5	4
Heavy Tank Company	7	19	–
Medium Tank Company	13	30	–
Light Tank Company x 2, each	7	16	–
Train Elements	5	12	47

Tank Regiment – Vehicle Strength (November 1941)	Strength
Headquarters:	
T-34	1
Motorcycle	2
Truck	1
Heavy Tank Company:	
KV tank	5
Medium Tank Company:	
T-34 tank	10
Light Tank Company:	2
T-40	10
Train Elements:	
Motorcycle	1
Car	1
Cargo truck	22
Shop truck	6
Tractor	4

regiment had a heavy company with KVs, a company of T-34s and a third company equipped with whatever light tanks were available. By September, combat casualties had forced a reduction in the paper strength of these units to 67 tanks, although very few had that many.

On the other side of the lines, the Panzer divisions were in better shape, but their tanks and other vehicles were in need of major overhauls after covering thousands of kilometres across country or over appalling dirt roads. The infantry divisions (which had virtually no motor vehicles) were exhausted by the epic marches needed to keep up with the rapidly advancing Panzers, but all were buoyed up by the sheer scale of their victories and the thought that Moscow was now within reach.

The *Panzergruppen* quickly broke through the Soviet lines and by 9 October had pulled off two more major encirclements, one between Smolensk and Vyazma and the other around Bryansk. These netted a total of 657,000 prisoners, 1241 AFVs plus 5396 guns and effectively opened the road to Moscow. As early as 6 October, a new factor began to help the Red Army's defence of the capital – the first snows fell. At first these rapidly melted, turning the roads to thick, clinging mud that slowed the momentum of the German advance and increased

the already alarming rate of breakdowns. (Hard-pressed *Luftwaffe* transport units were diverted to drop tow-ropes to supply columns floundering along mud-clogged roads.)

Winter halt

Despite the logistical and mechanical problems they faced, Hoth's *Panzergruppe* IV had captured Kalinin by 14 October, cutting the Moscow–Leningrad highway and the main north–south railway. This unwelcome development for the Soviets sparked off a temporary panic in the capital and it was lucky for

▶ **T-40 BM-8-24 'Katyusha' salvo rocket launcher**
9th 'Dzerzhinsky' NKVD Division / Artillery Regiment
One of the 44 T-40 light tanks that were converted to mount BM-8-24 'Katyusha' salvo rocket launchers in the autumn of 1941.

Specifications	
Crew: 3	Height: 2.12m (6ft 11in)
Weight: 5.6 tonnes (5.5 tons)	Engine: 70kW (52hp) GAZ-202 petrol
Length: 4.43m (13ft 6in)	Speed: 45km/h (28mph)
Width: 2.51m (8ft 3in)	Range: 350km (215 miles)

Stalin that the German airborne forces were unable to exploit the situation after their heavy losses in the assault on Crete.

By mid-November, sharp frosts had frozen the thick mud solid and restored the Panzers' mobility, which allowed them to make a renewed drive on Moscow. During the next two weeks, the Germans came tantalizingly close to taking the city – *Panzerguppen* III and IV swung north of Moscow, breaching the Volga Canal defence line on 28 November, while away to the south, Guderian's Second Panzer Army had taken Stalinogorsk and cut the capital's main railway link with the south. It looked as it a German victory was in the making.

By 4 December, leading German units were within 45km (28 miles) of Moscow when plummeting temperatures finally brought the advance to a halt. It was so cold that guns could not be fired because oiled parts froze solid. Fires had to be lit under vehicles at night to prevent their engines freezing. Very few German units had proper winter clothing and cases of severe frostbite soared, rapidly exceeding the

Snow camouflage tended to be simple and was usually just an overall coat of water-soluble white paint, although once again a minority of tanks sported disruptive camouflage, with the white paint applied in irregular bands or patches. A few vehicles had small red stars on the turret sides and quite a number had various patriotic slogans painted or chalked on hull or turret sides. The slogan on this turrent translates as 'For the Homeland!'.

number of battlefield casualties. Red Army equipment was far less severely affected by the intense cold and deep snow, the virtue of long experience dealing with Arctic-grade winters. The T-34 was fitted with a compressed air starting system that could operate even in the temperatures of -28°C (-19°F) which were not uncommon that winter. The wide tracks of the KV-1 and T-34 resulted in low ground pressure, which allowed them to operate far more easily in powdery, deep snow than German AFVs with their narrower tracks and consequent higher ground pressure.

▲ **Infantry support**

The dire shortages of KV-1s and T-34s during the winter of 1941/42 compelled the Red Army to use even thinly armoured T-40 Model 1940 amphibious light tanks in the infantry support role.

▶ **T-26 Model 1933 light tank**

Western Front / Fifth Army / 20th Tank Brigade

The T-26s, especially older versions such as this, were vulnerable to even the
lightest German AT weapons and suffered heavy losses.

Specifications

Crew: 2	Speed: 45km/h (28mph)
Weight: 5.8 tonnes (5.7 tons)	Range: 360km (224 miles)
Length: 4.29m (14ft 1in)	Radio: N/A
Width: 2.32m (7ft 7in)	Armament: 1 x 45mm (1.8in) Model 38 gun;
Height: 2.04m (6ft 7in)	1 x 7.62mm (0.3in) coaxial DT MG
Engine: 2 x GAZ-202 52+52kW (70+70hp)	

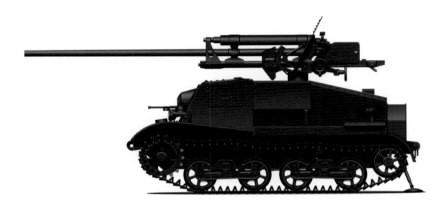

▲ **ZiS-30 tank destroyer**

9th 'Dzerzhinsky' NKVD Division / Anti-tank Battery

Roughly 100 Komsomolyets artillery tractors were converted to ZiS-30 tank
destroyers in 1941 by the installation of the powerful ZiS-2 57mm anti-tank gun
on a shielded limited traverse mounting. These vehicles equipped the anti-tank
batteries of tank brigades taking part in the defence of Moscow in 1941/42, but
very few survived these winter battles.

Specifications

Crew: 5	Width: 1.86m (6ft)
Weight (estimated): 4.5 tonnes (4.43 tons)	Engine: 37kW (50hp) GAZ-M 4-cylinder
Height (estimated): 2.44m (8ft)	Speed: 47km/h (29mph)
Length: 3.45m (11ft 1/2in)	Range: 250km (155miles)

▶ **T-26 Model 1938 light tank**

Fifth Army / 20th Tank Brigade

T-26s that survived the summer battles played an important role in the
defence of Moscow.

Specifications

Crew: 3	Speed: 28km/h (17mph)
Weight: 10.4 tonnes (10.3 tons)	Range: 200km (124 miles)
Length: 4.8m (15ft 8in)	Radio: N/A
Width: 2.39m (7ft 10in)	Armament: 1 x 45mm (1.8in) AT gun;
Height: 2.33m (7ft 8in)	1 x 7.62mm (0.3in) DT MG; additional
Engine: 68kW (91hp) GAZ T-26	7.62mm (0.3in) DT MG ball-mounted into
8-cylinder petrol	turret rear

▾ Medium Tank Battalion (October 1941)

The Red Army's inability to handle the massive mechanized corps effectively became clear in the opening stages of *Barbarossa*. As an initial step, all remaining tanks were concentrated in smaller tank divisions, each with two tank regiments. Each regiment fielded a small HQ, together with a single medium tank battalion and two light tank battalions.

HQ (3 x BA ACs, 1 x T-34)

Heavy Tank Company 1 (10 x KV-1)

Medium Tank Company 2 (10 x T-34)

Medium Tank Company 3 (10 x T-34)

Losses

The overall losses on both sides were staggering. The German casualties may well have totalled 800,000 plus 2300 AFVs. These figures were dwarfed by the enormous Soviet losses – roughly 3,000,000 prisoners, 20,000 AFVs and 25,000 guns. Operation *Barbarossa* was failing, and Germany was now trapped into fighting a war on several fronts. The situation was worsened by Hitler who, on hearing of the Japanese attack on Pearl Harbor, chose to declare war on the United States, adding its enormous potential strength to Germany's existing enemies.

 Individual vehicle and unit tactical markings were generally applied in white or yellow to the standard dark green summer camouflage scheme. In winter, they were normally replaced with red markings.

▲ **T-34 Model 1941 medium tank**

Forty-Third Army / 24th Tank Brigade

A T-34 Model 1941 in winter camouflage. The Model 1941 was a marked advance on the Model 1940 – mechanical reliability, armament and armour were all significantly improved.

Specifications

Crew: 4	Speed (road): 53km/h (33mph)
Weight: 26.5 tonnes (26.2 tons)	Range: 400km (250 miles)
Length: 5.92m (19ft 5in)	Radio: N/A
Width: 3.00m (9ft 8in)	Armament: 1 x 76mm (3in) F-34 gun;
Height: 2.44m (8ft)	2 x 7.62mm (0.3in) DT MGs (bow and coaxial)
Engine: 373kW (500hp) V-2-34 V-12 cylinder diesel	

Specifications

Crew: 5	Speed: 35km/h (22mph)
Weight: 45 tonnes (44.3 tons)	Range: 335km (208 miles)
Length: 6.75m (22ft 2in)	Radio: N/A
Width: 3.32m (10ft 10in)	Armament: 1 x 76mm (3in) F-32 gun;
Height: 2.71m (8ft 9in)	3 x 7.62mm (0.3in) DT MGs
Engine: 450kW (600hp) V-2 12-cylinder diesel	

▲ **KV-1 Model 1940**

Sixteenth Army / 4th Tank Brigade

A KV-1 Model 1940 – with armour up to 75mm (2.9in) thick, it proved almost impervious to German tank and AT guns in the first few months of *Barbarossa* – 88mm (3.5in) Flak guns or medium artillery frequently had to be deployed to guarantee a kill at anything other than suicidally short ranges.

The Moscow counter-offensives
DECEMBER 1941 – MARCH 1942

As the German advance ground to a halt in early December, the Soviet war machine was beginning to show signs of recovery.

DESPITE MASSIVE SOVIET casualties, a ruthless mobilization programme had brought the Red Army's strength up to 4,196,000 men. However, this measure resulted in a further reduction in industrial manpower, which had already been hit by the loss of population (35,000,000) in territories overrun by Axis forces. Coupled with the disruption caused by the evacuation of war industries, the newly raised and sketchily trained military forces suffered from a dire shortage of all types of weaponry, ranging from tanks to small arms.

In this crisis, there was no chance to rebuild the grandiose mechanized corps with their official tank strengths of over 1000 tanks apiece – the tanks simply did not exist and most surviving commanders were too inexperienced to cope with anything other than the simplest units. The small tank brigades that had replaced all larger formations from August 1941 shrank steadily – in December, they were reduced to 46 tanks apiece, with a further reduction to 42 in January 1942 and a final cut to 27 tanks in February 1942. (These were all 'official strengths' – in practice, many brigades were significantly weaker.)

Winter attack

By 5 December 1941, average temperatures around Moscow had dropped to -12°C (-10°F) and the *Wehrmacht* lay horribly exposed at the end of tenuous

▲ **First winter offensive**
Whitewashed T-34/76 Model 1941 tanks move through the town of Izyum near Kharkov, January 1942.

supply lines, with frostbite casualties climbing to 100,000 during the month. It was the ideal time for a Soviet counterattack and the Red Army had managed to assemble a force totalling 8 tank brigades, 15 rifle divisions and 3 cavalry divisions, many of which had been transferred from the Far East. Stalin was prepared to risk weakening his forces in Siberia and Mongolia as intelligence reports indicated that Japanese attention was indeed focused on South-East Asia and the Pacific.

His innate caution, however, led him to keep substantial formations in the Far East, including roughly 2000 of the 4500 operational AFVs left in the Red Army.

Shortages

Shortages of tanks and artillery, combined with sheer inexperience, led to heavy Soviet casualties, but the initial counterattacks succeeded in pushing back Army Group Centre and eliminating the immediate threat to Moscow. Buoyed up by this success, Stalin started to become over-confident. On 17 December, he ordered more attacks:

■ The Leningrad, Volkhov and North-West Fronts were to break the siege of Leningrad.
■ An offensive by Fourth Shock Army was to split Army Groups North and Centre and then retake Smolensk.

▲ **T-40 Model 1940 Amphibious Light Tank**

Western Front / Sixteenth Army / 4th Tank Brigade

Despite steadily declining numbers of combat-worthy Soviet AFVs in the winter of 1941/42, Stalin threw the bulk of the Red Army's surviving tanks into a series of offensives. T-40s were highly vulnerable to even the lightest German AT weapons and suffered heavy losses in these actions.

Specifications

Crew: 3	Speed: 45km/h (28mph)
Weight: 5.6 tonnes (5.5 tons)	Range: 350km (215 miles)
Length: 4.43m (13ft 6in)	Radio: N/A
Width: 2.51m (8ft 3in)	Armament: 1 x 12.7mm (0.5in) DShK MG plus
Height: 2.12m (6ft 11in)	1 x 7.62mm (0.3in) DT MG
Engine: 70kW (52hp) GAZ-202 petrol engine	

Specifications

Crew: 3	Speed: 72km/h (44mph)
Weight: 11.5 tonnes (11 tons)	Range: 200km (124 miles)
Length: 5.58m (18ft 3in)	Radio: 71-TK-1
Width: 2.23m (7ft 3in)	Armament: 1 x 45mm (1.8in) Model 1932 gun;
Height: 2.25m (7ft 5in)	1 x 7.62mm (0.3in) coaxial DT MG
Engine: 298kW (400hp) Model M-5	

▲ **BT-5TU Model 1934 Fast Tank**

Western Front / Thirtieth Army / 21st Tank Brigade

A BT-5TU command tank with its prominent 'clothes line' radio aerial that made such vehicles a prime target for German AT guns.

ARMIES, KALININ FRONT	Tank and Mechanized Units
Twenty-Ninth	8 Tank Bde
Thirtieth	58 Tank Div
	107 Motorized Rgt
	21 Tank Bde
	2, 11 Motorcycle Rgt
Front HQ	46 Motorcycle Rgt

ARMIES, WESTERN FRONT	Tank and Mechanized Units
Fifth	18, 19, 20, 22, 25 Tank Bde,
	27 STB, 36 Motorcycle Rgt
Sixteenth	4, 27, 28 Tank Bde
	22 Armoured Train Btn
Thirty-Third	5 Tank Bde
Forty-Third	9, 17, 24 Tank Bde
	31 STB
Front HQ	23, 26 Tank Bde

ARMIES, BRYANSK FRONT	Tank and Mechanized Units
Third	42, 121, 133 Tank Bde
Thirteenth	141, 150 Tank Bde
	38 Motorcycle Rgt
Fiftieth	108 Tank Div
	5, 11, 32 Tank Bdes

Jan 1942	TD	Bgde	Rifle	Mtcl	STB	Train
Kalinin Front	1	2	1	3	–	–
Western Front	–	14	–	1	2	1
Bryansky Front	1	7	–	1	–	–

- An amphibious operation to seize the Kerch Peninsula in the Crimea as a prelude to raising the Axis siege of Sevastopol.

To say the least, these were highly ambitious objectives, but on 5 January Stalin went further, announcing to a horrified meeting of *Stavka* (the Soviet High Command) that the current operations were to be supplemented by a general offensive from the Baltic to the Black Sea with the objectives of decisively defeating Army Group North, destroying Army Group Centre, recapturing the Donbass and the Crimea. Zhukov protested that the necessary resources were not there, but he was overruled.

Throughout the rest of January and February, the offensive was maintained at the cost of appalling casualties, pushing Axis forces back between 80km (50 miles) and 300km (186 miles), despite hopelessly inadequate numbers of tanks (including the first Lend-Lease Matildas and Valentines.)

▲ KV-1 Model 1941

Kalinin Front / Third Shock Army / 146th Tank Battalion

By the beginning of 1942, the Red Army's tank strength had fallen to dangerously low levels – even the official establishment of the tank brigade had dropped to five KV-1s. This one has had winter camouflage applied.

Specifications

Crew: 5

Weight: 45 tonnes (44.3 tons)

Length: 6.75m (22ft 2in)

Width: 3.32m (10ft 10in)

Height: 2.71m (8ft 9in)

Engine: 450kW (600hp) V-2 12-cylinder diesel

Speed: 35km/h (22mph)

Range: 335km (208 miles)

Radio: N/A

Armament: 1 x 76mm (3in) F-32 gun;

3 x 7.62mm (0.3in) DT MGs

Rzhev–Vyaz'ma offensive
JANUARY–APRIL 1942

The Rzhev-Vyaz'ma offensive was intended to be the blow that would destroy Army Group Centre, building on earlier Soviet progress in gaining ground towards Rzhev.

THE MAIN OPERATION was launched on 8 January with pincer attacks by the Western and Kalinin Fronts, and threatened the Warsaw–Moscow highway within a few days. This was one of the few all-weather roads in the region and was vital since it formed the Fourth Panzer Army's *Rollbahn* (main supply route). By 19 January, Soviet forces had cut this route and were preparing for the next stage in the operation.

While the Western and Kalinin Fronts were pushing their armoured forces to the limit, it was clear, even to Stalin, that these were not strong enough to achieve decisive results. It was decided to drop a full parachute corps – IV Airborne Corps – south of Vyaz'ma to link up with Soviet partisans and

▶ **Zhukov with staff**
Marshal Georgi Zhukov (1896–1974) was the archetypal Red Army commander, who rose from serving as a trooper in a Tsarist cavalry regiment in World War I to become a Marshal of the Soviet Union. One of the great commanders of World War II, he was one of the most decorated heroes in the history of both Russia and the Soviet Union.

▲ **BT-5 Model 1934 Fast Tank**

Western Front / Sixteenth Army / 33rd Tank Brigade
Large numbers of thinly armoured BT-5s were among the obsolescent AFVs committed to the Soviet offensives in January and February 1942.

Specifications	
Crew: 3	Speed: 72km/h (44mph)
Weight: 11.5 tonnes (11 tons)	Range: 200km (124 miles)
Length: 5.58m (18ft 3in)	Radio: N/A
Width: 2.23m (7ft 3in)	Armament: 1 x 45mm (1.8in) Model 1932 gun;
Height: 2.25m (7ft 5in)	1 x 7.62mm (0.3in) coaxial DT MG
Engine: 298kW (400hp) Model M-5	

seal off the Rzhev–Vyaz'ma salient, trapping the German Ninth Army and Fourth Panzer Army.

Such airborne operations were always highly risky, even with the benefit of complete air superiority, and in early 1942 it was the *Luftwaffe* that ruled the skies, threatening to massacre the slow, unwieldy Soviet transport aircraft.

Airborne operations

Two battalions from 21st Parachute Brigade and 250th Air Assault Regiment formed the first wave of this part of the operation, but had to be dropped over a period of several days (18–22 January). After I Guards Cavalry Corps cut the Warsaw-Moscow

highway on 27 January, the most that could be done was to drop 8th Airborne Brigade in support – only a third of the intended force. Ironically this was not due to the *Luftwaffe,* but to the diversion of Soviet aircraft to supply Red Army formations, notably Thirty-Ninth Army, which had been cut off by German counter-attacks.

The limited airborne forces that could be deployed were too weak to be effective – immense efforts reopened supply routes to Ninth Army and Fourth Panzer Army. Well-executed German counter-attacks were able to turn the tables, eliminating the threat from 8th Airborne Brigade and trapping a number of other Soviet formations (the final tally included the

Battalion HQ (1 x T-34, 2 x motorcycles, 1 x truck)

Heavy Tank Company (5 x KV1)

Medium Tank Company (10 x T-34)

1 Light Tank Company (10 x T-40)

1 Light Tank Company (10 x T-40)

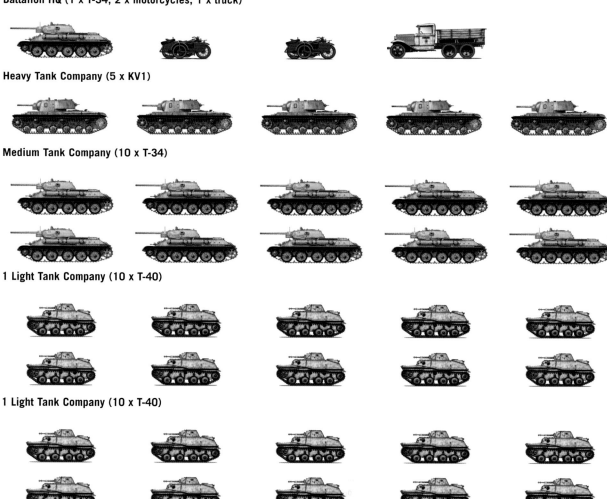

Twenty-Second, Twenty-Ninth and Thirty-Ninth Armies) until the front became a complex mass of isolated pockets separated by wide gaps that neither side had the strength to exploit. (The encircled Red Army forces were not finally eliminated until July 1942, when Army Group Centre was able to launch a new offensive, Operation Seydlitz, which netted 50,000 prisoners in addition to capturing 230 tanks and 760 guns.)

Results

As the Soviet operation wound down, it was possible to make some assessment of the results. Army Group Centre had been mauled and had been pushed back by between 80km (50 miles) and 250km (150 miles), but had inflicted over 750,000 casualties, three to four times its own losses. Soviet forces had also lost 957 tanks, almost 7300 guns and 550 aircraft.

Several factors contributed to the Red Army's failure to achieve a decisive victory, including the dire equipment shortages following the loss of so much materiel in the summer and autumn battle, the crisis in weapons production caused by the evacuation of much of the Soviet arms industry to the Urals, and the inexperience – coupled with poor, sometimes non-existent training – which led to units launching costly and unneccessary frontal attacks on well-fortified German positions.

Train (1 x motorcycle, 1 x car, 22 x cargo trucks, 6 x workshop vehicles, 4 x tractors)

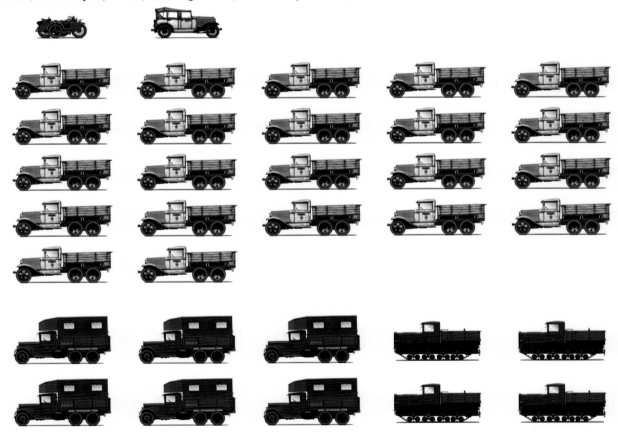

◢ Separate Tank Battalion (1942)

Separate tank battalions (STBs) began to be formed in late 1941, and 100 such units were raised within a few months. They were intended to operate in the infantry support role, freeing the tank brigades for breakthrough and exploitation operations. In practice, logistical support proved difficult due to the mix of tank types, while operational planning was complicated by their differing mobility.

▶ **M3A5 medium tank (early production model)**
Bryansk Front / XXIII Tank Corps / 114th Tank Brigade
The first M3 Lee medium tanks were delivered to the Red Army in late 1941. They were unpopular due to their high silhouette and vulnerability – their seven-man crews soon dubbed them 'Coffins for Seven Brothers'.

Specifications
Crew: 7	Speed: 29km/h (18mph)
Weight: 29.1 tonnes (32.1tons)	Radio: N/A
Length: 5.64m (18.5ft)	Armour: 57–12mm (2.24–0.47in)
Width: 2.72m (8.9ft)	Armament: 1 x 75mm (2.9in) main
Height: 3.12m (10.24ft)	gun; 1 x 37mm (1.5in) gun;
Engine: 253kW (340hp) General	3 x 7.62mm (0.3in) MGs
Motors 6046 12-cylinder diesel	

Specifications
Crew: 1	Height: 2.16m (7ft 1in)
Weight: 3.1 tonnes (3.42 tons)	Engine: 54/57kW (73/76hp) ZIS-5/ZIS-5M
Length: 6.1m (20ft)	Speed: 60km/h (37.3mph)
Width: 2.25m (7ft 4.5⁵in)	

▲ **ZiS-5V 4x2 3-ton truck**
Bryansk Front / Twenty-First Army / 10th Tank Brigade / AA Battery
In common with many other Soviet trucks, the ZiS-5 was modified soon after the German invasion to simplify production, the most obvious change being the adoption of a wooden cab. This vehicle serving with an AA battery has been fitted with a 12.7mm (0.5in) DShK HMG.

▶ **STZ-5 Medium Tractor**
Bryansk Front / Twenty-First Army / 1st Motorized Rifle Brigade / Artillery Battalion
More than 10,000 STZ-5 medium tractors were produced for the Red Army. The type was one of the few tracked artillery tractors specifically designed for the role – the vast majority of were modified agricultural machines.

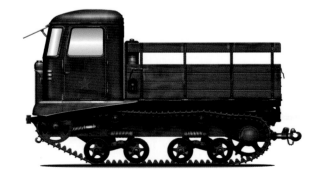

Specifications
Crew: 1	Engine: 69.68Kw (52hp) 1MA 4-cylinder petrol
Weight: 5.84 tonnes (5.75 tons)	Range: not known
Length: 4.15m (13ft 7in)	Radio: n/a
Height: 2.36m (8ft 9in)	

▶ **M3 light tank**

Bryansk Front / XXIV Tank Corps / 130th Tank Brigade

A small number of US M3 light tanks were dispatched from British stocks to the Red Army in 1941. Most of these were lost in the abortive 'Timoshenko Offensive' and the subsequent German advances in the summer of 1942.

Specifications
Crew: 4

Weight: 14.7 tonnes (14.4 tons)

Length: 4.45m (14ft 10in)

Width: 2.22m (7ft 4in)

Height: 2.30m (7ft 7in)

Engine: 185kW (250hp) Continental W-670
7-cylinder radial petrol

Speed: 58km/h (36mph)

Range: 113km (70miles)

Armament: 1 x 37mm (1.5in) gun;
2 x 7.62mm (0.3in) Browning MGs

◀ **T-60 BM-8-24 'Katyusha' salvo rocket launcher**

Bryansk Front / XIII Tank Corps / 309th Guards / Mortar Battalion

As the supply of T-34s improved, they began to supplant the ineffective T-60s in tank battalions. Many surplus T-60 hulls were then converted to launchers for 82mm (3.22in) M-8 rockets.

Specifications
Crew: 2

Weight: 5.8 tonnes (5.7 tons)

Length: 4.1m (13ft 5in)

Width: 2.46m (8ft 1in)

Height: 2.0m (6ft 6in)

Engine: 2 x GAZ-202 52+52kW (70+70hp)

Speed: 45km/h (28mph)

Range: 450km (280 miles)

Radio: N/A

Armament: 1 x 82mm (3.22in) rocket launcher

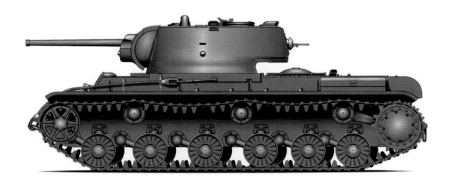

▲ **KV-1 Model 1941**

South-Western Front / Twenty-Eighth Army / 90th Tank Brigade

As large-scale production began in tank factories evacuated from Western Russia in 1941, the strength of tank formations began to rise. In March 1942, new tank corps began to form, each with an official strength of 20 KV-1s.

Specifications
Crew: 5

Weight: 45 tonnes (44.3 tons)

Length: 6.75m (22ft 2in)

Width: 3.32m (10ft 10in)

Height: 2.71m (8ft 9in)

Engine: 450kW (600hp) V-2 12-cyliinder diesel

Speed: 35km/h (22mph)

Range: 335km (208 miles)

Radio: N/A

Armament: 1 x 76mm (3in) F-32 gun;
3 x 7.62mm (0.3in) DT MGs

Disaster at Kharkov
MAY 1942

The spring thaws of 1942 gave both sides a chance to take stock and plan their summer campaigns. Stalin turned his attention to the south and ordered Marshal Timoshenko to prepare an attack to recapture Kharkov and disrupt German preparations for their own offensive.

THESE OBJECTIVES were ambitious enough, but Timonshenko was soon expanding them to include the recapture of a great swathe of territory as far west as the Dnieper – a total advance of roughly 250km (155 miles). German intelligence was aware of the build-up of Soviet forces, coming up with an accurate estimate of 620,000 men, 1300 AFVs, 10,000 guns and mortars, supported by 926 aircraft. (The majority of the tanks were concentrated in new tank corps, each with 20 KV-1s, 40 T-34s and

Ninth Army (May 1942)	KV-1	T-34	T-60	Pz III
12th Tank Battalion	2	8	0	0
15th Tank Battalion	1	2	5	0
121st Tank Battalion	3	8	20	3

40 light tanks of various types. Shortly before the offensive, many of these corps were strengthened and grouped into tank armies, which were supposed to have 200–300 tanks each.)

▲ **Matildas at Kharkov**
While the British Matilda was out-classed by later Soviet tanks, surviving vehicles remained in service in the infantry support role until 1944/45.

The Soviet offensive opened on 12 May, with a thrust by South-Western Front from Volchansk to the north of Kharkov, while the Southern Front attacked from the Barvenkovo Salient to the south of the city. The operation was spearheaded by 15 of the Red Army's 20 operational tank brigades, whose initial objective was to envelop Kharkov before driving westwards to the Dnieper. Timoshenko achieved initial successes by sheer weight of numbers, but after making advances averaging 25km (15.5 miles) in the first 48 hours, he was unable to maintain the tempo of the offensive.

One factor in delaying the Soviet progress was a plethora of local counterattacks by Axis forces, backed up by repeated *Luftwaffe* air strikes. However, the Red Army's poor logistical support and planning also played a part, as was apparent on 15 May, when an opportunity to achieve a decisive breakthrough was missed because XXI and XXIII Tank Corps were 25km (15.5 miles) behind the frontline.

They took a further 48 hours to assemble and move up, by which time German reinforcements had arrived to stabilize the threatened sector and the opportunity was lost.

▲ Infantry Tank Mark II 'Matilda'

South-Western Front / Thirty-Eighth Army / XXII Tank Corps / 13th Tank Brigade

Matildas were among the first British tanks to be sent to Russia in 1941 under the Lend-Lease programme. A total of 1084 Matildas were shipped, of which 252 were lost in transit on the Arctic convoys.

Specifications

Crew: 4	Engine: Two petrol 6-cylinder AEC engines,
Weight: 26.9 tonnes (29.7 tons)	64.8kW (87bhp)
Length: 5.61m (18ft 5in)	Speed: 24km/h (15mph)
Width: 2.59m (8ft 6in)	Range: 257km (160 miles)
Height: 2.5m (8ft 3in)	Armament: 1 x 40mm (1.57in) gun;
	1 x 7.92mm (0.31in) Besa MG

▶ Universal Carrier Mark I

Bryansk Front / XVI Tank Corps / 107th Tank Brigade

An initial consignment of 330 Universal Carriers arrived in Soviet ports during the autumn of 1941, with deliveries totalling over 2500 vehicles by 1945. This example retains its Boys AT rifle, although the Bren Gun in the rear compartment has been replaced with a DP MG.

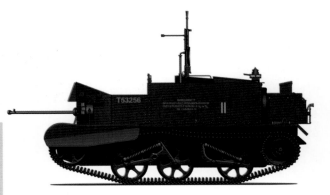

Specifications

Crew: 2/3	Speed: 48km/h (30mph)
Weight: 3.81 tonnes (3.75 tons)	Range: 250km (150miles)
Length: 3.65m (12ft)	Radio: N/A
Width: 1.92m (6ft 4in)	Armament: 1 x Boys AT rifle, plus 1 x 7.62mm
Height: 1.57m (5ft 2in)	(0.3in) Degtyarev DP MG
Engine: 85kW (85hp) Ford V-8 petrol	

Nonetheless, Timoshenko's forces were still advancing on 17 May when Kleist's Army Group A (First Panzer Army and Seventeenth Army) launched a devastating counter-offensive against the southern flank of the Barvenkovo Salient. Over the next few days, Stalin rejected increasingly urgent requests from Timoshenko to call off the offensive and a bizarre situation developed as Soviet armour continued to advance westwards as Kleist's Panzers were cutting through the neck of the salient.

By the time that Timoshenko received belated authorization to retreat, it was too late – the salient was sealed off on 23 May and during the next six days the bulk of the trapped units were virtually wiped out. Red Army losses probably totalled 208,000 men – 22 rifle divisions, 7 cavalry divisions and 15 tank brigades were destroyed. Equipment losses were equally severe – some 1200 tanks, 1600 guns, 3200 mortars and 540 aircraft.

Inexperience and fear

The disaster at Kharkov vividly demonstrated the fragility of the Red Army at this stage of the war. Its ranks were full of barely trained conscripts and the officer corps, emasculated by the purges, was struggling to learn the basics of armoured warfare while campaigning against a sophisticated enemy.

All ranks went in fear of the NKVD – whose malign influence was personified by Lev Mekhlis, the *Stavka* representative to the Crimean Front, who was also Head of the Main Political Administration of the Red Army. He was an arrogant bully who quarrelled with General Kozlov, the Front commander, and engineered the dismissal of his highly competent chief of staff, the future Marshal Tolbukhin.

Mekhlis was largely responsible for the Soviet failure to attack von Manstein's force besieging Sevastopol when it was at its most vulnerable in early 1942 and, when the Germans counter-attacked on

▶ **T-60 Model 1941**

South-Western Front / Twenty-Eighth Army / 90th Tank Brigade, Kharkov,
May 1942

This immobilized and abandoned T-60 has distinctive air recognition markings on the turret hatch. Such markings were temporarily applied for specific operations to minimize the risk from friendly fire.

Specifications

Crew: 2	Speed: 45km/h (28mph)
Weight: 5.8 tonnes (5.7 tons)	Range: 450km (280 miles)
Length: 4.1m (13ft 5in)	Radio: N/A
Width: 2.46m (8ft 1in)	Armament: 1 x 20mm (0.79in) TNSh gun;
Height: 1.89m (6ft 2in)	1 x 7.62mm (0.3in) coaxial DT MG
Engine: 2 x GAZ-202 52+52kW (70+70hp)	

▶ **T-60 Model 1942**

South-Western Front / Fifth Army / I Tank Corps

The T-60 Model 1942 was up-armoured in an attempt to improve its battlefield survivability. Disc pattern road wheels replaced the spoked type fitted to the Model 1941.

Specifications

Crew: 2	Speed: 45km/h (28mph)
Weight: 5.8 tonnes (5.7 tons)	Range: 450km (280 miles)
Length: 4.1m (13ft 5in)	Radio: N/A
Width: 2.46m (8ft 1in)	Armament: 1 x 20mm (0.79in) TNSh gun;
Height: 1.89m (6ft 2in)	1 x 7.62mm (0.3in) coaxial DT MG
Engine: 2 x GAZ-202 52+52kW (70+70hp)	

8 May, his incompetence contributed to the destruction of the Crimean Front in barely 10 days.

Uncoordinated response

As at Kharkov, there was little coordination between the Soviet tank brigades, whose 350 AFVs were committed to action piecemeal, negating their numerical superiority over the sole German armoured formation, the under-strength 22nd Panzer Division, which was largely equipped with obsolescent Panzer 38(t)s.

Once again, Soviet losses were staggering – three armies (Forty-Fourth, Forty-Seventh and Fifty-First) totalling 21 divisions had been broken and von Manstein's forces had taken 170,000 prisoners, as well as capturing 258 tanks and over 1100 guns.

▲ KV-1 Model 1941

South-Western Front / Twenty-First Army / 10th Tank Brigade

Although Soviet tank production dramatically increased in the first half of 1942, this was not matched by comparable improvements in strategic or tactical skill. A high proportion of the new Red Army armoured formations were destroyed in Timoshenko's over-ambitious Kharkov offensive in May 1942.

Specifications	
Crew: 5	Speed: 35km/h (22mph)
Weight: 45 tonnes (44.3 tons)	Range: 335km (208 miles)
Length: 6.75m (22ft 2in)	Radio: N/A
Width: 3.32m (10ft 10in)	Armament: 1 x 76mm (3in) F-32 gun;
Height: 2.71m (8ft 9in)	3 x 7.62mm (0.3in) DT MGs
Engine: 450kW (600hp) 12-cylinder V-2 diesel	

Specifications	
Crew: 4	GMC 6004 diesel
Weight: 16 tonnes (17.6 tonnes)	Speed: 24km/h (15mph)
Length: 5.4m (17ft 9in)	Range: 145km (90 miles)
Width: 2.6m (8ft 8in)	Armament: 1 x 40mm (1.57in) gun;
Height: 2.2m (7ft 6in)	1 x 7.92mm (0.31in) Besa MG
Engine: 131–210hp (97–157kW)	

▲ Infantry Tank Mark III, Valentine Mark V

South-Western Front / Sixth Army / XXI Tank Corps / 64th Tank Brigade

The Valentine was regarded by the Red Army as the best British tank supplied under Lend-Lease. A total of 3782 Valentines of all Marks were shipped to Soviet Russia between 1941 and 1945, of which 320 were lost en route.

Retreat to the Don

In April 1942, Hitler had chosen to make his main effort in the south with the aim of taking Stalingrad and driving deep into the Caucasus to seize the oilfields of Maikop, Grozny and Baku.

TIMOSHENKO'S OFFENSIVE at Kharkov had disrupted preparations for the offensive, but the sheer scale of the Soviet disaster (almost 75 per cent of the Red Army's tanks were destroyed) meant that there was very little left to oppose the Panzers as they struck deep into southern Russia on 28 June.

By 5 July, Hoth's Fourth Panzer Army had taken Voronezh, reinforcing Stalin's instinctive belief that Moscow was still the primary German objective. While *Stavka* concentrated on directing reserves to counter the illusory threat to Moscow, von Paulus' Sixth Army was making for Stalingrad and Kleist's First Panzer Army was well on its way to the oilfields of the Caucasus.

The psychological impact of these events was sharpened by the first indications that the *Panzerwaffe* was regaining lost ground in the gun/armour race. After the triumphant advances of 1941 ground to a halt in the winter snows, German planners realized that radical measures were needed to meet the threat of the T-34 and KV-1. As a first step, production of the 50mm (2in) L/60 and its tungsten-cored ammunition was stepped up to ensure that the Panzer III stood some chance against these opponents. Frantic efforts also went into replacing the 75mm (2.9in) L/24 of the Panzer IV with a long-

SW FRONT					
Tank Brigades	KV1	T-34	M3 Light	T-60	Total
6th Gds	5	7	–	16	28
65th	24	–	–	23	47
90th	7	3	15	15	40
Total	36	10	15	54	115

NINTH ARMY						
Tank Brigades	T-34	BT5/T-26	T-60	Matilda	Valentine	Total
12th	2	–	–	–	–	2
71st STB	–	20	24	2	5	51
132nd STB	3	–	3	1	4	11
Total	5	20	27	3	9	64

barrelled L/43 version, but this took time and it was mid-1942 before the first deliveries were made to front-line units. At the same time, work was in hand to rearm the StuG III with the L/43 and up-gunned versions were produced alongside the new Panzer IVs.

New armoured tactics

At the end of June, General Fedorenko, the head of the Red Army's armoured force, issued a directive on the principles for its future employment. Whilst

▶ **M3A5 medium tank (late production vehicle)**

Voronezh Front / Thirty-Eighth Army / 192nd Tank Brigade

This late production M3A5 has a long-barrelled M3 75mm (2.9in) gun. Both the gun and the turret armament have early stabilization systems fitted to improve accuracy when firing on the move.

Specifications

Crew: 7

Weight: 29.1 tonnes
(32.1 tons)

Length: 5.64m (18.5ft)

Width: 2.72m (8.9ft)

Height: 3.12m (10.24ft)

Engine: 254kW (340hp) General
Motors 6046 12-cylinder diesel

Speed: 29km/h (18mph)

Range: 193km (120 miles)

Armour: 57–12mm (2.2–0.47in)

Armament: 1 x 75mm (2.9in)
main gun; 1 x 37mm (1.5in)
gun; 3 x 7.62mm (0.3in) MGs

hardly original, they represented a willingness to learn from German practice, calling for the use of armour *en masse* against strategic targets. There was a new emphasis on the importance of surprise, the exploitation of favourable terrain and a call for logistical support capable of sustaining prolonged advances. For the time being, these were little more than hopes for the future – the pressing issue was whether the Red Army could survive long enough to put them into practice.

As the Germans advanced, a few of the remaining Soviet tank units fought effective delaying actions, such as that at the River Resseta in July, where the 11th and 19th Panzer Divisions had to tackle well dug-in AT guns while fending off repeated counterattacks directed against their flanks by small groups of T-34s.

However, across most of the vast front, the impression was one of the Red Army almost on the point of collapse. The First Tank Army and Sixty-Second Army were pinned against the Don in a classic double envelopment by Paulus' Sixth Army. Both the Stalingrad Front and the Southern Front temporarily collapsed, with the loss of 350,000 men and over 2000 AFVs.

Premature triumphalism

On 20 July, Hitler joyously announced 'The Russian is finished!' and even the commander of the

Thirty-Eighth Army (April 1942)						
Tank Brigades	KV1	T-34	T-60	Matilda	Valentine	Total
3rd	1	2	4	0	0	7
13th	0	0	0	0	1	1
36th	5	1	13	1	9	29
133rd	0	0	0	0	0	0
156th	2	0	0	0	0	2
159th	0	0	20	0	28	48
168th	3	10	17	0	0	30
92nd STB	7	0	7	0	0	14
Total	18	13	61	1	38	131

Oberkommando des Heeres (Army High Command; OKH), the cautious, scholarly General Halder, agreed. 'I must admit, it looks like it.' Such impressions were not confined to the high command – a Panzer NCO commented that the situation on the ground was different than in 1941. 'It's more like Poland. The Russians aren't nearly so thick on the ground. They fire their guns like madmen, but they don't hurt us.'

Order 227

Stalin was certainly conscious that the string of defeats and a seemingly unstoppable German advance had seriously affected morale – on 28 July, he issued Order No. 227, which instructed commanders

▲ **ZiS-6-BZ Fuel Tanker**

Voronezh Front / XVIII Tank Corps / 180th Tank Brigade / Transport Company

The Red Army's supply columns suffered heavy losses throughout much of 1942, both from air attacks and the rapid German advances to the Don and the Caucasus.

Specifications

Crew: 1

Weight: 4.23 tonnes (4.66 tons)

Length: 6.06m (19.9ft)

Width: 2.23m (7.33ft)

Height: 2.16m (7ft 1in)

Engine: 54kW (73hp) 6-cylinder

Speed: 55km/h (34mph)

to 'decisively eradicate retreat attitude in the troops' and to 'remove from office and send to *Stavka* for court-martial those army commanders who allowed their troops to retreat without authorization'.

Each Front was instructed to form penal battalions and companies for the punishment of offenders and create well-armed guard units (*zagradotryads*), deploying them in the rear of unreliable divisions

with power to execute 'panic-mongers and cowards' on the spot. An estimated 13,500 Soviet troops were executed in the three months following Stalin's order, while the number of penal companies grew until there were 1049 in the Red Army as a whole. The overall total of those sentenced to often fatal service in penal units throughout the war may well have exceeded 400,000.

▲ **KV-1 Model 1942**

Voronezh Front / XVIII Tank Corps / 180th Tank Brigade

Following the loss of 1200 tanks in the abortive Kharkov offensive, Soviet armour was in no condition to do more than fight delaying actions in the summer and autumn of 1942.

Specifications

Crew: 5	Speed: 35km/h (22mph)
Weight: 45 tonnes (44.3 tons)	Range: 335km (208 miles)
Length: 6.75m (22ft 2in)	Radio: N/A
Width: 3.32m (10ft 10in)	Armament: 1 x 76mm (3in) F-32 gun;
Height: 2.71m (8ft 9in)	3 x 7.62mm (0.3in) DT MGs
Engine: 450kW (600hp) 12-cylinder diesel Model V-2	

Specifications

Crew: 4	Speed (road): 53km/h (33mph)
Weight: 26.5 tonnes (26.2 tons)	Range: 400km (250 miles)
Length: 5.92m (19ft 5in)	Radio: N/A
Width: 3.0m (9ft 8in)	Armament: 1 x 76mm (3in) F-34 gun;
Height: 2.44m (8ft)	2 x 7.62mm (0.3in) DT MGs (bow and coaxial)
Engine: 373kW (500hp) V-2-34 V-12 diesel	

▲ **T-34 Model 1942**

Voronezh Front / XVIII Tank Corps / 181st Tank Brigade

The T-34 Model 1942 was essentially the same as the Model 1941, but incorporated numerous small changes to simplify production.

Specifications

Crew: 1	Height: 2.17m (7.12ft)
Weight: 5.25 tonnes (5.79 tons)	Engine: 57kW (76hp) ZiS-5m 6-cylinder
Length: 6.09m (20ft)	Speed: 45km/h (28mph)
Width: 2.36m (7.74ft)	Range: 500km (311miles)

▲ **ZiS-42M 2½-ton cargo halftrack**

Voronezh Front / Thirty-Eighth Army / 192nd Tank Brigade / Supply Company

Roughly 5000 ZiS-42M halftracks were produced between 1942 and 1945, although Lend-Lease US halftracks were much preferred for their armour protection and the superior cross-country capability conferred by their powered front axles.

Defending Stalingrad and Caucasus
JUNE–NOVEMBER 1942

Despite Stalin's orders forbidding retreat and surrender, the Germans continued their advance as the *Fall Blau* (Case Blue) offensive ground its way towards south-east Russia.

THE SHEER SCALE of the advance soon began to cause problems for the Germans as the Panzers outran their supply lines. Hitler's interference had also delayed the advance. The Fourth Panzer Army had been temporarily diverted from its assigned role of spearheading the advance on Stalingrad to 'assist the early passage of the lower Don'.

Logistical problems were causing far more delay to the First Panzer Army than the shaky Soviet defence, and these were compounded by the arrival of the Fourth Panzer Army, which created a monumental traffic jam at the Don crossings. In Hoth's absence, the advance on Stalingrad slowed, allowing the Soviets just enough time to reinforce the city's garrison before the Germans arrived in August. The Sixty-Second Army defending Stalingrad had 54,000 men, 900 guns and 110 tanks. Thus, instead of taking a largely undefended city, more and more

German forces were sucked into fierce street fighting, in which their rate of advance slowed to no more than a few hundred metres a day.

As the German Sixth Army and Fourth Panzer Army became ever more deeply committed to fighting in Stalingrad itself, responsibility for protection of their long, vulnerable flanks had to be assigned to comparatively weak and ill-equipped satellite armies. The Eighth Italian Army and Third Rumanian Army held a long sector of front north-

XXII TANK CORPS (July 1942)	T-34	T-60	T-70	Total
173rd TK Bde	32	13	21	66
176th TK Bde	32	0	16	48
182nd TK Bde	32	13	21	66
Total	96	26	58	180

SOUTH-EASTERN FRONT – operational tanks (Aug 1942)				
Sixty-Fourth Army, XIII Tank Corps	Registered	Operable	In Repair	Lost
6th Gd Bde				
T-34	44	13	17	14
13th Tank Bde				
T-34	44	11	12	21
254th Tank Bde				
T-34	32	6	15	11
T-70	16	4	7	5
133rd Tank Bde				
KV-1	40	38	2	0
Total Corps	136	34	51	51

Tank Brigade (July 1942)	Men	T-34	T-60/70
Brigade HQ and Company	24	1	–
Medium Tank Battalion:	151	–	–
Battalion HQ and Platoon	23	1	–
Medium Tank Company x 3	132	30	–
Supply and Trains Group	39	–	–
Light Tank Battalion:	146	–	–
Battalion HQ and Platoon	–	–	1
Light Tank Company x 2	–	–	20
Supply and Trains Group	–	–	–

west of the city, whilst the Fourth Rumanian Army held the line south of Stalingrad.

At first, Kleist's drive into the Caucasus achieved spectacular results – the First Panzer Army took the first of the oilfields at Maikop on 9 August and pushed on towards Grozny and Baku. Stalin was conscious of the potentially disastrous political implications of the German advance – Turkey might well join the Axis and launch an attack that would almost certainly destroy the hard-pressed Trans-Caucasus Front. There was also the possibility of a revolt against Soviet rule throughout the region, which was taken so seriously that Beria was sent there to supervise an urgent programme of repression.

However, the dire consequences of Hitler's decision to advance on Stalingrad and the Caucasus simultaneously rapidly became apparent. Essential supplies could only be brought up by continual improvisation – harassed quartermasters resorted to a motley collection of pack animals to transport vital supplies. Distances in this region were so vast that in many areas there were no conventional front-lines. Armoured patrols from both sides roamed the Kalmyk Steppe, the Soviets seeking Kleist's vulnerable supply lines, while the Germans attacked targets such as the Baku–Astrakhan railway. Ultimately, so many resources were diverted to Stalingrad that Kleist was robbed of any chance of taking the remaining oilfields.

▲ **KV-1S heavy tank**

South-Eastern Front / Front HQ / 133rd Independent Tank Brigade

The KV-1S (*Skorostniy:* Speedy) was a final attempt to update the KV-1, which was rapidly becoming out-classed by improved German AFVs and AT guns. The turret layout was re-arranged and the transmission up-rated to improve road speed and cross-country performance.

Specifications

Crew: 5

Weight: 42.5 tonnes (41.8 tons)

Length: 6.75m (22ft 2in)

Width: 3.32m (10ft 10in)

Height: 2.71m (8ft 9in)

Engine: 450kW (600hp) Model V-2
12-cylinder diesel

Speed: 45km/h (28mph)

Range: 250km (155 miles)

Radio: N/A

Armament: 1 x 76mm (3in) ZIS-5 gun;
3 x 7.62mm (0.3in) DT MGs

Specifications

Crew: 4

Weight: 30.9 tonnes (30 tons)

Length: 5.92m (19ft 5in)

Width: 3.00m (9ft 8in)

Height: 2.44m (8ft)

Engine: 373kW (500hp) V-2-34 V-12 cylinder diesel

Speed (road): 53km/h (33mph)

Range: 465km (290 miles)

Radio: N/A

Armament: 1 x 76mm (3in) L-40 gun;
2 x 7.62mm (0.3in) DT MGs (bow and coaxial)

▲ T-34 Model 1943

South-Eastern Front / Sixty-Fourth Army / XIII Tank Corps

Despite its designation, the T-34 Model 1943 actually entered service in 1942. The most obvious change from earlier versions was the enlarged turret, which gave welcome extra space for the crew. This T-34 has all-metal road wheels, a result of the dire shortage of rubber that affected Soviet war industries for much of 1942.

▲ T-34 Model 1943

South-Eastern Front / Sixty-Second Army / XXIII Tank Corps / 6th Tank Brigade

The use of all-metal road wheels was soon found to create harmonic vibrations when the T-34 was running at high speed, which loosened parts and caused engine damage. Rubber-rimmed road wheels had to be reinstated in the first and fifth positions to solve the problem.

Specifications

Crew: 4

Weight: 30.9 tonnes (30 tons)

Length: 5.92m (19ft 5in)

Width: 3.00m (9ft 8in)

Height: 2.44m (8ft)

Engine: 373kW (500hp) V-2-34 V-12 diesel

Speed (road): 53km/h (33mph)

Range: 465km (290 miles)

Radio: N/A

Armament: 1 x 76mm (3in) L-40 gun;
2 x 7.62mm (0.3in) DT MGs (bow and coaxial)

▶ Harley-Davidson 42WLA motorcycle

Stalingrad Front / Sixty-Fourth Army / HQ XIII Tank Corps

The Red Army greatly appreciated the reliability of the WLA and received a total of 26,000 machines by 1945.

Specifications

Crew: 1/2

Weight: 191kg (512lb)

Engine: 17kW (23hp) V-2

Speed: 105km/h (65.2mph)

Range: 201km (125miles)

STALINGRAD FRONT (Oct 1942)	Operable	Inoperable
62 Army, 6 Gds Tk Bde:		
T-34	9	5
T-60	–	2
T-70	4	1
64 Army, XIII TK Corps, 13 Tk Bde:		
T-34	11	2
T-60	–	–
T-70	2	1
64 Army, XIII Corps, 56 Tk Bde:		
T-34	4	2
T-60	1	1
T-70	4	1
Total XIII Corps:		
T-34	15	4
T-60	1	1
T-70	6	2
51 Army, 254 Tk Bde:		
T-34	1	–
T-60	9	–
T-70	–	–
57 Army, 155 Tk Bde:		
T-34	3	–
T-60	9	–
T-70	–	–
Total for four armies:		
T-34	28	9
T-60	19	3
T-70	10	2

▲ **Appliqué armour**
T-34 Model 1941s with appliqué armour fitted to the hull front and driver's hatch in response to the threat posed by increasing numbers of German towed and SP 75mm (2.9in) AT guns.

▶ **Light Tank Mark VII 'Tetrarch'**

North Caucasus Front / Forty-Fifth Army / 151st Tank Brigade

A consignment of 20 Tetrarchs from British Army stocks were supplied to the Red Army via Iran in 1941. They were deployed in the Caucasus, where their cross-country agility could be put to good use and there was little threat from heavier Axis AFVs.

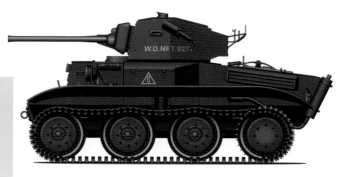

Specifications

Crew: 3

Weight: 7.5 tonnes (7.4t)

Length: 4.04m (13ft 3in)

Width: 2.31m (7ft 7in)

Height: 2.12m (6ft 11in)

Engine: 123kW (165hp) Meadows 12-cylinder petrol

Speed: 42km/h (28mph) off-road

Range: 224km (140miles)

Radio: N/A

Armament; 1 x 40mm (1.57in);

   1 x 7.92mm (0.3in) Besa MG

▼ Tank Brigade (July 1942)

At this stage of the war, there were still insufficient T-34s and light tanks had to be used to make up numbers. Tactical handling of the brigade was hampered by a shortage of radios, which were normally issued only to platoon commanders and above, leaving two-thirds of all tanks without radios. In addition to the tanks illustrated, each tank brigade included a 400-strong motorized rifle battalion, an AT battery and a mortar company.

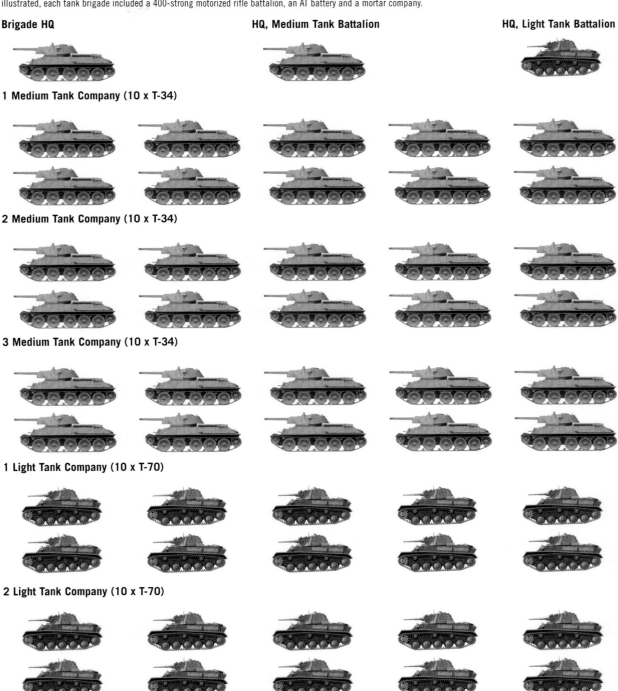

Brigade HQ

HQ, Medium Tank Battalion

HQ, Light Tank Battalion

1 Medium Tank Company (10 x T-34)

2 Medium Tank Company (10 x T-34)

3 Medium Tank Company (10 x T-34)

1 Light Tank Company (10 x T-70)

2 Light Tank Company (10 x T-70)

▶ T-70 Model 1942 light tank

Stalingrad Front / Sixty-Second Army / XIII Tank Corps / 56th Tank Brigade

The T-70 was the final Soviet light tank to enter service in quantity during the war. While the 45mm (1.8in) gun and thicker armour were welcome advances on earlier designs, the retention of a one-man turret severely limited the type's battlefield performance.

Specifications

Crew: 2	Speed: 45km/h (28mph)
Weight: 5.8 tonnes (5.7 tons)	Range: 360km (224 miles)
Length: 4.29m (14ft 1in)	Radio: N/A
Width: 2.32m (7ft 7in)	Armament: 1 x 45mm (1.8in) Model 38 gun;
Height: 2.04m (6ft 7in)	1 x 7.62mm (0.3in) coaxial DT MG
Engine: 2 x GAZ-202 52+52kW (70+70hp)	

▶ Harley-Davidson 42WLA motorcycle with M72 side car

South-Eastern Front / Sixty-Second Army / XXIII Tank Corps / 13th Tank Brigade / Motorized Rifle Battalion / Mortar Company

Most of the Red Army's WLAs were fitted with M72 sidecars and a proportion of these combinations were modified to mount the standard 82mm (3.2in) mortar.

Specifications

Crew: 3	Armament: 1 x 82mm (3.2in) mortar;
Engine: 17kW (23hp) V-2 cylinder 750cc (45ci)	1 x 7.62mm (0.3in) DP MG
Speed: 0km/h (0mph)	

Operation *Uranus*
NOVEMBER 1942

In September 1942, Stalin approved plans for Operation *Uranus*, an ambitious counter-offensive intended to punch through the Third and Fourth Rumanian armies, before enveloping the German Sixth Army and Fourth Panzer Army around Stalingrad.

THROUGHOUT THE autumn of 1942, the Red Army built up reserves around Stalingrad while feeding in just enough reinforcements to prevent any decisive German breakthrough. General Chuikov's Sixty-Second Army held the city itself, steadily wearing down the attacks of the Sixth Army and Fourth Panzer Army in an expert campaign of attrition. At the same time, Zhukov steadily assembled his forces, including 894 tanks and 13,500 guns, to strike at the Rumanians both north and south of Stalingrad.

When the South-West Front launched its attack on the Third Rumanian Army on 19 November, the 80-minute Soviet barrage by at least 3000 guns could be heard 50km (31 miles) away. A 12km (8-mile) gap was ripped in the Rumanian defences, which was rapidly exploited by the Fifth Tank Army. Twenty-four hours later, the Stalingrad Front's offensive hit the Fourth Rumanian Army, tearing a 30km (20-mile) hole in its line before launching IV Mechanized Corps and IV Cavalry Corps into the breach to link up with Fifth Tank Army.

Surprised and unprepared

Most German planners had simply not believed that the Red Army had the resources or the skill to conduct an offensive on this scale. Soviet armour was

▲ Winter offensive

Infantry of the South-West Front's Twenty-First Army advance past a knocked-out T-70 light tank on the banks of the Don at Kalach, November 1942. It was here that the Fifth Tank Army broke through the Fourth Panzer Army's defences to link up with the Fourth Mechanized Corps and trap the Sixth Army in Stalingrad. (The transport and spectators on the bridge make it highly likely that this is a staged propaganda photograph.)

Specifications

Crew: 4

Weight: 26.5 tonnes (26.2 tons)

Length: 5.92m (19ft 5in)

Width: 3.00m (9ft 8in)

Height: 2.44m (8ft)

Engine: 373kW (500h) V-2-34 V-12 diesel

Speed (road): 53km/h (33mph)

Range: 400km (250 miles)

Radio: N/A

Armament: 1 x 76mm (3in) F-34 gun;

2 x 7.62mm (0.3in) DT MGs (bow and coaxial)

▲ T-34 Model 1942
South-Western Front / Fifth Tank Army / XXVI Tank Corps

On 23 November, IV and XXVI Tank Corps linked up with IV Mechanized Corps to complete the encirclement of Stalingrad. The two tank corps had covered 130km (81 miles) since crossing the start line four days earlier.

Tank Corps – vehicle strength (late 1942)	Weapons
HQ:	
Medium tank	3
Tank Brigade x 3:	
Light tank	21
Medium tank	32
LMG	18
MG	4
ATR	6
82mm (3.22in) mortar	6
76mm (3in) guns	4
Motorized Rifle Brigade:	
LMG	110
MG	18
HMG	3
ATR	54
82mm (3.2in) mortar	30
120mm (4.7in) mortar	4
45mm (1.8in) AT	12
37mm (1.5in) AA	12
76mm (3in) guns	12
Reconnaissance Battalion:	
Armoured car	20
Rocket Launcher Battalion:	
Rocket launcher	8

Tank Corps – personnel/small arms strength (late 1942)	Officers	NCOs	Other	SMGs	Rifles
HQ	56	38	36	5	27
Brigade x 3	229	423	464	490	225
Mot Rifle	390	1187	1960	1364	1396
Recon	41	146	21	50	56
Rocket Lch	30	56	164	5	104
Pioneer Mine	9	20	77	36	60
Fuel Trans	8	9	58	0	51
Maintenance Coy x 2	9	13	53	10	20
NKVD	11	6	32	10	20
Total	1250	2757	3846	2068	3126

now being employed – and most effectively – in accordance with the principles laid down by General Fedorenko earlier in the year.

In contrast, the German response was clumsy and ineffective. XLVIII Panzer Corps had been assigned to act as an armoured reserve for the Third Rumanian Army, but it was an exceptionally weak formation, comprising the 22nd Panzer Division with only 45 operational tanks and the 1st Rumanian Tank Division with 40 R-2 tanks (obsolete Panzer 35(t)s). Despite being massively outnumbered by Soviet armour, these two divisions managed to break out to the West. The under-strength elements of the Fourth Panzer Army that attempted to block the Fifth Tank Army's advance at the Don crossings near Kalach were not so fortunate. They were inadequately briefed and committed to an understandably rushed deployment with low fuel and ammunition. Although they reached Kalach just ahead of Soviet forces, their small combat teams lacked infantry support to hold vital ground and were quickly overrun by Soviet armour operating *en masse*.

On 23 November, the Red Army pincers closed at Sovietskiy, 20km (12.4 miles) south-east of Kalach, trapping an estimated 300,000 Axis troops in Stalingrad. The tables had been decisively turned.

◄ **Tank crews**

Tank crewmen of the South-West Front relax after completing the encirclement of the Sixth Army in Stalingrad. At this stage of the war, many Soviet tank crews went into action with as little as 72 hours classroom training, a deficiency that contributed to their high casualty rates.

⏶ T-34 platoon

November 1942 – a platoon of T-34 Model 1943 tanks awaits orders to move up to the front. Access to the enlarged turret of the T-34 Model 1943 was improved by the installation of twin hatches instead of the clumsy single hatch of previous models.

Specifications

Crew: 1 driver
Weight: 1.55 tonnes (1.5 tons)
Length: 5.33m (17ft 6in)
Width: 2.1m (7ft)
Height: 1.97m (6ft 6in)
Engine: 29.8kW (40hp) 4-cylinder
 SV petrol
Speed: 70km/h (43.5mph)

⏷ ZiS-6 BM-8-48

Stalingrad Front / Sixty-Second Army / XXVI Tank Corps / Rocket Launcher Battalion

The ZiS-6 was the first type of truck to be converted to carry the various versions of the 'Katyusha' salvo rocket launcher. Although largely superseded in this role by Lend-Lease trucks, surviving vehicles remained in service throughout the war.

⏶ GAZ-65 1½-ton halftrack

South-Western Front / Fifth Tank Army / XXVI Tank Corps / Supply Battalion

The GAZ-65 was a conversion to allow the GAZ-AA truck to operate as a halftrack whenever required. The tracks were readily removable and the small roadwheels could be raised so that the truck could be used in the conventional wheeled mode.

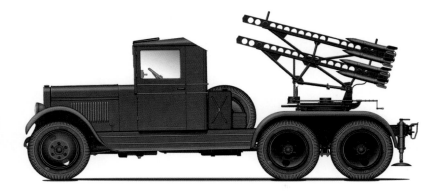

Specifications

Crew: 1
Weight: 4.31 tonnes (4.756 tons)
Length: 6.06m (19.9ft)
Width: 2.23m (7.33ft)
Height: 2.16m (7ft 1in)
Engine: 54kW (73hp) 6-cylinder
Speed: 55km/h (34mph)
Armament: 48 x 82mm M-8 rockets with a maximum
 range of 5.9 km (3.66 miles)

Chapter 3

False Dawn: Kharkov to Kursk

During much of the winter of 1942–43, it seemed
that the Red Army was on the verge of achieving a decisive
victory. Hitler had characteristically refused to allow the
Sixth Army to break out from Stalingrad and insisted that
Kleist's Army Group A should remain in the Caucasus.
Even von Manstein's genius could not compensate for this
folly – his attempt to relieve Stalingrad was beaten back and
the last remnants of the garrison surrendered on
2 February 1943. The Soviet advance threatened to cut off
Army Group A, which was forced to retreat to the Taman
Peninsula. Within a week of the surrender at Stalingrad,
the Voronezh and South-Western Fronts had retaken Kursk
and Belgorod. Kharkov fell on 14 February and
Soviet armour was threatening the Dnieper
crossings at Zaporozhe.

◀ **Transient victory**
A T-34 Model 1943 of the Voronezh Front enters Kharkov, 16th February 1943. Manstein's masterly
counter-offensive re-took the city on 15 March.

Reverse at Kharkov

FEBRUARY–MARCH 1943
The seemingly irresistible Red Army offensive was pushed too far, out-running its supply lines and providing an opportunity for a devastating German counterattack.

B Y MID-FEBRUARY, there was very little time left before the mud of the spring thaw made major operations impossible, but von Manstein showed just what could be achieved in the most threatening situation. By getting a shaken Hitler to authorize a mobile defence and release the necessary resources

(the SS Panzer Corps, five *Wehrmacht* Panzer divisions and the elite *Grossdeutschland* Division), he was able to shorten his front and concentrate the Panzers to take advantage of Soviet overconfidence. This overconfidence was understandable – Soviet armour had advanced as much as 300km (186 miles) in a month and seemed poised to re-conquer the entire Ukraine. Such spectacular successes brought their own problems as the tanks outran their supply lines and had to struggle forward with totally inadequate reserves of fuel and ammunition. By this time, Lieutenant-General Popov's 'mobile group' of four tank corps spearheading the advance had been reduced to 53 serviceable tanks.

On 20 February, von Manstein unleashed four Panzer corps supported by a 'maximum effort' from the *Luftwaffe*, which rapidly established air

◀ **Objective Kharkov**
T-34s of the Voronezh Front advance on Kharkov in the depths of the winter of 1942/43. The T-34's wide tracks gave it good mobility across snow and ice.

▲ **T-34 Model 1943**
South-Western Front / Lieutenant-General Popov's Mobile Group
This T-34 was one of only 53 operational tanks left in all four tank corps comprising Popov's Mobile Group when it was destroyed by Manstein's counter-offensive in February 1943.

Specifications	
Crew: 4	Engine: 373kW (500hp) V-2-34 V-12
Weight: 30.9 tonnes (30 tons)	cylinder diesel
Length: 5.92m (19ft 5in)	Speed (road): 53km/h (33mph)
Width: 3.00m (9ft 8in)	Range: 465km (290 miles)
Height: 2.44m (8ft)	Armament: 1 x 76mm (3in) L-40 gun;
	2 x 7.62mm (0.3in) DT MGs (bow and coaxial)

superiority over the battlefield, flying up to 1000 sorties per day. The concentrated Panzer thrusts achieved massive local superiority over the scattered and depleted Red Army armoured forces, rapidly defeating each in detail. The SS Panzer Corps recaptured Kharkov on 15 March, going on to take Belgorod three days later before the thaw and the exhaustion of the German forces combined to end the counter-offensive.

After coming tantalizingly close to winning a major victory, the Red Army had been badly mauled – the South-Western Front had lost 23,000 men, 615 AFVs and 354 guns, whilst the Voronezh Front's casualties were even worse, totalling 40,000 men, 600 tanks and 500 guns. German forces once again held much of the territory lost during the winter except for a large salient centred on the small provincial city of Kursk.

▲ SU-12 self-propelled gun

North Caucasus Front / 1448th Artillery Regiment

Initially designated the SU-12, the first model of the SU-76 was an early attempt to produce a light self-propelled gun by mounting the 76.2mm (3in) ZiS-3 gun on a lengthened T-70 chassis. The power-train was nearly identical to that of the early T-70 light tank, with two commercial GAZ-202 engines each powering one track through separate, unsynchronized transmissions. Unsurprisingly, this proved to be a mechanical nightmare and was a major factor in cancelling production in March 1943 after only 360 units had been completed.

Specifications	
Crew: 4	Engine: 2 x GAZ 6-cylinder petrol 52+52kW
Weight: 10.8 tonnes (11.9 tons)	(70+70hp)
Length: 4.88m (16ft)	Speed (road): 45km/h (28mph)
Width: 2.73m (8ft 11.5in)	Range: 450km (280miles)
Height: 2.17m (7ft 1.4in)	Armament: one 76mm (3in) gun and one
	7.62mm (0.3in) MG

▲ T-38 light tank

Southern Front / HQ 28th Army / Reconnaissance Company

A total of 1340 T-38s were produced between 1936 and 1939 and were widely used by reconnaissance units. Some of these vehicles were fitted with a 20mm (0.79in) ShVAK cannon in place of the usual DT MG, but few survived the first months of the war.

Specifications	
Crew: 2	Engine: 30 kW (40hp) GAZ-AA
Weight: 3.3 tonnes (3.25 tons)	Speed: 40 km/h (24.86mph)
Length: 3.78m (12ft 5in)	Range: 170km
Width: 3.33m (10ft 11in)	Radio: N/a
Height: 1.63m (5ft 4in)	Armament: 1 x 7.62mm (0.3in) DT MG

Specifications

Crew: 1 driver	Engine: 54.39 kW (73hp) 6 cylinder
Weight: 4.66 tonnes (4.59 tons)	ZiS-5 petrol
Length: 6m (19ft 8in)	Speed: 36 km/h (22.37mph)
Width: 2.4m (7ft 10in)	Range: 300km (186.4 miles)
Height: 2.23m (7ft 4in)	Radio: N/A

▲ **ZiS-22(M) halftrack**

Voronezh Front / HQ Forty-Sixth Army / Supply Battalion

In common with many other Soviet-produced halftracks, the front wheels of this ZiS-22(M) have been fitted with wooden 'skis' to improve its performance while moving across snow.

Kursk: the last *Blitzkrieg*
JULY 1943

From the German perspective, the Kursk salient was an obvious target for a summer offensive in 1943 – unfortunately for them, it was just as obvious to the Red Army.

AN ATTACK TO 'PINCH OUT' the Kursk salient would shorten the German front by 250km (155 miles), freeing up to 20 divisions for use elsewhere, besides destroying what was seen as a 'gateway for the invasion of the Ukraine'. Typically, von Manstein proposed a radical alternative, a new offensive on the same principles as his recent operations that had led to the recapture of Kharkov and Belgorod. He

intended to tempt the Southern and South-Western Fronts into attacks against the newly reconstituted Sixth Army, drawing them into eastern Ukraine. A counter-offensive would then be launched from the Kharkov area towards Rostov, to trap most of the two Fronts against the Sea of Azov.

Predictably, this 'Manstein plan' was vetoed by Hitler, who ordered an offensive against the Kursk

▶ **BA-64B Model 1943 light armoured car**

Voronezh Front / Fifth Guards Tank Army / XVIII Tank Corps

The BA-64B gradually replaced pre-war types of armoured cars in reconnaissance units from 1943. It first saw action during the Kursk offensive.

Specifications

Crew: 2	Engine: 37kW (50hp) GAZ-64 4-cylinder
Weight: 2.3 tonnes (2.54 tons)	Speed: 80km/h (50mph)
Length: 3.66m (12ft)	Range: 540km (869 miles)
Width: 1.53m (5ft)	Armament: 7.62mm (0.3in) DT MGn
Height: 1.90m (6ft 3in)	

salient, which seemed to invite the sort of Panzer-led pincer attack that had been so successful in the past. This was equally obvious to the Soviets, who were busily fortifying the area, and Hitler was urged to strike quickly before the odds became too great.

New technology

Fortunately for the Red Army, Hitler was convinced that only the new *Elefants* and Panthers could guarantee to break the strengthening Soviet defences and imposed delay after delay until he felt that the

SOVIET TANK ARMIES, KURSK (July 1943)		
Front	Army	Corps
Central	Second Tank	III Tank
		XVI Tank
Voronezh	First Tank	VI Tank
		XXXI Tank
		III Mechanized
Steppe	Fifth Guards Tank	V Guards Mechanized
		XXIX Guards Tank

▲ T-34 Model 1943
Voronezh Front / Fifth Guards Tank Army / XXIX Tank Corps
This T-34 Model 1943 incorporates the final updates applied to the type, notably the commander's 360-degree vision cupola and 'drum type' long-range fuel tanks.

Specifications
Crew: 4
Weight: 30.9 tonnes (30 tons)
Length: 5.92m (19ft 5in)
Width: 3.00m (9ft 8in)
Height: 2.44m (8ft)

Engine: 373kW (500hp) V-2-34 V-12 diesel
Speed (road): 53km/h (33mph)
Range: 465km (290 miles)
Armament: 1 x 76mm (3in) L-40 gun;
        2 x 7.62mm (0.3in) DT MGs (bow and coaxial)

Specifications
Crew: 5
Weight: 50.16 tonnes (45.5 tons)
Length: 8.95m (29ft 4in)
Width: 3.25m (10ft 7in)
Height: 2.45m (8 ft)

Engine: 450kW (600hp) 12-cylinder V-2K diesel
Speed: 43 km/h (27mph)
Range: 330km (205miles)
Armament: 152mm (5.9in) ML-20S
        gun-howitzer

▲ SU-152 heavy self-propelled gun
Voronezh Front / Fifth Guards Tank Army / XXIX Tank Corps
The SU-152 was developed under a crash programme to produce a heavy tank destroyer on the KV-1S chassis. In the type's first actions at Kursk, the 152mm (5.9in) ML-20's 48.7kg (107lb) armour-piercing rounds proved capable of dealing with even the latest German AFVs at normal battle ranges.

Panzerwaffe was strong enough for the task. German commanders were appalled at the prospect of a head-on attack against the deep belts of minefields and *Pakfronts* – the massed AT gun batteries – which showed up all too clearly in air reconnaissance photographs. They were also well aware of the security risks that grew with each successive delay. (In fact, the so-called Red Orchestra spy ring was busily sending Moscow complete details of the German plans).

German attack

On 5 July, the German attack, code-named *Zitadelle* ('Citadel') went in against the flanks of the salient. Model's Ninth Army struck south to meet Hoth's Fourth Panzer Army moving north on Kursk. A total

Specifications

Crew: 5	Engine: 1450kW (600hp) Model V-2
Weight: 45 tonnes (44.3 tons)	2-cylinder diesel
Length: 6.75m (22ft 2in)	Speed: 35km/h (22mph)
Width: 3.32m (10ft 10in)	Range: 335km (208 miles)
Height: 2.71m (8ft 9in)	Armament: 1 x 76mm (3in) F-32 gun;
	3 x 7.62mm (0.3in) DT MGs

▲ **KV-1A heavy tank**

Voronezh Front / First Tank Army / III Mechanized Corps / 203rd Separate Heavy Tank Regiment

By mid-1943, it was clear that the KV-1 was being overtaken by newer German AFVs such as the Tiger and Panther. Soviet design teams began work on a successor, the JS-2, which finally entered service in the spring of 1944.

Specifications

Crew: 4	Engine: 223.5 kW (300hp) 12 cylinder Maybach
Weight: 23.9 tonnes (23.52 tons)	HL120 TRM petrol
Length: 6.77m (22ft 2in)	Speed: 40km/h (24.86mph)
Width: 2.95m (9ft 8in)	Range: 155km (96.32 miles)
Height: 2.38m (7ft 10in)	Radio: 9R (when fitted)
	Armament: 1 x 76.2mm (3in) ZiS-3 gun

▲ **SU-76i assault gun**

Voronezh Front / Fifth Guards Tank Army / 1902nd Self-Propelled Artillery Regiment

The SU-76i was brought into service in 1943 to provide an interim assault gun pending the arrival of the SU-76M. Just over 200 were produced, using captured Panzer III and Stug III hulls fitted with a 76mm (3in) F-34 or ZiS-5 tank gun in a limited traverse mounting.

▲ **Loading up**

T34/76 tanks of the Sixth Guards Tank Army of the Voronezh Front prepare to move out, July 1943. These are older model T-34s, with the single-turret hatch.

▲ **T-34 Model 1943**

Voronezh Front / First Tank Army / VI Tank Corps / 22nd Tank Brigade

Almost 35,000 T-34s were built between 1940 and 1944, when production tapered off in favour of the T-34/85. This example has a combination of all-steel and rubber-rimmed road wheels, as rubber supplies were still limited in 1943.

Specifications

Crew: 4	Engine: 373kW (500hp) V-2-34 V-12 diesel
Weight: 30.9 tonnes (30 tons)	Speed (road): 53km/h (33mph)
Length: 5.92m (19ft 5in)	Range: 465km (290 miles)
Width: 3.0m (9ft 8in)	Armament: 1 x 76mm (3in) L-40 gun;
Height: 2.44m (8ft)	2 x 7.62mm (0.3in) DT MGs (bow and coaxial)

of 16 Panzer and *Panzergrenadier* divisions with 2700 AFVs were fielded with the support of 10,000 guns and 2000 aircraft. Despite these numbers, the offensive soon ran into trouble – the first attacks quickly bogged down in massive minefields averaging over 3000 mines per kilometre, which were swept by the fire of up to 100 guns and mortars per kilometre.

The attackers frequently used the *Panzerkeil*, or armoured wedge, a formation in which *Elefants* or Tigers formed the point of the wedge and were followed by the lighter AFVs. Even this formation was only partially successful in the face of such

▲ **Dodge T-110 L-5 D-60L 3-ton truck**

Voronezh Front / Forty-Eighth Army / HQ / Supply Battalion

A total of 1700 of these Canadian vehicles were shipped to Soviet forces via Iran.

Specifications

Crew: 1	Engine: six cylinder 70.84kW (95hp) engine
Weight: not known	Speed: 70km/h (43mph)
Length: 6.55m (21ft 6in)	Range: not known
Width: 2.286m (7ft 7in)	Armament: none
Height: 3.15m (10ft 4in)	

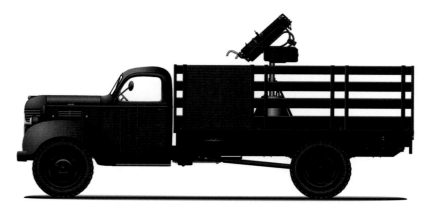

Specifications

Crew: 1 driver + 3 MG crew	Engine: 6 cylinder 73.82kW (99hp) petrol
Weight: not known	engine
Length (wheel base): 4.064m (13ft 4in)	Speed: 70km/h (43mph)
Width: not known	Range: not known
Height: not known	Armament: Quadruple 7.62mm (0.3in) Maxim
	Maxim anti-aircraft MG

▲ **Dodge WF-32 4x2 1½-ton Truck (Maxim 4M AA MG Mount)**

Voronezh Front / Fifth Guards Tank Army / XXIX Tank Corps / AA Company

Roughly 9500 of these trucks were sent to Soviet Russia in 1942/43 to replace the massive losses suffered by transport units during the German offensives. In common with many other Lend-Lease trucks, a proportion of these vehicles were issued to AA units.

▶ **Surrender**
Red Army tank crew surrender to a *Waffen*-SS soldier during the bloody battle of
Kursk in 1943.

massive Soviet defences – the Tigers and *Elefants*
might well get through, but all too often the lighter
vehicles and infantry were destroyed as they
attempted to follow. This left the 'heavies'
unsupported and horribly vulnerable to Soviet
infantry AT teams using demolition charges
or flamethrowers.

Soviet counterattack
Rokossovsky's Central Front holding the north of the
salient launched a counterattack by the Second Tank
Army on 6 July, which broke down after taking heavy
losses (in part from Soviet minefields, which had
been strengthened by German engineers). In
contrast, General Vatutin's Voronezh Front in the
south did not commit major armoured formations
against the initial German attacks, relying on the
minefields and *Pakfronts*.

Although Model's advance was halted after little
more than 15km (9.3 miles) – far short of Kursk –
Hoth managed to penetrate rather deeper, beating off
all counterattacks and threatening to make a decisive
breakthrough.

▲ **Tank column**
T-34s advance through the Ukraine in the wake of the successful counter-offensive at Kursk, summer 1943.

▼ Soviet Tank Brigade (November 1943)

By late 1943, Soviet tank brigades had evolved into powerful formations. The vulnerable light tanks had now been replaced by T-34s and battlefield communications were improved by the increasing numbers of radio-equipped tanks.

Brigade HQ, Staff Section (2 x T-34)

Brigade HQ, Reconnaissance Section (3 x ACs)

Battalion 1, HQ (1 x T-34)

Battalion 2, HQ (1 x T-34)

Reconnaissance Platoon (3 x APCs)

Reconnaissance Platoon (3 x APCs)

Company 1, HQ (1 x T-34)

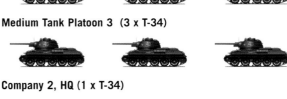

Company 1, HQ (1 x T-34)

Medium Tank Platoon 1 (3 x T-34)

Medium Tank Platoon 1 (3 x T-34)

Medium Tank Platoon 2 (3 x T-34)

Medium Tank Platoon 2 (3 x T-34)

Medium Tank Platoon 3 (3 x T-34)

Medium Tank Platoon 3 (3 x T-34)

Company 2, HQ (1 x T-34)

Company 2, HQ (1 x T-34)

Medium Tank Platoon 1 (3 x T-34)

Medium Tank Platoon 1 (3 x T-34)

Medium Tank Platoon 2 (3 x T-34)

Medium Tank Platoon 2 (3 x T-34)

Medium Tank Platoon 3 (3 x T-34)

Medium Tank Platoon 3 (3 x T-34)

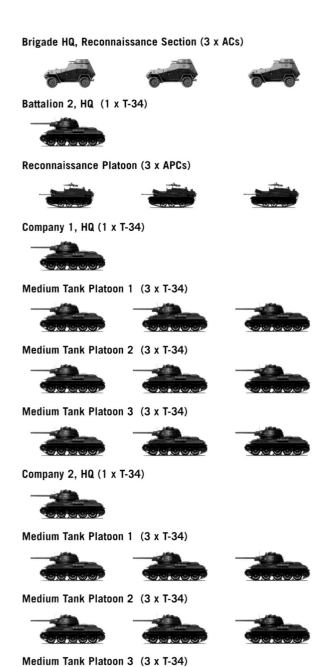

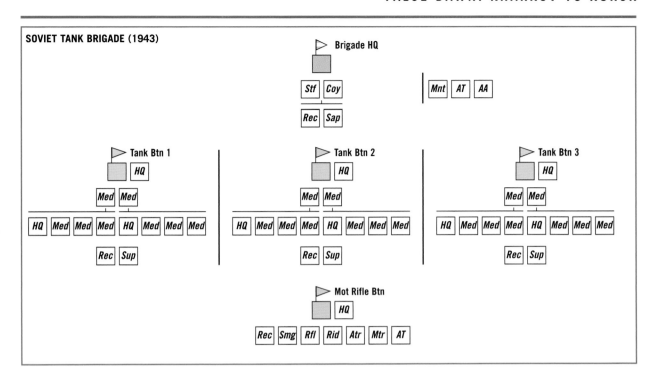

SOVIET TANK BRIGADE (1943)

Battalion 3, HQ (1 x T-34)

Reconnaissance Platoon (3 x APCs)

Company 1, HQ (1 x T-34)

Company 2, HQ (1 x T-34)

Medium Tank Platoon 1 (3 x T-34)

Medium Tank Platoon 1 (3 x T-34)

Medium Tank Platoon 2 (3 x T-34)

Medium Tank Platoon 2 (3 x T-34)

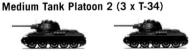

Medium Tank Platoon 3 (3 x T-34)

Medium Tank Platoon 3 (3 x T-34)

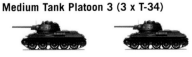

Prokhorovka
12–13 JULY 1943

Despite halting the German advance from the north of the Kursk salient, Hoth's attack from the south was making steady progress and desperate measures were called for.

B Y 11 JULY, HOTH'S FOURTH PANZER ARMY was threatening to capture Prokhorovka and secure a bridgehead over the River Psel, the last natural barrier between the Panzers and Kursk. The German attack was led by Hausser's II SS Panzer Corps, which had begun the offensive with over 300 tanks.

Vatutin believed that the situation was critical and committed the 650 tanks of Rotmistrov's 5th Guards

▲ **Infantry Tank Mark IV, Churchill Mark III**
Voronezh Front / Fifth Guards Tank Army / 36th Independent Guards Breakthrough Heavy Tank Regiment
Almost 250 Churchills were issued to Soviet tank units, including Fifth Guards Tank Army, which took part in the action at Prokhorovka.

Specifications

Crew: 5	Engine: 261kW (350hp) Bedford Twin Six
Weight: 38.5 tonnes (42 tons)	12-cylinder liquid-cooled petrol
Length: 7.3m (24ft 5in)	Speed: 24km/h (15mph)
Width: 3.0m (10ft 8in)	Range: 140km (88 miles)
Height: 2.8m (8ft 2in)	Armament: 1 x 57mm (2.2in) gun;
	1 or 2 x 7.92mm (0.31in) MG

Specifications

Crew: 5	Engine: 350hp (261kW)
Weight: 38.5 tonnes (42 tons)	Bedford twin-six petrol
Length: 7.3m (24ft 5in)	Speed (road): 24km/h (15mph)
Width: 3m (10ft 8in)	Range: 90km (56 miles)
Height: 2.8m (8ft 2in)	Armament: 1 x 75mm (2.9in) or 94mm (3.7in)
	gun; 2 x Besa 7.92mm (0.31in) MGs

▲ **Infantry Tank Mark IV, Churchill Mark IV**
Voronezh Front / Fifth Guards Tank Army / 49th Guards Heavy Tank Regiment
The Churchill was never popular with the Red Army, who compared it unfavourably with the KV-1.

▲ **Advance from Prokhorovka**
Churchill Mk.IV of the Fifth Guards Tank Army, 49th Guards Heavy Tank Regiment
passes a destroyed German SdKfz 232 armoured car, Kursk area, July 1943.

Tank Army, which had been intended to spearhead
the Soviet 'post-Kursk' offensive, Operation
Rumyantsev. On 11 July, the Fifth Guards Tank Army
arrived in the Prokhorovka area, after a four-day
march from assembly areas 300km (186 miles) to
the east. It was reinforced by II Tank Corps and
II Guards Tank Corps, increasing its strength to
about 850 tanks, 500 of which were T-34s.

These forces were opposed by 211 operational
German tanks, including only 15 Tigers, when the
battle opened on 12 July with massed Soviet tank

attacks from Prokharovka. Waves of 40–50 T-34s and
T-70s carrying infantry were launched in frontal
charges against the German armour, which were
broken up with heavy losses. The Germans resumed
their advance on Prokharovka and were engaged by
Rotmistrov's reserves, including the 181st Tank
Regiment, which was virtually wiped out when it
attempted to charge a handful of Tigers of the 1st SS
Panzer Regiment. It was only late in the day that the
intervention of the Soviet V Mechanized Corps
finally stabilized the situation.

The first day's fighting had resulted in massive
Soviet casualties – almost 650 tanks were destroyed,
while II SS Panzer Corps' losses totalled 70 AFVs, of
which 22 were repaired and serviceable on the

▶ **Universal Carrier Mark I with AT rifle**
Voronezh Front / Fifth Guards Tank Army / 12th Guards Mechanized Brigade /
Reconnaissance Company
Many of the Red Army's 2000-plus Universal Carriers were issued to
reconnaissance units, sometimes, as here, retaining their original armament
of a Boys AT rifle and a Bren Gun.

Specifications

Crew: 2/4	Engine: 63.4 kW (85hp) 8-cylinder Ford V8
Weight: 4.06 tonnes (4 tons)	Speed: 52km/h (32 mph)
Length: 3.76m (12ft 4in)	Range: 258km (160 miles)
Width: 2.11m (6ft 11in)	Armament: 1 x 14mm (0.55in) Boys AT rifle,
Height: 1.63m (5ft 4in)	1 x 7.7mm (0.303in) Bren Gun

following day. When combat resumed on 13 July, the Fifth Guards Tank Army was reduced to 150–200 operational tanks and was incapable of effective offensive action. Hausser's forces continued to attack, but were unable to make a decisive breakthrough. There was still a chance of a German victory – von Manstein urged Hitler to commit the three experienced Panzer divisions of 24th Panzer Corps, which he believed could destroy the Fifth Guards and take Kursk itself. Despite these forceful arguments, Hitler called off the operation to free units for Italy,

as the Allied landings in Sicily were on the point of causing the collapse of Mussolini's regime.

Although the Kursk offensive had failed, it demonstrated that the Red Army was in danger of losing the technological battle – the T-34 and KV were out-gunned by the Tiger and Panther, and their 76mm (3in) armament was ineffective against both German types, except at suicidally short ranges. The new SU-152 had proved to be a highly effective tank destroyer, but was, at best, only a partial solution to the problem.

Counterattack

JULY–AUGUST 1943

Soviet forces in the north of the Kursk salient recovered quickly from the German attack and launched their own offensive – Operation *Kutuzov* – against Orel on 12 July.

O REL WAS STRONGLY DEFENDED – only falling on 3/4 August after the Third Guards Tank Army and 4th Tank Army had been committed to the assault. Further south, the battering that Hoth's highly capable Fourth Panzer Army had inflicted meant that Operation *Rumyantsev*, the Soviet attack directed towards Belgorod and Kharkov, could not begin until 3 August. Belgorod fell on 5 August, but

Kharkov was far more strongly defended, its garrison reinforced by the 2nd SS Panzer Division *Das Reich*, with 96 Panthers, 32 Tigers and 25 assault guns. When Rotmistrov's newly re-equipped Fifth Guards attacked in an attempt to encircle the city, its initial assaults were beaten off with the loss of 420 tanks. It was only on 22 August that the defenders withdrew to avoid being cut off.

▲ Infantry Tank Mark III, Valentine Mark IV
Central Front / HQ Second Tank Army

The Red Army greatly appreciated the Valentine's reliability and large numbers remained in service throughout the war. The cranelike structure on the turret here is the Lakeman AA mount for a Bren Gun. The whole assembly could be folded away – the Bren Gun was normally stowed in the turret.

Specifications	
Crew: 3	Engine: 103kW (138bhp) GMC diesel
Weight: 17.69 tonnes (19.5 tons)	Speed (road): 24km/h (15mph)
Length: 5.41m (17ft 9in)	Range: 145km (90 miles)
Width: 2.63m (8ft 7.5in)	Armament: 1 x 40mm (1.57in) gun;
Height: 2.27m (7ft 5.5in)	1 x 7.92mm (0.31in) Besa MG

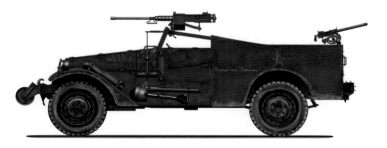

Specifications

Crew: 2, plus up to 6 passengers

Weight: 5.618 tonnes (5.53 tons)

Length: 5.62m (18ft 5in)

Width: 2.03m (6ft 8in)

Height: 2m (6ft 6in)

Engine: 71 kW (95hp) 6-cylinder White Hercules
JXD petrol

Speed: 105 km/h (65 mph)

Range 400km (250 miles)

Armament: 1 x 12.7mm (0.5in) Browning HMG,
1 x 7.62mm (0.3in) Browning MG

▲ Scout Car M3A1

Voronezh Front / HQ Fifth Guards Tank Army

The speed and light armour of the M3A1 made it popular as a command vehicle. This example was used by General Rotmistrov,
commander of the Fifth Guards Tank Army.

Specifications

Crew: 5

Weight: 32.28 tonnes (35.58 tons)

Length: 5.92m (19ft 5in)

Width: 2.62m (8ft 7in)

Height: 2.74m (9ft)

Engine: 280kW (375hp) General Motors 6046
12-cylinder diesel

Speed: 48km/h (30mph)

Range: 240km (150 miles)

Armament: 1 x 75mm (2.9in) M3 L/40 gun;
1 x 12.7mm (0.5in) I Browning M2HB MG

▲ M4A2 Sherman medium tank (early production)

Central Front / Forty-Eighth Army / 229th Independent Tank Regiment

Shermans began to appear in significant numbers in Red Army units during 1943. Initially they were mainly issued to
Independent Tank Regiments to ease the logistic support burden.

Specifications

Crew: 5

Weight: 32.28 tonnes (35.58 tons)

Length: 5.92m (19ft 5in)

Width: 2.62m (8ft 7in)

Height: 2.74m (9ft)

Engine: 280kW (375hp) General Motors 6046
12-cylinder diesel

Speed: 48km/h (30mph)

Range: 240km (150miles)

Armament: 1 x 75mm (2.9in) M3 L/40 gun;
1 x 12.7mm (0.5in) I Browning M2HB MG,
1 x turret mounted 12.7mm 0.50 cal MG

▲ M4A2 Sherman medium tank

Central Front / Forty-Eighth Army / 229th Independent Tank Regiment

Although not as well suited to Russian conditions as the T-34, the Sherman's mechanical reliability was greatly appreciated.

Specifications

Crew: 6

Weight: 31 tonnes (30.51 tons)

Length: 5.64m (18ft 6in)

Width: 2.72m (8ft 11in)

Height: 3.05m (10ft)

Engine: 279.38kW (375hp) General Motors 6046 12-cylinder twin in-line diesel

Speed: 48 km/h (30mph)

Range: 240km (150 miles)

▲ **M31B2 (T48) armoured recovery vehicle (ARV)**

Voronezh Front / 245th Tank Regiment

120 Lend-Lease M31s were the only purpose-built ARVs issued to Soviet tank units during the war years.

West to the Dnieper and beyond
AUGUST–DECEMBER 1943

The Red Army now held the strategic initiative, but its advances were to be costly affairs as German forces fought a series of highly effective rearguard actions.

IN THE AFTERMATH of the Red Army's capture of Orel and Kharkov, even Hitler recognized that there was little chance of holding any line east of the Dnieper. Orders to construct the Dnieper defence line, which formed part of the Panther-Wotan Line or the Eastern Wall, had been issued as early as 11 August 1943 and work began immediately. In theory, fortifications were to be erected along the length of the Dnieper, but the resources did not exist to undertake such a massive project and defence works were concentrated in sectors where Soviet assault crossings were most likely to be attempted, especially Kremenchug, Zaporozhe and Nikopol.

On 15 September 1943, Hitler finally authorized Army Group South to fall back to the Dnieper

defence line and a deadly race ensued, with the Red Army attempting to beat the German retreat. *Stavka* assigned the Third Tank Army to spearhead the drive to the river, which it reached on the night of 21/ 22 September. Small bridgeheads were secured, but were very vulnerable and it was decided to expand them by an airborne operation using the 1st, 3rd and 5th Guards Airborne Brigades. The operation on the night of 24/25 September was rushed and ill-planned, with transport aircraft taking off as they were ready, rather than in properly organized formations. This was a major factor in scattering the 10,000 paratroops over a wide area on the west bank of the Dnieper. Most of the 5th Guards Airborne Brigade was slaughtered when it was dropped on the

▲ KV-85 Heavy Tank

1st Ukrainian Front / Twenty-Eighth Army / 34th Guards Heavy Tank Breakthrough Regiment

Only 130 KV-85s were produced because the type was essentially an interim design to provide an up-dated heavy tank pending the introduction of the Josef Stalin (JS) series. The hull of the KV-1S was fitted with the turret of the JS-1, armed with an 85mm (3.3in) gun.

Specifications

Crew: 4/5	Engine: 450kW (600hp) Model V-2
Weight: 46 tonnes (45.3 tons)	12-cylinder diesel
Length: 8.6m (28ft 2in)	Speed: 42km/h (26mph)
Width: 3.25m (10ft 8in)	Range: 330km (205 miles)
Height: 2.8m (9ft 2in)	Armament: 1 x 85mm (3.3in) D-5T gun;
	2 x 7.62mm (0.3in) DT MGs

▲ SU-76M self-propelled Gun

1st Ukrainian Front / Third Guards Tank Army / IX Mechanised Corps

The SU-76M was a re-designed SU-76. A revised power-train dramatically improved the type's mechanical reliability and the replacement of the SU-76's enclosed fighting compartment by an open-topped design cured the problems with engine and gun fumes. It was more frequently used as an assault gun than for long-range artillery fire.

Specifications

Crew: 4	Engine: 2 x GAZ-203 6-cylinder petrol,
Weight: 10.2 tonnes (11.2 tons)	103kW (138bhp)
Length: 5m (16ft 5in)	Speed: 45km/h (28mph)
Width: 2.7m (8ft 10in)	Range: 320km (199 miles)
Height: 2.1m (6ft 11in)	Armament: 1 x 76mm (3in) ZiS-3 L/41 gun

19th Panzer Division, which was moving up to reinforce the Dnieper defences. While the operation was a disaster, German efforts to eliminate the scattered pockets of airborne forces did distract attention from the build-up of Soviet forces for a decisive breakthrough on the Panther-Wotan Line.

The handful of initial bridgeheads were slowly enlarged and new ones secured until by the end of September, there were no less than 23, some of them 10km (6.2 miles) wide and 2km (1.2 miles) deep. All these attracted fierce German counterattacks, but managed to hold out with massive fire support from Soviet artillery on the east bank of the river.

By mid-October, the forces assembled in the bridgeheads were strong enough to go over to the offensive, coupled with diversionary attacks in the

MECHANIZED BRIGADE (1943)				
AFVs	Arm Truck	AC	Lt Tk	Med Tk
Reconnaissance Coy	10	7	–	–
Tank Rgt	–	3	7	32

Mechanized Brigade (light veh)	Mot cycl	Field Car	Truck
Brigade HQ	–	2	4
HQ Coy	6	–	5
Reconnaissance Coy	6	–	4
Tank Rgt	4	2	70
Motorized Rifle Btn x3	1	1	26
Submachine-Gun Coy	1	–	1
Anti-Tank Rifle Coy	–	–	–
Mortar Btn	–	–	20
Artillery Btn	–	1	25
Anti-Aircraft MG Coy	–	–	12
Pioneer Mine Coy	–	–	6
Trains Coy	1	–	31
Medical Platoon	–	–	5

Mechanized Brigade (personnel)	Officers	NCOs	Other
Brigade HQ	39	15	26
HQ Coy	5	17	51
Reconnaissance Coy	7	72	62
Tank Rgt	89	194	187
Motorized Rifle Btn x3	48	212	389
Submachine Gun Coy	4	22	68
Anti-Tank Rifle Coy	4	20	45
Mortar Btn	23	47	127
Artillery Btn	24	67	123
Anti-Aircraft MG Coy	4	23	21
Pioneer Mine Coy	8	23	90
Trains Coy	6	28	38
Medical Platoon	8	5	19

▶ **Crowded target**

A heavily laden T-34 advances through Kiev shortly after its liberation in
November 1943. Crowded onto a tank's decks with few secure hand-holds, tank
riders ran a high risk of accidental death or injury, as well as being highly
vulnerable to enemy fire.

Mechanized Brigade	Sub MG	Carbines	Aut-rifles	Light MG	Med MG	Heavy MG	Anti-Tank	82mm	120mm	45mm AT	76mm Fld
Brigade HQ	3	8	19	2	–	–	–	–	–	–	–
HQ Coy	0	60	–	–	–	–	–	–	–	–	–
Reconnaissance Coy	79	14	–	–	–	–	–	–	–	–	–
Tank Rgt	143	95	57	2	–	–	–	–	–	–	–
Motorized Rifle Btn x3	273	99	138	36	15	–	18	6	–	4	–
Submachine Gun Coy	88	5	–	–	–	–	–	–	–	–	–
Anti-Tank Rifle Coy	37	–	–	–	–	–	27	–	–	–	–
Mortar Btn	2	–	147	–	–	–	–	12	6	–	–
Artillery Btn	60	100	9	–	–	–	–	–	–	–	12
Anti-Aircraft MG Coy	–	32	–	–	–	9	–	–	–	–	–
Pioneer Mine Coy	53	10	50	–	–	–	–	–	–	–	–
Trains Coy	1	43	–	–	–	–	–	–	–	–	–
Medical Platoon	–	9	–	–	–	–	–	–	–	–	–

south to draw German forces away from Kiev. At the end of the offensive, the Red Army controlled a bridgehead 300km (186 miles) wide and up to 80km (50 miles) deep, while in the far south, Army Group A was now cut off in the Crimea.

German tactical expertise could still impose serious delays – throughout much of October 1943, Vatutin's forces were penned into the 'Bukrin Bend' of the Dnieper and had to be redeployed northwards to the tiny bridgehead across the Dnieper at Lyutlezh, just

upstream of Kiev. By 3 November, the move was complete and VII Artillery Breakthrough Corps unleashed a bombardment by 2000 guns, mortars and rocket launchers before the Third Tank Army went in to the attack. The German forces screening the bridgehead were smashed, and Kiev was liberated on 6 November.

Fourth Panzer Army attempted to halt the Soviet advance, but Vatutin's newly re-designated 1st Ukrainian Front took Zhitomir and Korosten,

Specifications	
Crew: 3	Engine: 97–157kW (131–210hp) GMC
Weight: 18.6 tonnes (20.5 tons)	6004 diesel
Length: 5.4m (17ft 9in)	Speed: 24km/h (15mph)
Width: 2.6m (8 ft 8in)	Range: 145km (90miles)
Height: 2.2m (7ft 6in)	Armament: 1 x 57mm (2.2in) gun

▲ **Infantry Tank Mark III, Valentine Mark IX**

2nd Ukrainian Front / 27th Guards Tank Brigade

The Valentine's popularity with the Red Army was such that production was continued into 1944 solely to meet its requirements.

▲ **SU-152 heavy self-propelled gun**

1st Ukrainian Front / Eighteenth Army / 5th Guards Tank Brigade

The SU-152 was highly valued for its effectiveness both as a tank destroyer and assault gun. Over 700 vehicles were completed during 1943 before production switched to the JSU-152.

Specifications	
Crew: 5	Speed: 43km/h (26.72mph)
Weight 45.5 tonnes (44.78 tons)	Range: 330km (205 miles)
Length: 8.95m (29ft 4in)	Radio: 9R (when fitted.)
Width: 3.35m (10ft 8in)	Armament: 1 x 152mm (5.98in)
Height: 2.45m (8ft)	ML-20S howitzer
Engine: 372.5kW (500hp) V-2 12-cylinder diesel	

cutting the rail link between Army Groups Centre and South.

At this critical point, von Manstein counterattacked with LVIII Panzer Corps (1st, 7th, 19th and 25th Panzer Divisions, plus 1st SS Panzer Division and elements of the 2nd SS Panzer Division.) This force recaptured Zhitomir, fighting a fierce battle with the VII Guards Tank Corps before the deep mud created by the autumn rains temporarily halted operations. Both sides took advantage of the enforced lull to refit, but LVIII Panzer Corps took the initiative. As soon as the ground froze in early December, it launched an attack north of Zhitomir with the aim of encircling the Sixtieth Army, which hurriedly withdrew from Korosten. The situation was so critical that *Stavka*

▲ **Chevrolet 3116, 1½-ton, 4x2 Truck, with stake-and-platform body**

4th Ukrainian Front / Fifty-First Army / Supply Battalion

Lend-Lease transport vehicles rarely lasted long in Red Army service. Apart from the risks of enemy action, they were commonly overloaded, fuelled with very low octane petrol and driven for thousands of kilometres over appalling terrain.

Specifications

Crew: 1 driver
Weight: not known
Length: 5.69m (18ft 7in)
Width: 2.18m (7ft 2in)
Height: 2m (6ft 6in)

Engine: 6 cylinder 63.38kW (85hp) 4F1R petrol engine
Speed: 70km/h (43mph)
Range: not known
Radio: none

TANK BRIGADE (1943)	Mot cycl	Field Car	Trucks	Men	Arm Car	Med Tank
Brigade HQ	3	–	1	54	–	2
HQ Company	9	–	10	164	3	–
Tank Battalion x 3	–	1	12	148	–	21
Mot Submachine Gun Btl	–	–	30	507	–	–
Anti-Air Machine Gun Coy	–	–	9	48	–	–
Trains Coy	–	1	58	123	–	–
Medical Pltn	–	–	2	14	–	–

Tank Brigade	Sub MG	Rifle/Carbine	Light MG	Medium MG	Heavy MG	AT Rifle	82mm Mort	45mm AT
Brigade HQ	–	8	–	–	–	–	–	–
HQ Company	41	97	4	–	–	–	–	–
Tank Battalion x3	30	43	0	–	–	–	–	–
Mot Submachine Gun Btl	280	50	18	4	–	18	6	4
Anti-Air Machine Gun Coy	1	37	–	–	9	–	–	–
Trains Coy	10	113	–	–	–	–	–	–
Medical Pltn	–	14	–	–	–	–	–	–

▶ **Tank train**

Winter 1943/44 – a trainload of T-34 Model 1943 tanks en route to the front. The Soviet rail network was vitally important for all strategic movements of armoured forces.

transferred the First Tank Army and the Eighteenth Army to the 1st Ukrainian Front. These reinforcements allowed Vatutin to halt the German attack and return to the offensive – by mid-December, it seemed that both sides were exhausted and LCVIII Panzer Corps was withdrawn to rest and refit. However, Vatutin was determined to exploit his numerical superiority and renewed his attacks on 24 December – these made good progress and as the year ended, his forward units were approaching the 1939 Polish frontier.

Soviet AFV production totalled just under 20,000 vehicles in 1943 compared to almost 6000 in Germany. However, this did not give the Red Army the overwhelming numerical superiority that might have been expected, as the Germans destroyed 22,400 Soviet tanks in the course of the year – approximately four times their own losses.

▶ **Light Tank M3A1 'Stuart', early production series**

Central Front / Forty-Eighth Army / 45th Separate Tank Regiment

Over 1600 Lend-Lease Stuarts were shipped to the Red Army. This vehicle has the riveted hull of early production runs and has been fitted with two auxiliary fuel tanks, which virtually doubled its operating range.

Specifications

Crew: 4	Engine: Continental W-970-9A 7-cylinder
Weight: 14.7 tonnes (32,400lb)	radial petrol
Length: 4.54m (14ft 10.75in)	Speed (road): 58km/h (36mph)
Width: 2.24m (7ft 4in)	Range: 112.6km (70miles)
Height: 2.30m (7ft 6.5in)	Armament: 37mm (1.5in) M6 L/56 gun;
	3 x 7.62mm (0.3in) Browning M1919A4 MGs

▶ **Light Tank M3A1 'Stuart', standard production series**

Central Front / Forty-Eighth Army / 45th Separate Tank Regiment

This M3A1 from a late production batch has an all-welded hull. Although Soviet tank crews disliked the tank's high silhouette, the Stuart's two-man turret was far superior to the one-man turret of the T-70.

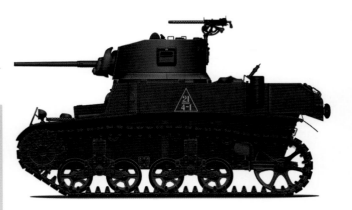

Specifications

Crew: 4	Engine: Continental W-970-9A 7-cylinder
Weight: 14.7 tonnes (32,400lb)	radial petrol
Length: 4.54m (14ft 10.75in)	Speed (road): 58km/h (36mph)
Width: 2.24m (7ft 4in)	Range: 112.6km (70miles)
Height: 2.30m (7ft 6.5in)	Armament: 37mm (1.5in) M6 gun; 3 x
	7.62mm (0.3in) Browning M1919A4 MGs

▲ SU-57 tank destroyer

1st Ukrainian Front / Third Guards Tank Army / 16th Tank Destroyer Brigade

A total of over 600 US T-48 tank destroyers – M3 halftracks armed with the 57mm (2.2in) M1 AT gun – were supplied to the Red Army, which knew it as the SU-57. These were concentrated in tank destroyer brigades, each with 60–65 SU-57s.

Specifications	
Crew: 5	Engine: 109.5kW (147hp) White 160AX
Weight: 8.6 tonnes (8,46 tons)	6- cylinder in-line petrol
Length: 6.42m (21ft)	Speed: 72km/h (45mph)
Width: 1.962m (6ft 5in)	Range: 320km (200 miles)
Height: 2.3m (7ft 6in)	Armament: 1 x 57mm (2.24in) M1 gun

▲ M2 halftrack

4th Ukrainian Front / Twenty-Eighth Army / HQ

The 342 M2 halftracks received by the Red Army were used mainly as command vehicles.

Specifications	
Crew: 2, plus up to 8 passengers	Engine: 109.5kW (147hp) White 160AX
Weight: 8.7 tonnes (8.56 tons)	6- cylinder in-line petrol
Length: 5.96m (19ft 6in)	Speed: 72km/h (45mph)
Width: 1.962m (6ft 5in)	Range: 320km (200 miles)
Height: 2.3m (7ft 6in)	Armament: 1 x 12.7mm (0.5in) Browning HMG,
	plus 1 x 7.62mm (03in) Browning MG

▶ Willys MB 'Jeep'

3rd Ukrainian Front / HQ

At least 50,000 Lend-Lease jeeps were issued to Red Army units between 1942 and 1945.

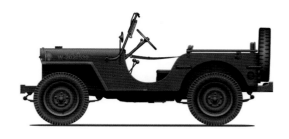

Specifications	
Crew: 1 driver	Engine: 44.7kW (60hp) 4-cylinder petrol
Weight: 1.04 tonnes (1.02 tons)	Speed: 88.5km/h (55mph)
Length: 3.33m (10ft 11in)	Range: not known
Width: 1.575m (5ft 2in)	Radio: N/A
Height: 1.83m (6ft)	

▼ GAZ-MM 4x2 1½-ton Truck Model 1943 with 25mm (1in) 72-K Model 1940 AA Gun

4th Ukrainian Front / Twenty-Eighth Army / 1693rd AA Regiment

The increasing threat from *Luftwaffe* armoured ground-attack aircraft such as the Henschel HS129B, which were largely invulnerable to MG fire, prompted the development of these more powerful self-propelled AA guns.

Specifications

Crew: 1 driver, 4 gun crew

Weight: 18.1 tonnes (19.96 tons) (without gun)

Length (hull): 5.35m (17ft 6in)

Width: 2.04m (6ft 8in)

Height: 1.97m (6ft 5½in)

Engine: 37kW (50hp) Gaz-MM 4-cylinder

Speed: 70km/h (43.5mph)

Armament: 1 x 25mm (1in) 72-K Model 1940 AA gun

Motorized Rifle Battalion, personnel/weapons (1943)				
	Officers	NCOs	Other	Main Weapons
Battalion HQ	13	3	5	–
SMG Coy x2	5	22	74	9 LMG, 2 MG
SMG Coy	4	10	81	–
Mortar Coy	3	13	26	6 82mm Mortars
AT Rifle Coy	–	–	–	18 AT Rifles
AT Battery	4	15	25	4 45mm AT
Trains Ptn	2	14	29	–
Medical Det	1	1	3	–

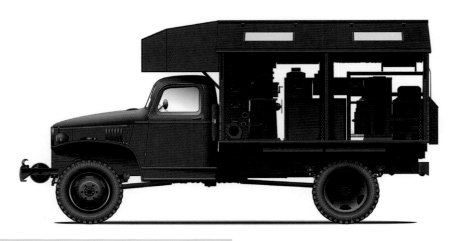

Specifications

Crew: 1 driver

Weight: 1.53 tonnes (1.5 tons)

Length: 5.69m (18ft 7in)

Width: 2.28m (7ft 6in)

Height: 2.64m (8ft 8in)

Engine: 69.3kW (93hp) 6 cylinder 4F1R petrol engine

Speed: not known

Range: not known

Armament: none

▲ Chevrolet G-7117 4x4 1½-ton truck with PARM-1 Type B field repair workshop

4th Ukrainian Front / HQ / Maintenance Battalion

Substantial numbers of Lend-Lease trucks were converted to fulfil a range of specialist functions. A proportion of those allocated to maintenance units were fitted with field repair workshop bodies.

Chapter 4

The Destruction of the *Wehrmacht*

As 1944 began, the balance of power on the
Eastern Front swung more strongly in favour of the Red
Army. Five Tank Armies, each comprising two tank and one
mechanized corps, were already in existence and a sixth
was forming. A uniquely Soviet addition to the more
conventional forces was the cavalry mechanized
group (KMG), a combination of a cavalry corps and a
mechanized corps. This formation proved to be ideal for
'deep-penetration' missions to exploit breakthroughs across
thickly forested areas or swamps, which were marginal
terrain for tanks. The *Luftwaffe*'s demonstration of effective
close air support operations in 1941–43 led to increased
resources being devoted to the Red Air Force. An expansion
and re-equipment programme provided each Front with
its own air army of 700–800 fighters and
ground-attack aircraft.

◀ **New Year, new victories**
A column of T-34 Models 1943 and their tank riders advance across the Ukraine in early 1944.

Korsun Pocket
DECEMBER 1943 – FEBRUARY 1944

By 24 December 1943, the 4th Ukrainian Front had sealed off 150,000 German and Rumanian troops in the Crimea. As the New Year began, cavalry of the 1st Ukrainian Front crossed the 1939 Polish frontier and turned southwards in an attempt to trap the German forces in the Dneiper bend south of Kiev.

THE BULK OF these forces (elements of 11 divisions of the Eighth Army) held a salient centred on Korsun, west of Cherkassy. *Stavka* quickly appreciated the salient's vulnerability, assigning Vatutin's 1st Ukrainian Front and Konev's 2nd Ukrainian Front to strike at its flanks. By this stage of the war, both the Fronts were powerful formations, with each fielding three tank armies, plus three to four other armies.

Konev's Fifth Guards Tank Army and Sixth Tank Army sealed off the salient on 3 February 1944 despite appalling weather conditions (intense cold spells broken by brief thaws that turned the region's dirt roads to thick, clinging mud.) Approximately 60,000 men under General Stemmermann (*Gruppe Stemmermann*) were trapped in this newly formed Korsun Pocket. A rescue attempt was made by the

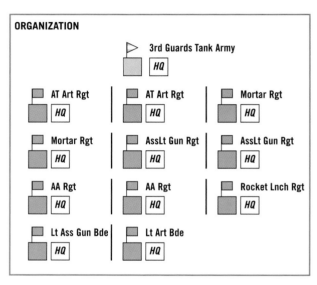

ORGANIZATION

3rd Guards Tank Army — HQ

AT Art Rgt — HQ	AT Art Rgt — HQ	Mortar Rgt — HQ
Mortar Rgt — HQ	AssLt Gun Rgt — HQ	AssLt Gun Rgt — HQ
AA Rgt — HQ	AA Rgt — HQ	Rocket Lnch Rgt — HQ
Lt Ass Gun Bde — HQ	Lt Art Bde — HQ	

▲ **KV-85 heavy tank**

1st Ukrainian Front / Thirty-Eighth Army / 7th Independent Guards Heavy Tank Regiment

The KV-85 was produced by fitting the hull of the KV-1S with the turret of the JS-1, armed with an 85mm (3.3in) gun. Only 130 KV-85s were produced, as the type was essentially an interim design to provide an up-dated heavy tank pending the introduction of the Josef Stalin (JS) series.

Specifications

Crew: 4/5	Engine: 450kW (600hp) Model V-2
Weight: 46 tonnes (45.3 tons)	12-cylinder diesel
Length: 8.6m (28ft 2in)	Speed: 42km/h (26mph)
Width: 3.25m (10ft 8in)	Range: 330km (205 miles)
Height: 2.8m (9ft 2in)	Armament: 1 x 85mm (3.3in) D-5T gun;
	2 x 7.62mm (0.3in) DT MGs

First Panzer Army, which managed to seize small bridgeheads across the River Gniloy Tikich on 11 February, but was unable to break through to the pocket 30km (19 miles) away to the east. During the next few days, the First Panzer Army was locked in fierce combat with the Sixth Tank Army, but the relief force could do no more than hold its ground in the face of such strong opposition.

By 15 February, it was clear that the trapped forces would have to attempt a breakout. They had already

Tank Corps (January 1944)	Strength
Personnel	12,010
Armour:	
T-60 light tank	–
T-70 light tank	–
T-34 medium tank	208
KV heavy tank	1
SU-76	21
SU-85	16
SU-152/ISU-152	12
Guns and Mortars:	
82mm (3.2in) mortars	52
120mm (4.7in) mortars	42
45mm (1.8in) AT guns	12
57mm (2.2in) AT guns	16
37mm (1.5in) AA guns	18
76mm (3in) guns	12
M-13 rocket launchers	8

Mechanized Corps (January 1944)	Strength
Personnel	16,370
Armoured Vehicles:	
Light tanks	21
Medium tanks	176
Heavy tanks	–
Light assault guns	21
Medium assault guns	16
Heavy assault guns	12
Guns and Mortars:	
82mm (3.2in) mortars	100
120mm (4.7in) mortars	54
45mm (1.8in) AT guns	36
57mm (2.2in) AT guns	8
37mm (1.5in) AA guns	18
76mm (3in) guns	36
BM-13 rocket launchers	8

▲ T-34/85 Medium Tank

2nd Ukrainian Front / Fifth Guards Tank Army

The T-34/85's 85mm (3.3in) gun was a major factor in restoring the technological balance between Soviet and German armoured forces. Although it was not as effective as the guns of the Panther or the Tiger, its armour-piercing performance was almost twice as good as the 76.2mm weapons of earlier T-34s.

Specifications

Crew: 5

Weight: 32 tonnes (31.5 tons)

Length: 6m (19ft 7in)

Width: 3m (9ft 9in)

Height: 2.60m (8ft 6in)

Engine: 1 x V-2 V-12 cylinder 372 kW (493hp) diesel engine

Speed (road): 55km/h (33mph)

Range: 360km (223 miles)

Radio: 9R (When fitted)

Armament: 1 x 85mm (3.4in) ZiS-S-53 cannon; 2 x 7.62mm (0.3in) DT MGs (bow and coaxial)

▲ **Tank riders**
Soviet infantry hitch a lift on a T-34 as troops from the 1st Ukrainian Front push through the Ukraine, spring 1944.

edged closer to the stalled relief force and launched their main effort on the night of 16/17 February. Elements of three Soviet tank armies lay between *Gruppe* Stemmermann and the forward elements of the First Panzer Army only 12km (7.5 miles) away.

Konev furious

Konev reacted furiously to the German breakout attempts – he had rashly promised Stalin a second Stalingrad – and threw in all available units, including the new JS-2s of XX Tank Corps. Lacking infantry support, Soviet tanks initially stood off, firing into the escaping units from a distance, but as it became obvious that there were very few AT weapons to oppose them, the T-34s charged into the German columns. Although as many as 35,000 German troops eventually fought their way clear after abandoning all their artillery and heavy equipment, the Eighth Army had been badly mauled and the First Panzer Army had lost large numbers of AFVs, which were increasingly difficult to replace.

Headquarters

▼ **Light Assault Gun Regiment**

Light assault gun regiments were generally used in the infantry support role and suffered particularly heavy losses, as their thinly armoured, open-topped SU-76Ms were highly vulnerable to even light AT weapons.

Battery 1   **Battery 2**   **Battery 3**   **Battery 4**

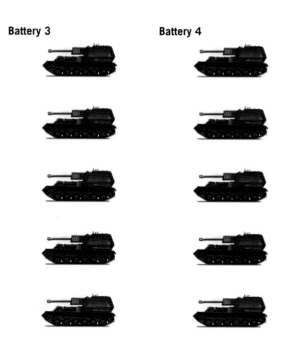

Specifications

Crew: 4	Engine: 2 x GAZ 6-cylinder petrol 52+52kW
Weight: 10.8 tonnes (11.9 tons)	(70+70hp)
Length: 4.88m (16ft)	Speed (road): 45km/h (28mph)
Width: 2.73m (8ft 11.5in)	Range: 450km (280miles)
Height: 2.17m (7ft 1.4in)	Armament: one 76mm (3in) gun and one
	7.62mm (0.3in) MG

▲ **SU-76M SP assault gun**

2nd Ukrainian Front / Fifth Guards Tank Army / 1223rd Light Self-Propelled Artillery Regiment

When operating in the indirect-fire role, the SU-76M's ZiS-3 76mm (3in) gun had a maximum range of over 13,000m (42,650ft).

Operation *Bagration*
22 JUNE – 19 AUGUST 1944

Throughout April and May 1944, *Stavka* planned Operation *Bagration*, a massive offensive intended to destroy Army Group Centre and drive German forces from Soviet territory.

ELABORATE DECEPTION measures were employed to convince the Germans that the forthcoming offensive would exploit earlier Soviet advances in the south by retaking the remaining occupied areas of the Ukraine and driving into the Balkans to knock Rumania out of the war.

These measures were highly successful and the offensive achieved complete surprise when it opened on 22 June, the third anniversary of the start of Operation *Barbarossa*. The balance of forces was very much in favour of the Red Army (see table opposite for figures).

By this stage of the war, the Soviet Air Force had gained air superiority and flew 153,000 combat sorties in support of the offensive. Almost 1000 aircraft of Soviet Long Range Aviation based in southern Russia supplemented these operations with

Operation *Bagration*	Soviet Forces	Army Group Centre
Troops	2,400,000	1,200,000
AFVs	5200	900
Artillery and mortars	36,400	9500
Aircraft	5300	1350

Operation *Bagration*	Armies employed
1st Baltic Front	4th Shock, 6th Guards, 43rd
3rd Byelorussian Front	11th Guards, 5th, 39th, 31st, 5th Guards Tank
2nd Byelorussian Front	33rd, 49th, 50th, 4th Air
1st Byelorussian Front	3rd, 28th, 48th, 65th

bombing raids on targets such as German HQs and
Luftwaffe airfields. In crucial sectors of the front, the
Soviets had local numerical superiority of up to 10:1
and quickly broke through the German defences.
Within days, the three tank armies assigned to the
operation were able to exploit the breakthroughs and
advance deep into the German rear areas, while a
KMG moved through the Pripet Marshes to cut off
the German Ninth Army's line of retreat.

Encirclement operations

On 25 June, Vitebsk was surrounded by a second
KMG and Soviet forces pressed on, cutting off
Mogilev, Bobruisk and Minsk by 3 July. In each case,
large German forces were trapped, the haul increased
by Hitler's refusal to authorize timely retreats. By this
time, Army Group Centre had lost 25 of its 63
divisions (including the bulk of the Ninth Army) and
the Soviet offensive was still far from over.

The second stage of Operation *Bagration* began on
5 July. The German pocket around Minsk was
destroyed between 5 and 11 July, before the advance

▶ **Marshall Rokossovsky**

Rokossovsky survived imprisonment and torture during Stalin's purges to
become a Marshal of the Soviet Union in recognition of his victories during
Operation *Bagration*.

▲ **JS-2m heavy tank**

***1st Ukrainian Front / First Guards Tank Army / 72nd Independent Guards
Heavy Tank Regiment***

By late 1944, a total of at least 34 independent heavy tank regiments had been
formed, each with 21 JS-2s.

Specifications

Crew: 4	Speed: 37km/h (23mph)
Weight: (46 tonnes) 45.27 tons	Range: 240km (149miles)
Length: 9.9m (32ft 6in)	Armament: 1 x 122mm (4.8in) D-25T gun,
Width: 3.09m (10ft 2in)	3 x 7.72mm (0.3in) DT MGs (1 coaxial, 1 fixed
Height: 2.73m (8ft 11in)	in bow, 1 ball-mounted in turret rear)
Engine: 383kW (513hp) V-2 12-cylinder diesel	

resumed, taking Vilnius on 13 July. Throughout this period, the tank armies and the KMGs formed the spearhead of the advance, frequently out-running their artillery support.

For the first time, the Red Air Force proved capable of providing effective close air support to these formations and resupplying them. (During the operation, it delivered 1182 tonnes/1163 tons of fuel,

1240 tonnes/1220 tons of ammunition and around 1000 tonnes/984 tons of equipment and spare parts to forward units.)

Soviet progress was, in fact, so rapid that the German front-line entirely disintegrated – so many defensive pockets were formed that there was no chance of any organized relief efforts. In fact, there were insufficient reserves to re-establish any proper

▲ SU-122 SP gun

Voronezh Front / Fifth Guards Tank Army / 1446th Self-Propelled Gun Regiment

The SU-122 was the first successful assault gun design based on the T-34 and was armed with the 122mm (4.7in) M-30 howitzer in a fully enclosed fighting compartment. Medium SP gun regiments, each with 16 SU-122s, began to enter service early in 1943. (A total of 638 vehicles were completed before production ended in November 1943.)

Specifications

Crew: 5	Speed: 55km/h (34.18mph)
Weight: 30.9 tonnes (11.02 tons)	Range: 300km (186.4miles)
Length: 6.95m (22ft 9in)	Radio: 9R (When fitted – even by
Width: 3m (9ft 8in)	1945, not all Soviet AFVs had radios.)
Height: 2.32m (7ft 7in)	Armament: 122mm (4.8in) M30-S howitzer
Engine: 373kW (500hp) V-2 diesel	

▲ M10 'Wolverine' tank destroyer

3rd Byelorussian Front / Fifth Guards Tank Army / 29th Tank Corps / 1223rd Self-Propelled Artillery Regiment

The Red Army received no more than 52 Lend-Lease M10s, which seem to have seen action only with Fifth Guards Tank Army during 1944.

Specifications

Crew: 5	Engine: 277.89kW (375hp) General Motors
Weight: 29.6 tonnes (29.13 tons)	6046; 12 cylinder, twin in-line diesel
Length: 5.82m (19ft 1in)	Speed: 48km/h (30mph)
Width: 3.05m (10ft)	Range: 320km (200miles)
Height: 2.49m (8ft 2in)	Armament: 1 x 76mm M7 gun, plus 1 x pintle-
	mounted 12.7mm (0.5in) Browning HMG

▼ Tank Brigade (June 1944)

By 1944, Soviet tank brigades were far more effective formations than they had been earlier in the war. Increasing standardization of vehicle types eased maintenance and support problems, while the more widespread issue of radios greatly improved operational command and control.

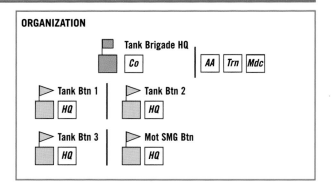

ORGANIZATION

Brigade HQ (3 x MCs, 1 x truck, 2 x T-34/85s)

HQ Company (3 x ACs, 9 x MCs, 10 x trucks)

Tank Battalion 1 (1 x staff car, 21 x T-34/85s, 12 x trucks)

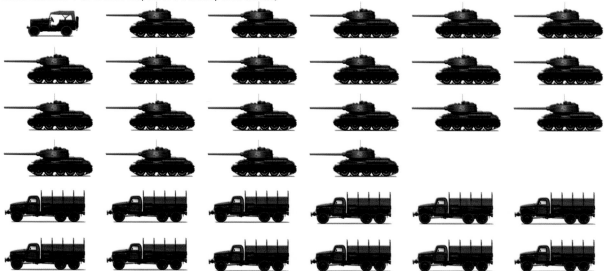

front-line and the isolated units were left to their own devices. A minority managed to break out to the west, but most were destroyed by the Red Army or partisan bands.

Inevitably, supply problems and sheer exhaustion took their toll as the advance continued, but by the time that the offensive finally wound down in the third week of August, Soviet forces had crossed the frontier of East Prussia, were on the point of reaching the Baltic and had advanced to the gates of Warsaw. German forces were in a state of utter chaos, with on-paper units and formations bearing little resemblance to the forces on the ground.

Army Group Centre had indeed been practically

Tank Battalion 2 (1 x staff car, 21 x T-34/85s, 12 x trucks)

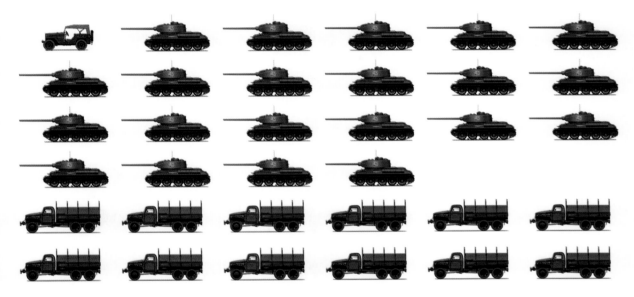

Tank Battalion 3 (1 x staff car, 21 x T-34/85s, 12 x trucks)

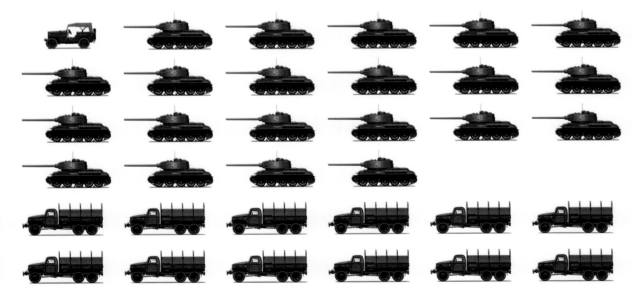

▲ Crushing Army Group Centre

Summer 1944 – a JS-2 of the 1st Ukrainian Front operating in the infantry support role during Operation *Bagration*.

Operation *Bagration* Losses	German	Soviet
Tanks	2000	2957
Other Vehicles	57,000	–
Artillery Pieces	–	2447
Aircraft	–	822
Dead	300,000	60,000
Wounded	250,000	110,000
Captured	120,000	–
Missing	–	8000
Overall Casualties	670,000	–

annihilated with 2000 AFVs and 57,000 other vehicles destroyed or captured. German casualties may well have been as high as 300,000 dead, 250,000 wounded and about 120,000 prisoners. The *Wehrmacht* simply could not afford casualties on this scale – experienced NCOs were vital in restoring the effectiveness of units that had to absorb large numbers of replacement personnel and their loss gradually reduced the tactical superiority that German units had previously taken for granted.

Red Army losses were also high, with 60,000 killed, 110,000 wounded and about 8000 missing. In terms of equipment, Soviet forces lost 2957 tanks, 2447 guns and 822 aircraft, but Soviet war production and Lend-Lease supplies meant that these losses could readily be replaced.

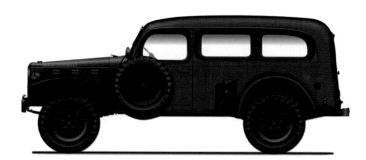

Specifications

Crew: 1 driver

Weight: 2.6 tonnes (5750lb) fully laden

Length: 4.72m (15ft 6in)

Width: 2m (6ft 6in)

Height: 2.03m (6ft 7in)

Engine: 6 cylinder 68.6kW (92hp) petrol engine

Speed: not known

Range: not known

Armament: none

▲ WC-53 Truck, ¾-ton 4x4 Dodge Carryall

HQ 1st Belorussian Front

Roughly 200 Lend-Lease WC-53s were supplied to the Red Army. Their six-seat capacity and 4x4 configuration made them ideal staff cars.

Lvov–Sandomir Offensive
13 July – 29 August 1944

This offensive towards Lvov was intended to ensure the success of Operation *Bagration* by preventing the Germans from reinforcing Army Group Centre.

THE OPERATION WAS assigned to Konev's 1st Ukrainian Front, which could deploy over 1,200,000 troops, 2050 tanks, about 16,000 guns and mortars and over 3250 aircraft of the Second Air Army. They were opposed by General Harpe's Army Group North Ukraine, totalling roughly 370,000 men with 420 AFVs.

The 1st Ukrainian Front's offensive was launched on two axes. Three armies were to attack towards Rava-Ruska, whilst a further four advanced on Lvov. The attacks were to be made on a front of only 26km (16 miles). The attack towards Rava-Ruska began on 13 July 1944 and by nightfall the Thirteenth Army had advanced 20km (12.4 miles). On the following day, the advance on Lvov began, which left the German XIII Corps in a dangerously exposed salient around Brody.

The southern arm of the Soviet offensive achieved a decisive breakthrough on a front of only 3–4km (1.8–2.5 miles; the Koltiv Corridor) between XIII Corps and XLVIII Panzer Corps. Fierce German counterattacks on the corridor were beaten off, and on 16 July Konev took the risk of committing the Third Guards Tank Army to an attack through the Corridor, which was still under heavy bombardment from German artillery. By 18 July, 45,000 men of XIII Corps were trapped around Brody, and a 200km (124-mile) breach had been created in the German front. The Brody pocket was destroyed on 22 July and Lvov was captured four days later, completing the reconquest of Ukraine.

The second stage of the offensive opened on 29 July, aimed at a seizing a bridgehead across the Vistula and taking Sandomierz in southern Poland. The bridgehead was taken, but Sandomierz did not fall until 18 August.

The badge is the Piast eagle, the symbol of the *Ludowe Wojsko Polskie* (LWP) – the People's Army of Poland, which was adopted as the unit insignia of the 1st Polish Armoured Brigade.

▲ **PT-34 engineer tank**

1st Byelorussian Front / Polish First Army / 1st Armoured Brigade

This late-production T-34 Model 1943 was converted to a PT-34 by the installation of a Mugalev mine-clearing roller, which could withstand between eight and 10 detonations of AT mines before requiring replacement. The system equipped seven Red Army Engineer Tank Regiments from 1943 onwards.

Specifications

Crew: 5

Weight: 3.90 tonnes (30.41 tons) (without roller)

Length: 6.75m (22ft 1in) (without roller)

Width: 3m (9ft 8in) (without roller)

Height: 2.45m (8ft 0in)

Engine: 373kW (500hp) V-2 diesel

Speed: 55km/h (34.2mph)

Range: (road) 465km (289 miles);

(terrain) 365km (227miles)

Radio: 9R (When fitted)

Armament: Main: 76.2mm (3in) F-34 gun,

Secondary: 2 x 7.62mm (0.3in) DT machine

guns (coaxial and bow)

◀ **Into Poland**

A GAZ-MM truck passes a column of SU-152s in Lvov, July 1944. Despite the introduction of the JSU-152, surviving SU-152s remained in service throughout the war. These vehicles are heavily laden with spare fuel drums to extend their range.

Specifications

Crew: 5

Weight: 46 tonnes (45.27 tons)

Length: 9.2m (30ft 1in)

Width: 3.07m (10ft 1in)

Height: 2.48m (8ft 1in)

Engine: 447kW (600hp) V-2 diesel

Speed: 37km/h (23mph)

Range: (Road) 220km (136.7miles);

(Terrain) 80km (49.7miles)

Radio: 10RF (When fitted)

Armament: 152mm (5.9in) ML-20S howitzer

▲ **JSU-152 heavy SP gun**

1st Ukrainian Front / Third Guards Tank Army / Independent Heavy Self-Propelled Artillery Regiment

The SU-152 was a highly effective assault gun, but as production of the KV series was scheduled to end in late 1943, the design had to be adapted to fit the hull of the JS-2. The new JSU-152, which entered service in 1944, had an enlarged fighting compartment and thicker armour.

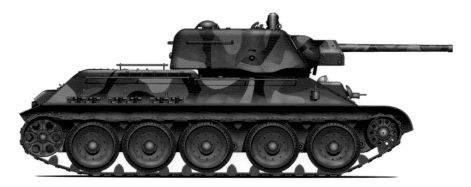

▲ **T-34 Model 1943**

1st Ukrainian Front / Fourth Tank Army / XI Tank Corps

This unusual four-tone camouflage pattern, applied to some Red Army AFVs during the Lvov–Sandomir operation of July–August 1944, is in striking contrast to the far more common overall dark-green finish.

Specifications

Crew: 4

Weight: 30.9 tonnes (30 tons)

Length: 5.92m (19ft 5in)

Width: 3.00m (9ft 8in)

Height: 2.44m (8ft)

Engine: 373kW (500hp) V-2-34 V-12 cylinder

diesel

Speed (road): 53km/h (33mph)

Range: 465km (290 miles)

Armament: 1 x 76mm (3in) L-40 gun;

2 x 7.62mm (0.3in) DT MGs (bow and coaxial)

▼ Tank Regiment (1944)

By 1944, these tank regiments were powerful units, especially when equipped with the new T-34/85 with its greatly improved protection and firepower. Such units provided close support for infantry formations, freeing the tank armies for deep-penetration operations.

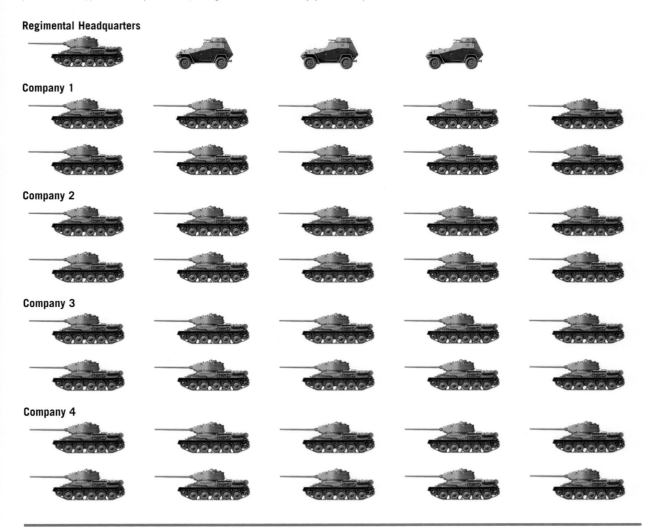

Regimental Headquarters

Company 1

Company 2

Company 3

Company 4

Operation *Jassy-Kishinev*
20–29 AUGUST 1944

By May 1944, German Army Group South Ukraine had been pushed back towards the Rumanian frontier along the River Dniester. The Red Army prepared for its next offensive.

THE RED ARMY HELD two bridgeheads across the river, and *STAVKA* now planned a double envelopment of the German and Rumanian armies by the 2nd and 3rd Ukrainian Fronts. The 2nd Ukrainian Front was to break through north of Jassy and then seize the crossings over the River Prut to cut

Specifications

Crew: 5	Speed: 48km/h (30mph)
Weight: 33.3 tonnes (32.77 tons)	Range: 161km (100miles)
Length: 7.6m (24ft 10in)	Radio: 9R (When fitted)
Width: 2.62m (8ft 7in)	Armament: 1 x 76mm (3in) M1A1 gun,
Height: 2.97m (9ft 9in)	1 x 12.7mm (0.5in) Browning HMG on turret
Engine: 279.4kW (375hp) General Motors	AA mount, 2 x 7.62mm (0.3in) Browning MGs,
12-cylinder in-line diesel	1 coaxial, 1 bow

▲ **M4A2 (76mm) Sherman medium tank**

2nd Ukrainian Front / Sixth Guards Tank Army / 5th Mechanized Corps.

By mid-1944, the M4A2 (76mm) formed the entire tank strength of V Mechanized Corps – several more mechanized and tank corps were entirely equipped with the type by the end of the war.

off the German Sixth Army. The Sixth Tank Army was to seize the bridges across the River Siret and the fortified Focsani Gap between the Siret and the Danube. The 3rd Ukrainian Front would break out from its bridgehead at Tiraspol, then head north to meet the 2nd Ukrainian Front and trap the German and Rumanian forces. After sealing the pocket, the Sixth Tank Army and IV Guards Mechanized Corps were to take Bucharest and the Ploesti oil fields.

Soviet forces were formidable – more than 1,340,000 men and at least 1800 AFVs to face about 500,000 Germans and 405,000 Rumanians supported by only 170 tanks and assault guns. The Red Army now had a huge qualitative superiority over the Rumanian forces, whose AFVs and AT weapons were unable to counter T-34/85s and JS-2s.

The attacks by the 2nd and 3rd Ukrainian Fronts were made on narrow frontages supported by the fire of almost 250 guns per kilometre. This superiority ensured rapid breakthroughs, leading to a double envelopment of the German Sixth Army and elements of the Eighth Army. By 22 August, the Axis front-line collapsed and VI Guards Mechanized Corps was inserted to exploit the breakthrough.

The next day, a *coup d'etat* led by King Michael of Rumania deposed the pro-German dictator, Marshal

Antonescu, and the country changed sides. German forces guarding the Ploesti oilfields were attacked by Rumanian troops and withdrew into Hungary.

The equivalent of 18 German divisions had been destroyed and Germany's last major source of crude oil was lost. Fuel shortages caused by the Allied bombing campaign had already badly affected the *Luftwaffe*'s operations and the loss of Rumanian oil would soon cripple the *Wehrmacht*'s efforts to repulse future Soviet offensives.

▲ **Tank ferry**

Red Army engineers ferry a T-34/85 across the Donetz River as part of the massive Soviet summer offensive in 1944.

Specifications

Crew: 7	Engine: 95kW (128hp) White 160AX
Weight: 10.16 tonnes (10 tons)	6-cylinder petrol
Length: 6.14m (20ft 3in)	Speed: 64km/h (45mph)
Width: 2.49m (8ft 2in)	Range: 280km (200miles)
Height: 2.44m (8ft)	Armament: 1 x 37mm (1.46in) M1A2 gun,
	2 x coaxial 12.7mm (0.5in) Browning HMGs

▲ **Combination Gun Motor Carriage M15A1**

3rd Ukrainian Front / Thirty-Seventh Army / AA Regiment

As late as 1944/45, the *Luftwaffe*'s ground-attack units still posed a significant threat to Soviet armoured forces. (It has been estimated that air attacks were responsible for 6 per cent of the Red Army's tank losses, equating to 90 tanks a month during 1944.) Roughly 100 M15A1s were supplied under Lend-Lease and were enthusiastically received, as their armour protection and cross-country mobility allowed them to operate far more effectively with armoured and mechanized units than earlier truck-mounted AA guns.

▶ **GAZ-67 4X4 command car**

HQ 3rd Ukrainian Front

Intended as a Soviet equivalent of the Lend-Lease jeep, the GAZ-67 was never as popular, primarily due to its high fuel consumption and weak brakes.

Specifications

Crew: 1 driver	Engine: 37.25kW (50hp) 4-cylinder petrol
Weight: 1.32 tonnes (1.3 tons)	Speed: 90km/h (56mph)
Length: 3.35m (11ft)	Range: 450km (280miles)
Width: 1.685m (5ft 6in)	Radio: Name
Height: 1.7m (5ft 7in)	

To the Baltic
14 SEPTEMBER – 24 NOVEMBER 1944

In February 1944, the *Wehrmacht* was forced to retreat from the approaches of Leningrad to the Panther Line on the borders of Estonia. In June–August, Operation *Bagration* had decimated Army Group Centre and pushed it back into Poland.

THIS CREATED THE opportunity for a Red Army offensive (the Shyaulyay Offensive Operation) which reached the Baltic on 31 July, severing the land connection between the German Army Groups. Although Operation *Doppelkopf*, a German counter-offensive launched in August, temporarily reopened land links between the Army Groups, the 'corridor' was never more than 30km (18.6 miles) wide. It was always vulnerable and was quickly cut by a new Soviet offensive launched on 14 September by the

1st and 3rd Baltic Fronts. This made rapid progress towards Riga, despite counter-attacks by XXXIX Panzer Corps.

Memel offensive

On 5 October, the 1st Baltic Front launched the Memel Offensive Operation, which destroyed the Third Panzer Army and finally cut the land link between Army Groups North and Centre, isolating Schoerner's forces in Riga and Courland. Initially, it seemed that Memel would soon fall, but the German XXVIII Corps was able to hold a perimeter around the port, supported by naval gunfire from heavy units of the *Kriegsmarine,* including the pocket battleship *Lützow* and the heavy cruiser *Prinz Eugen.*

Insignia of the 1219th Self-Propelled Artillery Regiment. Many Soviet armoured units adopted similar simple geometric symbols.

▲ **JSU-122 heavy self-propelled gun**

1st Baltic Front / Fifth Guards Tank Army / 1219th Self-Propelled Artillery Regiment

The JSU-122 was developed purely to take advantage of the ready availability of 122mm (4.7in) guns and was identical to the JSU-152 except for the main armament and ammunition stowage.

Specifications

Crew: 5	Speed: 37km/h (23mph)
Weight: 45.5 tonnes (44.78 tons)	Range: (Road) 220km (136.7miles), (Terrain)
Length: 9.85m (32ft 3in)	80km (49.7miles)
Width: 3.07m (10ft 1in)	Radio: 10RF (When fitted)
Height: 2.48m (8ft 1in)	Armament: 1 x 122mm (4.7in) A-19S gun,
Engine: 447kW (600hp) V-2 diesel	plus 1 x 12.7mm (0.5in) DShK HMG

Specifications

Crew: 5	Engine: 106.54kW (143hp) International
Weight: 8.94 tonnes (8.8 tons)	Harvester RED-450-B; 6 cylinder, in-line petrol
Length: 6.49m (21ft 4in)	Speed: 68km/h (42mph)
Width: 2.17m (7ft 1in)	Range: 320km (200miles)
Height: 2.3m (7ft 6in)	Armament: 4 x 12.7mm (0.5in) Browning HMGs

▲ **M17 Multiple Motor Gun Carriage**

3rd Baltic Front / Sixty-First Army / AA Regiment / HQ

As many as 1000 M17s were issued to Soviet forces by 1945. The impressive firepower of the vehicle's four 12.7mm (0.5in) HMGs endeared it to the Red Army, which found it useful for infantry support as in its AA role.

Hitler did not accept Schoerner's proposal to use forces freed by evacuating Riga in an attack towards Memel to attempt to re-establish the land connection, but his position was rapidly becoming untenable. Soviet forces were advancing and Riga was taken by the 3rd Baltic Front on 13 October, forcing Army Group North to retreat into the Courland Peninsula (where it held out until May 1945).

The success of these operations prompted *Stavka* to attempt a new offensive into East Prussia by Chernyakhovsky's 3rd Belorussian Front. The plan was for the Fifth and Eleventh Guards Armies to break through the German defences, after which II Guards Tank Corps and the Twenty-Eighth Army would advance on Königsberg, with the Thirty-First and Thirty-Ninth Armies providing flank protection. *Stavka* was becoming over-confident, however, and it failed to appreciate that the defenders had been

▲ M5 halftrack
2nd Baltic Front / Third Shock Army / HQ

In common with the other US armoured personnel carrier (APC) halftracks, the majority of the 342 M5s sent to Soviet forces were appropriated by formation HQs for use as command vehicles.

Specifications

Crew: 2, plus 11 passengers	Engine: 106.54kW (143hp) International
Weight: 9.3 tonnes (9.15 tons)	Harvester RED-450-B; 6-cylinder, in-line petrol
Length: 6.33m (20ft 9in)	Speed: 68km/h (42mph)
Width: 2.2m (7ft 2in)	Range: 320km (200miles)
Height: 2.74m (9ft)	Armament: 1 x 12.7mm (0.5in) Browning HMG

▲ M2 halftrack
3rd Baltic Front / Second Shock Army / HQ

With only a canvas tilt for protection against the elements, the open-topped US halftracks were not ideally suited to the extreme conditions of Russian winters.

Specifications

Crew: 2, plus 8 passengers	Engine: 109.5kW (147hp) White 160AX;
Weight: 8.89 tonnes (8.75 tons)	6 cylinder, in-line petrol
Length: 6.14m (20ft 2in)	Speed: 72km/h (45mph)
Width: 2.22m (7ft 3in)	Range: 320km (200miles)
Height: 2.7m (8ft 10in)	Armament: 1 x 12.7mm (0.5in) Browning HMG

heavily reinforced and would be aided by substantial fortifications.

On 16 October, the Fifth and Eleventh Guards Armies began their attacks, making an 11km (6.8-mile) penetration of the outer German defences and crossing the East Prussian border within the first 24 hours. However, it soon became clear that the German defences had been underestimated – it took four days to break through the first defensive line and the second was so strong that II Guards Tank Corps had to be committed.

The second line was finally broken at the cost of very heavy casualties, but it took the addition of the Front's reserve, the Twenty-Eighth Army, to push back the defending units, which had been reinforced by the 18th Flak Division, whose guns inflicted heavy losses on the Soviet tanks. Gumbinnen was taken on 22 October, but was recaptured two days later.

There was equally fierce fighting around Goldap on the southern flank of the Soviet offensive. The town was retaken by the Germans on 25 October, successfully assaulted by the Soviet Thirty-First Army in a surprise attack on 28 October, and finally recaptured by the 5th Panzer Division on 3 November. The Soviet offensive had been a bloody failure, sustaining an estimated 79,500 casualties. The Red Army would not re-enter East Prussia in strength until January 1945.

▼ Heavy Assault Gun Regiment (1944)

The JSU-122 equipped regiments were formidable units, equally capable of acting as tank destroyers or in an infantry support role. Their high-velocity 122mm (4.8in) guns were capable of destroying even the heavily armoured Tiger IIs at normal combat ranges.

Regiment Headquarters

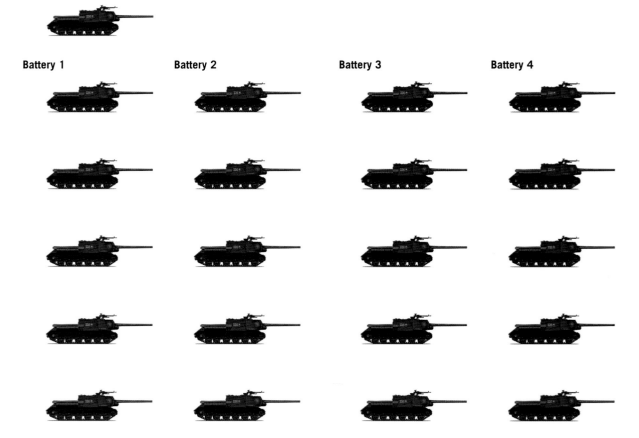

Battery 1 **Battery 2** **Battery 3** **Battery 4**

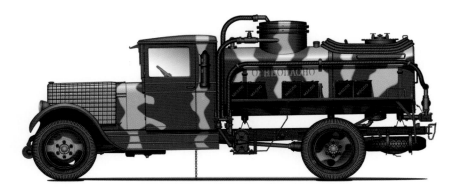

Specifications*

Crew: 1 driver

Weight: 3.1 tonnes (3.42 tons)

Length: 6.1m (20ft)

Width: 2.25m (7ft 4.5in)

Height: 2.16m (7ft 1in)

Engine: 54/57kW (73/76hp) ZiS-5M

Speed: 60km/h (37.3mph)

*Data for the basic ZiS-5 truck. Dimensions
 and weight of the tanker version are likely
 to be somewhat greater.

▲ **ZiS-5-BZ fuel tanker**

2nd Baltic Front / Supply Battalion

Even with the vast influx of Lend-Lease trucks, there were never enough supply vehicles, and priority always had to be given to ammunition and fuel.

Into the Balkans
14 SEPTEMBER – 24 NOVEMBER 1944

In September 1944, the two German Army Groups (E and F) in the Balkans were in danger of being cut off by the rapid advance of the Red Army and the defection of former German satellite forces. The Soviet victory at Jassy-Kishinev had forced Bulgaria and Romania to change sides, adding them to Germany's list of enemies. *Stavka* now planned to carry the war into Yugoslavia and take Belgrade.

B Y THE END OF September 1944, the 3rd Ukrainian Front (with the Second Bulgarian Army under command) had moved up to the Bulgarian-Yugoslav border in preparation for an advance on Belgrade. In Rumania, elements of the 2nd Ukrainian Front were assembling in readiness for an attack to cut the rail link between Belgrade and

Specifications

Crew: 2/3

Weight: 3.81 tonnes (3.75 tons)

Length: 3.65m (12ft)

Width: 1.92m (6ft 4in)

Height: 1.57m (5ft 2in)

Engine: 63.3kW (85hp) Ford V-8 petrol

Speed: 48km/h (30mph)

Range: 250km (150miles)

Armament: 1 x 12.7mm (0.5in) DShK HMG,
 plus 1 x 7.7mm (0.303in) Bren Gun

▶ **Universal Carrier Mark II**

3rd Ukrainian Front / Fourth Guards Army / IV Guards Mechanized Corps /
14th Mechanized Brigade

Although the Red Army preferred US halftracks due to their far greater carrying capacity, it employed 2500 Lend-Lease Universal Carriers in a variety of roles. While retaining its Bren Gun, this example has been fitted with a 12.7mm (0.5in) DShK HMG for the infantry fire support role.

▲ **Balkan victory**
A T-34/85 of the 3rd Ukrainian Front's IV Guards Mechanized Corps pauses for a halt in Belgrade, October 1944. The extra kit accumulated by tank crews on active service is much in evidence.

Hungary. Tito's partisans now controlled large swathes of territory in Yugoslavia and Tito himself flew to Moscow for a meeting with Stalin to co-ordinate plans for the offensive.

Before the start of ground operations, the 3rd Ukrainian Front's Seventeenth Air Army carried out a week-long series of air attacks against German units withdrawing from Greece and southern Yugoslavia. The offensive began in late September – the 2nd Bulgarian Army's advance was contested by the 7th SS Mountain Division *Prinz Eugen*, which was overwhelmed and forced to withdraw. The Bulgarian forces then moved on Kosovo in an attempt to cut Army Group E's line of retreat from Greece. The Soviet Fifty-Seventh Army led the 3rd Ukrainian Front's attack towards Belgrade, with considerable support from Tito's partisans and the gunboats of the

Danube Military Flotilla. By 12 October, IV Guards Mechanized Corps was moved up from Bulgaria in preparation for a breakthrough to Belgrade.

Further north, the 2nd Ukrainian Front's Forty-Sixth Army advanced in an attempt to outflank the German Belgrade defensive position from the north, by cutting the river and rail supply lines running along the River Tisa. With close air support from the Fifth Air Army, its X Guards Rifle Corps made rapid progress to threaten the main rail routes from Belgrade.

On 14 October, IV Guards Mechanized Corps and the Yugoslav XII Corps broke through the German defences south of Belgrade. Although the assault on the city was delayed by the need to clear German forces holding out in the surrounding area, Belgrade was finally liberated on 20 October by combined Soviet and Yugoslav forces. At this time, the Bulgarian Second Army and Yugoslav XIII Corps were still advancing from the south-east. Their operations had forced Army Group E to retreat through Montenegro and Bosnia, preventing it from reinforcing German formations in Hungary.

By late November, German forces had been cleared from virtually the whole of Yugoslavia and the Red Army was poised for its next offensives, riding high on a growing wave of victories. While its military successes had been spectacular, they were overshadowed by their political results – a new Soviet empire to rival that of the Tsars was rapidly being formed.

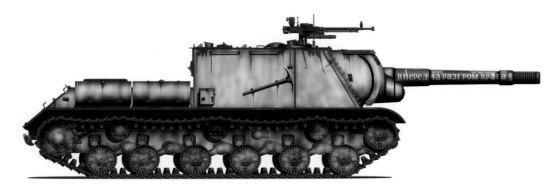

Specifications

Crew: 5

Weight: 46 tonnes (45.27 tons)

Length: 9.18m (30ft 1in)

Width: 3.07m (10ft 1in)

Height: 2.48m (8ft 1in)

Engine: 447kW (600hp) V-2 diesel

Speed: 37km/h (23mph)

Range: (Road) 220km (136.7 miles),
(Terrain) 80km (49.7 miles)

Radio: 10RF (When fitted)

Armament: 1 x 152mm (5.9in) ML-20S
howitzer, plus 1 x 12.7mm (0.5in) DShK HMG
on an AA mount

▲ JSU-152 heavy SP gun

2nd Ukrainian Front / Sixth Guards Tank Army / Independent Heavy Self-Propelled Artillery Regiment

Although officially designated as an artillery weapon, the JSU-152 was primarily used as a direct-fire assault gun, relying on its good armour protection to engage targets at close range.

Specifications

Crew: 4

Weight: 30.9 tonnes (30 tons)

Length: 5.92m (19ft 5in)

Width: 3.00m (9ft 8in)

Height: 2.44m (8ft)

Engine: 373kW (500hp) V-2-34 V-12 cylinder
diesel

Speed (road): 53km/h (33mph)

Range: 465km (290 miles)

Armament: 1 x 76mm (3in) L-40 gun;
2 x 7.62mm (0.3in) DT MGs (bow and coaxial)

▲ T-34 Model 1943

2nd Ukrainian Front / Sixth Tank Army

As the Red Army undertook increasingly large-scale offensives during 1944, ever-expanding numbers of its AFVs were fitted with 'drum type' long-range fuel tanks to extend their radius of action and ease demands on the supply columns.

Chapter 5

Victory in Europe

By 1945, the Red Army was rapidly closing the 'technology gap' that had opened up in 1943 with the *Panzerwaffe*'s introduction of the Tiger and Panther. The T-34/85 had entered service in 1944 and was steadily replacing earlier T-34s, while the JSU-122 and JSU-152 had proved to be exceptionally useful both as heavy assault guns and as tank destroyers. The Germans attempted to maintain their qualitative edge with improved versions of the Panther and new types such as the Tiger II, Jagdpanzer IV and Jagdpanther, but were unable to produce them in sufficient numbers to make a significant impact. Ironically, in the last months of the war one of the greatest threats to Soviet AFVs would not be the impressive German Jagdpanzers, but the simple, deadly *Panzerfausts* and *Panzerschrecks*.

◀ **Tank victory**
JS-2s roll through central Berlin, May 1945 – after the ceasefire, judging by the casual attitude of the tank commanders.

Vistula–Oder Offensive
12 January – 2 February 1945

The Vistula–Oder operation was originally intended as a major element of a series of offensives to be launched in late January 1945, with the objective of ending the war in 45 days.

HOWEVER, IN RESPONSE to US and British requests for action to ease the pressure from the Ardennes offensive, Stalin ordered a less ambitious operation, which was launched on 12 January. The Soviet objective was now limited to securing the line of the River Vistula, which would bring them to within 60km (37 miles) of Berlin.

Zhukov's 1st Byelorussian Front and Konev's 1st Ukrainian Front fielded 163 divisions for the offensive, with a total of 2,203,000 troops, 4529 tanks, 2513 assault guns, 13,763 field artillery weapons (76mm/3in or more), 14,812 mortars, 4936 AT guns, 2198 'Katyusha' salvo rocket launchers and 5000 aircraft.

They were opposed by Army Group A, which could muster no more than 400,000 troops, 4100 guns and 1150 AFVs. (As usual, the Soviet numerical superiority was increased by massive

Tank Corps, Personnel (1945)	Strength
Corps Headquarters	32
Signal Battalion	253
Motorcycle Battalion	451
Tank Brigade x 3	1362
Motorized Rifle Brigade	3222
Heavy Assault Gun Regiment (SU-152)	374
Assault Gun Regiment (SU-85/100)	318
Light Assault Gun Regiment (SU-76)	225
Light Artillery Regiment	625
Rocket Launcher Battalion	203
Mortar Regiment	596
Anti-Aircraft Regiment	397
Pioneer Battalion	455
Trains Elements	298

▲ **JS-1 heavy tank**

2nd Ukrainian Front / Sixth Guards Tank Army

Only small numbers of the JS-1 were built. It was quickly replaced by the JS-2 after combat experience showed that a better gun was needed to deal with the heavy armour of the Tiger II and Jagdpanther.

Specifications

Crew: 4

Weight: 46 tonnes (45.3 tons)

Length: 8.32m (27ft 3in)

Width: 3.25m (10ft 8in)

Height: 2.9m (9ft 6in)

Engine: 38.8kW (510hp) V-2 12-cylinder diesel

Speed: 40km/h (24.9mph)

Range: 250km (155miles)

Radio: 10R

Armament: 1 x 85mm (3.35in) D-5T gun,
  plus 2 x 7.62mm (0.3in) DT MGs, 1 coaxial,
  1 ball-mounted in turret rear

concentrations of troops and artillery at key sectors – Eighth Guards Army had 350 guns and mortars per kilometre, one gun every 3m (10ft).

The offensive was launched on 12 January 1945 by Konev's 1st Ukrainian Front from the Soviet bridgehead near Sandomierz. The assault quickly broke through the sketchy defences of the Fourth Panzer Army, which largely comprised isolated strongpoints since it lacked the infantry to hold a continuous front-line. Within 12 hours, Third Guards and Fourth Tank Armies with a combined strength of over 1700 tanks and SP guns were able to exploit the breakthrough and the Fourth Panzer Army had lost over 60 per cent of its artillery and 25 per cent of its troops.

Zhukov attacks

On 14 January, Zhukov's attack began with a 25-minute preliminary artillery barrage in which 315,000 rounds were fired (almost 5500 tonnes/ 5413 tons). Once again, the German defences virtually disintegrated: within a few hours, the First and Second Guards Tank Armies' 1635 tanks and SP guns were driving into the German rear areas, towards Lodz. Indeed, the speed of the Soviet advance was such that Panzer Corps *Grossdeutschland*, hastily transferred from East

▲ **Marshall Konev**

Konev (left) was an able and exceptionally ruthless commander. By 1944, his rivalry with Zhukov was exploited by Stalin to hasten the capture of key objectives.

▲ **T-34/85**

1st Ukrainian Front / Third Guards Tank Army / IX Mechanized Corps

By 1945, the T-34/85 was increasingly supplanting the earlier T-34s, especially in guards units, which tended to get priority for new equipment.

Specifications

Crew: 5

Weight: 32 tonnes (31.5 tons)

Length: 6m (19ft 7in)

Width: 3m (9ft 9in)

Height: 2.60m (8ft 6in)

Engine: 1 x V-2 V-12 cylinder 372 kW (493hp) diesel engine

Speed (road): 55km/h (33mph)

Range: 360km (223 miles)

Radio: 9R (When fitted)

Armament: 1 x 85mm (3.4in) ZiS-S-53 cannon; 2 x 7.62mm (0.3in) DT MGs (bow and coaxial)

Prussia, was brushed aside before it could fully deploy and was forced to retreat.

Warsaw was taken on 17 January by the 1st Byelorussian Front's First Polish Army, whilst Konev's forces overran the industrial area of Upper Silesia by the end of the month. (Stalin had personally briefed Konev on the vital importance of capturing the region's factories and mines intact. All Soviet operations in the area carefully left escape routes open for retreating German forces to avoid destructive combat in key industrial centres.) While many towns and cities were captured quickly, some by-passed centres held out for prolonged periods, considerably complicating the work of the over-stretched Soviet supply units. Nonetheless, by 31 January the 1st

Byelorussian Front's I Mechanized Corps had secured bridgeheads over the frozen Oder, roughly 30km (18.6 miles) apart, one south of Frankfurt-an-der-Oder and the other north of Kustrin. They were only 60km (37 miles) from Berlin.

Although both Zhukov and Konev pressed for permission to go on to Berlin, *Stavka* closed down the offensive on 2 February. Both Fronts had advanced roughly 500km (311 miles) on a 500km (311-mile) frontage in little more than three weeks and their supply lines were stretched to breaking point. Furthermore, despite their weakened state, German forces in East Pomerania posed a real threat to the exhausted Soviet troops and would have to be dealt with – Berlin would have to wait.

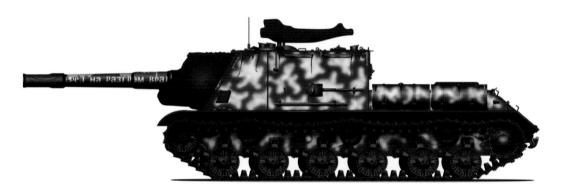

▲ **JSU-152 Heavy Self-Propelled Gun**

1st Ukrainian Front / Third Guards Tank Army / IV Guards Tank Corps / 385th
Guards Heavy Self-Propelled Artillery Regiment

This JSU-152 has unusually elaborate winter camouflage – roughly applied coats of whitewash were far more common.

Specifications

Crew: 5	Range: (Road) 220km (136.7miles),
Weight: 46 tonnes (45.27 tons)	(Terrain) 80km (49.7miles)
Length: 9.18m (30ft 1in)	Radio: 10RF (When fitted)
Width: 3.07m (10ft 1in)	Armament: 1 x 152mm (5.9in) ML-20S
Height: 2.48m (8ft 1in)	howitzxer, plus 1 x 12.7mm (0.5in) DShK HMG
Engine: 447kW (600hp) V-2 diesel	on an AA mount
Speed: 37km/h (23mph)	

▶ **Willys MB 4x4 ¼-ton Truck, Command Reconnaissance**

1st Ukrainian Front / Third Guards Tank Army / HQ

The extremes of the Russian climate led to many jeeps being fitted with 'hard tops' as a field modification.

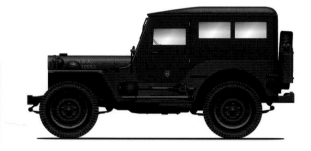

Specifications

Crew: 1 driver	Engine: 44.7kW (60hp) 4-cylinder petrol
Weight: 1.04 tonnes (1.02 tons)	Speed: 88.5km/h (55mph)
Length: 3.33m (10ft 11in)	Range: n/k
Width: 1.58m (5ft 2in)	Radio: n/a
Height: 1.83m (6ft)	

▲ **The war's last winter**

Soviet troops ride on the warm rear deck of an JSU-152, Poland, January 1945.

▲ **Studebaker US6 BZ-35S 6x4 2½-ton fuel tanker**

1st Ukrainian Front / Third Guards Tank Army / Special Transport Regiment

A proportion of the thousands of Lend-Lease Studebakers received by the
Red Army were converted to fuel tankers under the designation BZ-35S. The
advances of 1945 stretched logistics to the limit, as each tank army required
600–750 tonnes (591–738 tons) of fuel per day – 270 to 300 tanker loads.

Specifications

Crew: 2	Engine: JXD 6 cylinder Hercules
Weight: 4.33 tons (9555lbs)	Speed: not known
Length: 6.55m (21ft 6in)	Range: not known
Width: 2.23m (7ft 4in)	Radio: none
Height: 2.76m (9ft 1in)	

HQ 1 x T-70 light tank   **5 Batteries each with 4 x SU-76 assault guns**

HQ 1 x T-70 light tank   **5 Batteries each with 4 x SU-76 assault guns**

HQ 1 x T-70 light tank   **5 Batteries each with 4 x SU-76 assault guns**

◀ Light Assault Gun Brigade

Although their thinly armoured, open-topped SU-76Ms were very vulnerable to air-burst artillery, light assault gun brigades were highly mobile formations with considerable firepower.
(The low ground pressure of the SU-76M allowed it to cross swampy ground that was impassable to heavier AFVs.)

▲ SU-76M

1st Ukrainian Front / Third Guards Tank Army / VII Guards Tank Corps

The open-topped SU-76M was a particularly uncomfortable vehicle in the depths of an Eastern Front winter.

Specifications

Crew: 4	Engine: 2 x GAZ 6-cylinder petrol 52+52kW
Weight: 10.8 tonnes (11.9 tons)	(70+70hp)
Length: 4.88m (16ft)	Speed (road): 45km/h (28mph)
Width: 2.73m (8ft 11.5in)	Range: 450km (280miles)
Height: 2.17m (7ft 1.4in)	Armament: one 76mm (3in) gun and one
	7.62mm (0.3in) MG

▲ Forest cover

A JSU-122S moves up for the assault on Berlin, April 1945.

Austria and Hungary
FEBRUARY–APRIL 1945

By the summer of 1944, the Hungarian regime of Admiral Horthy was an increasingly reluctant German ally as the Red Army advanced towards the Carpathians. Hitler was determined to keep control of the oilfields around Lake Balaton, which were the Reich's last major source of oil.

GERMAN TROOPS HAD occupied key points throughout Hungary since March 1944, when Hitler had first learned of Admiral Horthy's initial 'peace feelers' to the Allies. On 16 October, renewed Hungarian attempts to negotiate with the Allies provoked Operation *Panzerfaust*, which deposed Admiral Horthy and set up a puppet fascist government led by Ferenc Szalasi.

Siege of Budapest

While the Germans had secured their rear areas, their defences in Hungary were rapidly crumbling as Malinovsky's 2nd Ukrainian Front advanced on Budapest. The first Red Army units penetrated the city's eastern suburbs on 7 November, but were halted by the German/Hungarian garrison that had just received major reinforcements, including the 1st, 3rd, 6th and 8th Panzer Divisions.

During the next six weeks, the Soviet forces were joined by Tobulkhin's 3rd Ukrainian Front and on 18 December both Fronts launched a new offensive to encircle Budapest. Despite fierce counter-attacks by several Panzer divisions, 3rd Ukrainian Front's XVIII Tank Corps linked up with 2nd Ukrainian Front on 26 December to seal off the city. Although the garrison of 76,000 was heavily outnumbered by the opposing 300,000 strong Soviet Fronts, the cover provided by the urban terrain went a long way towards balancing the odds. (The city was divided by the Danube – Buda lay on the hills of the river's west bank and Pest covered the relatively flat ground to the east of the river.)

▲ **JSU-122S heavy SP gun**

3rd Ukrainian Front / Sixth Guards Tank Army / V Guards Tank Corps / Independent Heavy Assault Gun Regiment

The JSU-122S was an updated JSU-122 that began to enter service in 1945. The main improvements were the D-25 122mm (4.8in) gun, with a revised breech mechanism to increase the rate of fire and a muzzle brake that reduced recoil. The D-25 was mounted in a new ball mantlet that improved traverse arcs.

Specifications

Crew: 5	Range: (Road) 220km (136.7miles),
Weight: 45.5 tonnes (44.78 tons)	(Terrain) 80km (49.7miles)
Length: 9.85m (32ft 3in)	Radio: 10RF (When fitted)
Width: 3.07m (10ft 1in)	Armament: 1 x 122mm (4.8in) D-25 gun,
Height: 2.48m (8ft 1in)	plus 1 x 12.7mm (0.5in) DShK HMG on
Engine: 447kW (600hp) V-2 diesel	an AA mount
Speed: 37km/h (23mph)	

Hungary, January 1945	T-34	IS-2	SU-76	SU-85	SU-100	ISU-122	ISU-152	M4A2 Sherman
XVIII Tank Corps	120	19	–	11	–	–	–	–
I Gds Mechanized Corps	–	–	–	–	62	–	–	184
II Gds Mechanized Corps	35	8	–	11	–	–	–	–
VII Mechanized Corps	–	65	12	14	10	–	–	–
I Gds Fortified Region	7	–	4	–	–	–	–	–
V Gds Cavalry Corps	2	–	13	–	–	–	–	–
XXIII Tank Corps	–	174	–	–	–	–	19	–

Specifications

Crew: 3

Weight: 17.27 tonnes (17 tons)

Length: 5.89m (19ft 4in)

Width: 2.64m (8ft 8in)

Height: 2.29m (7ft 6in)

Engine: 100kW (135hp) GMC 6004 diesel

Speed: 24km/h (14.9mph)

Range: 0km (0miles)

Radio: n/a

Armament: 1 x 2pdr (40mm), plus 1 x coaxial
7.92mm (0.31in) Besa MG

▲ **Infantry Tank Mark III, Valentine Mark VII**

2nd Ukrainian Front / 1st Guards Mechaniszd Cavalry Group

The Valentine was still in service with the Red Army in the final months of the war. As late as March 1945, a total of 41 Valentines were operational with the 1st Guards Mechanized Cavalry Group.

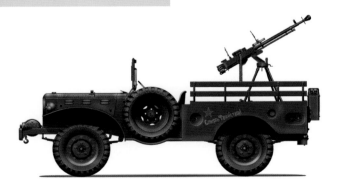

Specifications

Crew: 1 driver + 2/3 gun crew

Weight: 2.69 tonnes (5940lbs)

Length: 2.69m (14ft 8in)

Width: 2.10m (6ft 10in)

Height: 1.7m (5ft 7in)

Engine: 6 cylinder 68.6kW (92hp) petrol

Speed: not known

Range: not known

Armament: 1 x DShK 12.7mm (0.5in) HMG

▲ **Dodge WC52 4x4 ¾-ton weapons carrier with DShK 12.7mm (0.5in) HMG**

3rd Ukrainian Front / Sixth Guards Tank Army

From 1943 onwards, the Soviet Union received almost 25,000 of these vehicles, which were primarily used as gun tractors and troop carriers. However, a number were armed with the DShK 12.7mm (0.5in) HMG for use in the AA role and to protect AFVs against *Panzerfaust* ambushes.

The Soviet offensive began in the eastern suburbs, advancing into Pest itself along the broad main streets. The outnumbered German and Hungarian defenders fought delaying actions, slowly withdrawing to more defensible positions in the city centre. Soviet armoured units quickly discovered that *Panzerfausts* represented the greatest single threat to their tanks in street fighting. This was especially true when the defenders managed to pin down their accompanying infantry, before stalking the isolated tanks to make close range shots against their relatively

◀ **Waiting to advance**

A column of IS-2 heavy tanks from the 1st Byelorussian Front sits outside a town on the Polish-Hungarian border, March 1945.

AFV Units (Operational Strength), Hungary, March 1945	T-34	IS-2	SU-76	SU-85	SU-100	ISU-122	ISU-152	M4A2 Sherman
XVIII Tank Corps	42	–	12	–	–	16	6	–
208th SPGBr	2	–	3	–	63	–	–	–
XXIII Tank Corps	20	1	–	–	–	–	–	–
207th SPGR	2	–	–	–	20	–	–	–
366th Gds SPGR	–	2	–	–	–	–	4	–
I Gds Mechanized Corps	–	–	–	–	17	–	–	47
V Gds Cavalry Corps	7	–	8	–	–	–	–	2
1891st SPGR	–	–	2	–	–	–	–	–
1513rd SPGR	–	–	24	–	–	–	–	–
1523rd SPGR	–	–	25	–	–	–	–	–
1524th SPGR	–	–	25	–	–	–	–	–
SSPGB (4th Gds Army)	–	–	2	–	–	–	–	–
432nd SSPGB	–	–	7	–	–	–	–	–
1202nd SPGR	–	–	14	–	–	–	–	–
1201st SPGR	1	–	–	12	–	–	–	–
72nd SSPGB	–	–	–	–	–	–	–	–
32nd Gds Mot Rifle Bde	19	–	–	–	–	–	–	–
249th Tank Reg	–	10	–	–	–	–	–	–
854th SPGR	1	–	21	–	–	–	–	–
1094th SPGR	–	–	–	–	20	–	–	–
1922nd SPGR	–	–	–	–	16	–	–	–
3rd Gds SSPGB	10	–	–	–	–	–	–	–
58th SSPGB	10	–	–	–	–	–	–	–
SSPGB (27th Army)	–	–	22	–	–	–	–	–
209th SPGBr	2	–	–	–	46	–	–	–
XXII Tank Corps	6	–	–	2	–	–	–	–

KEY
SPGBr Self-Propelled Gun Brigade
SPGR   Self-Propelled Gun Regiment
SSPGB Separate Self-Propelled
        Gun Battalion

thin side and rear armour. Stalin was rapidly losing patience with the Red Army's slow progress and Malinovsky ordered the formation of a special combat group, including heavy weapons and assault engineers equipped with flamethrowers, to spearhead assaults. Rifle divisions were assigned attack sectors up to 700m (2297ft) wide, with regiments advancing fronts of no more than 300m (984ft). Large numbers of guns, including 122mm (4.8in), 152mm (5.9in), and 203mm (8in) howitzers, were brought up to support attacks with direct fire.

While Malinovsky was struggling to crush resistance in the city, three attempts by IV SS Panzer Corps to raise the siege (Operations *Konrad* I, II and III) came tantalizingly close to success before being blocked by hastily reinforced Soviet units. On 18 January, the corps launched a further attack after redeploying to the south, penetrating 32km (20 miles) in the first 24 hours, beating off a counterattack by VII Mechanized Corps.

The next day, further counterattacks by XVIII Tank Corps and CXXXIII Rifle Corps were broken up, largely due to the fire of the 3rd SS Panzer Division *Totenkopf*'s AT battalion, equipped with the new Jagdpanzer IV tank destroyers. Within three days, the leading German units had advanced 100km

▲ T-44 medium tank

Trials Unit

The T-44 entered production in 1945 as the replacement for the T34/85. Between 150 and 200 vehicles were produced by the end of the war, although it seems unlikely that any went into combat. (In 1947, the type was itself superseded by the T-54 which was armed with a 100mm gun.)

▼ M4A2 Sherman medium tank

3rd Ukrainian Front / I Guards Machanized Corps

By the end of the War, Shermans equipped three Guards mechanized corps and a Guards tank corps.

Specifications

Crew: 4	diesel
Weight: 31.9 tonnes (31.4 tons)	Speed: 51km/h (31.69mph)
Length: 7.65m (25ft 1in)	Range: 300km (186.4 miles)
Width: 3.15m (10ft 4in)	Armament: 1 x 85mm (3.35in) D-5T gun, plus
Height: 2.45m (8ft)	2 x 7.62mm (0.30in) DTM MGs, 1 coaxial and
Engine: 372.5kW (500hp) V-44 12-cylinder	1 fixed forward-firing

Specifications

Crew: 5
Weight: 32.28 tonnes (35.58 tons)
Length: 5.92m (19ft 5in)
Width: 2.62m (8ft 7in)
Height: 2.74m (9ft)
Engine: 280kW (375hp) General Motors 6046
    12- cylinder diesel
Speed: 48km/h (30mph)
Range: 240km (150miles)
Armament: 1 x 75mm (2.9in) M3 L/40 gun;
    1 x 12.7mm (0.5in) I Browning M2HB MG,
    1 x turret mounted 12.7mm 0.50 cal MG

(62 miles) and had reached the Danube, cutting into the rear of the 3rd Ukrainian Front's Fifty-Seventh Army. By 24 January, the force had advanced to within 24km (15 miles) of Budapest and inflicted heavy losses on I Guards Mechanized Corps and V Guards Cavalry Corps. It was only with the arrival of the last Soviet reserve formation, XXIII Tank Corps, that the German advance was halted.

By 28 January, IV SS Panzer Corps was forced to withdraw, abandoning Budapest. Amazingly, some parts of the city held out until 13 February, largely due to air-dropped supplies, supplemented by larger shipments brought in at night by small river craft. Losses on both sides were heavy – an estimated 100,000 Soviet casualties to set against over 75,000 Germans and Hungarians killed or captured. Only 785 survivors managed to safely cross the 40km (25 miles) to reach the German lines.

The Lake Balaton offensive
Code-named Operation *Frühlingserwachen* ('Spring Awakening'), this was the last significant German offensive of the war. It was ordered by Hitler in a typically unrealistic attempt not only to secure the Hungarian oilfields, but to retake Budapest and destroy the 3rd Ukrainian Front.

Good operational security (and an understandable Soviet belief that the Germans were incapable of launching any major offensive) ensured that complete surprise was achieved. Spearheaded by Sepp Dietrich's Sixth Panzer Army, the attack went in on 6 March and made good progress.

An early thaw, however, had turned the entire region into a muddy morass and the appalling ground conditions posed as many problems for the Panzers as the Soviet forces. In some sectors, Tiger IIs sank up to their turrets in the thick mud and at least 15 had to be abandoned. Delays imposed by these conditions gave time for Tolbukhin to call in reinforcements from the Ninth Guards Army and launch a counterattack on 16 March, which pushed the German forces back to their start-lines within 24 hours.

By the end of the month, the remnants of the Sixth Panzer Army had retreated into Austria in an attempt to protect Vienna. (Sepp Dietrich remarked with only slight exaggeration and no doubt a great

▲ **SU-85 and T-34**

The SU-85 was a well-designed tank destroyer based on the T-34 hull and armed with an 85mm (3.3in) gun, which entered service in late 1943. In the summer of 1944, production switched to the SU-100 armed with a far more powerful 100mm (3.9in) gun.

deal of bitterness that 'Sixth Panzer Army is well named — we have just six tanks left!')

Vienna

The 3rd Ukrainian Front followed up Sixth Panzer Army's retreat and quickly assembled around Vienna, which was garrisoned mainly by II SS Panzer Corps. The Soviet assault began on 2 April with attacks by Fourth and Ninth Guards Armies, but made only limited progress until Sixth Guards Tank Army was committed on 8 April. The additional pressure forced German units westwards to avoid being trapped and

the city surrendered on 13 April. (As II SS Panzer Corps withdrew on 12 April, a single Panther commanded by *Leutnant* Arno Giesen knocked out 14 T-34s and JS-2s while holding one of the Danube bridges – a sharp reminder of German AT talents.)

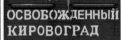 This inscription 'Liberated Kirovgrad' is typical of many carried on Soviet AFVs. While some were undoubtedly designed and applied by the crews themselves, it seems likely that many of the more 'political' slogans were the work of the NKVD.

▲ **JSU-152 heavy SP gun**

2nd Byelorussian Front / HQ Fiftieth Army / Independent Heavy Assault Gun Regiment

The JSU-152 proved invaluable in the fierce street fighting prevalent at the end of the war, as its 40kg (88lb) HE shells were highly effective against even heavily fortified strrongpoints.

Specifications

Crew: 5	Speed: 37km/h (23mph)
Weight: 46 tonnes (45.27 tons)	Range: (Road) 220km (136.71miles),
Length: 9.18m (30ft 1in)	(Terrain) 80km (49.71miles)
Width: 3.07m (10ft 1in)	Radio: 10RF (When fitted)
Height: 2.48m (8ft 1in)	Armament: 1 x 152mm (5.9in) ML-20S howitzer
Engine: 447kW (600hp) V-2 diesel	

▲ **SU-152 heavy SP gun**

1st Byelorussian Front / First Guards Tank Army / XI Guards Tank Corps / HQ 362nd Guards Assault Artillery Regiment

Although production of the SU-152 ended in late 1943, surviving vehicles remained in service until the end of the war.

Specifications

Crew: 5	Speed: 43km/h (26.72mph)
Weight: 45.5 tonnes (44.78 tons)	Range: (Road) 330km (205miles),
Length: 8.95m (29ft 4in)	(Terrain) 120km (74.57miles)
Width: 3.25m (10ft 8in)	Radio: 9R (When fitted)
Height: 2.45m (8ft 0in)	Armament: 1 x 152mm (5.9in) ML-20S howitzer
Engine: 447kW (600hp) V-2 diesel	

Seelow Heights and Berlin
APRIL–MAY 1945

During the second week of April 1945, a massive Soviet force was assembled in the small bridgehead on the west bank of the Oder near Kustrin. Zhukov's 1st Byelorussian Front was preparing to attack the Seelow Heights, the last natural defence line before Berlin.

THE 1ST BYELORUSSIAN Front had 908,000 men, 3155 AFVs and 16,934 guns and had stockpiled over 7,000,000 rounds of artillery ammunition. On its northern flank was Rokossovsky's 2nd

Byelorussian Front. Zhukov's forces were opposed by General Gotthard Heinrici's Army Group Vistula – its Ninth Army, which would bear the brunt of the assault on the Seelow Heights, fielded 14 divisions, 512 AFVs, 344 guns and 300–400 AA guns. Further south the front was held by the Fourth Panzer Army, which faced Konev's 1st Ukrainian Front.

Although heavily outnumbered, Heinrici had done much to reduce the odds against him. Correctly anticipating that the main Soviet attacks would be made on the Seelow Heights along the line of the main east–west autobahn, he had thinned out other sectors of the front to reinforce the area. The Heights themselves were well fortified, forming part of three defence lines up to 25km (15.5 miles) deep. The Oder's flood plain, already saturated by the spring thaw, was turned into a swamp by water released

▲ **Into the suburbs**
ISU-122 heavy assault guns move into the suburbs of Berlin, April 1945.

▲ T-34/85

1st Byelorussian Front / Second Guards Tank Army

This T-34/85 has been fitted with wooden-framed wire mesh panels as protection against German *Panzerfausts* and *Panzerschrecks*, which were responsible for almost 23 per cent of the T-34s lost during the battle of Berlin. It bears the white turret band adopted in April 1945 as a recognition marking to minimize the risk of friendly fire incidents between Western Allied tanks and Soviet AFVs.

Specifications

Crew: 5

Weight: 32 tonnes (31.5 tons)

Length: 6m (19ft 7in)

Width: 3m (9ft 9in)

Height: 2.60m (8ft 6in)

Engine: 1 x V-2 V-12 cylinder 372 kW (493hp) diesel engine

Speed (road): 55km/h (33mph)

Range: 360km (223 miles)

Radio: N/A

Armament: 1 x 85mm (3.4in) ZiS-S-53 cannon; 2 x 7.62mm (0.3in) DT MGs (bow and coaxial)

from a reservoir upstream and minefields were laid in to protect key points.

At 0500 on 16 April, the offensive began with a massive bombardment by thousands of guns and 'Katyushas' of the 1st Byelorussian Front before the main assault went in. Almost immediately, things started to go wrong – the debris and smoke from the massive bombardment meant that the glare of the 140-plus searchlights intended to blind the Germans was reflected and blinded the attackers. (It also turned them into easy targets, silhouetted against the light.) Worse still, the bombardment had been largely

Specifications

Crew: 5	Engine: 447kW (600hp) V-2 diesel
Weight: 42.5 tonnes (41.83 tons)	Speed: 45km/h (28mph)
Length: 6.8m (22ft 4in)	Range: (Road):250km (155miles), (Terrain)
Width: 3.25m (10ft 8in)	160km (99 miles)
Height: 2.64m (8ft 8in)	Radio: 9R (When fitted)

▲ **KV1S Heavy Tank**

1st Byelorussian Front / First Guards Tank Army / XI Guards Tank Corps / HQ / 362nd Guards Assault Artillery Regiment

A few KV heavy tanks survived until the end of the war, usually as command vehicles in JSU-122 or JSU-152 units.

Mechanized Corps (May 1945)	Strength
Personnel	16,438
Armoured Vehicles:	
Light tanks	–
Medium tanks	183
Heavy tanks	–
Light assault guns	21
Medium assault guns	21
Heavy assault guns	21
Guns and Mortars:	
82mm (3.2in) mortars	100
120mm (4.7in) mortars	54
45mm (1.8in) AT guns	36
57mm (2.2in) AT guns	8
37mm (1.5in) AA guns	16
76mm (3in) guns	36
BM-13 rocket launchers	8

Tank Corps (May 1945)	Strength
Personnel	11,788
Armoured Vehicles:	
T-60 light tanks	–
T-70 light Tanks	–
T-34 medium Tanks	207
KV heavy tanks	–
SU-76	21
SU-85	21
SU-152/ISU-152	21
Guns and Mortars:	
82mm (3.2in) mortars	52
120mm (4.7in) mortars	42
45mm (1.8in) AT guns	12
57mm (2.2in) AT guns	16
37mm (1.5in) AA guns	16
76mm (3in) guns	36
M-13 rocket launchers	8

wasted on empty defences – a Soviet prisoner had revealed the timing of the attack and Heinrici had pulled his forces back to their second defensive line. Taking advantage of the slow and confused Soviet advance, the Germans reoccupied their forward defences and brought down a murderous fire on the attackers. By the next day, the 1st Byelorussian Front had advanced no more than 8km (5 miles) and was still bogged down in the German defences.

An enraged Zhukov committed the 1337 AFVs of his two tank armies to the attack, but the huge number of vehicles deployed on a narrow front caused a massive traffic jam, providing more targets for the German artillery.

▲ JS-2 heavy tank

1st Ukrainian Front / Third Guards Tank Army / 57th Guards Heavy Tank Regiment

Even the heavily armoured JS-2 was vulnerable in the Berlin fighting, where hazards ranged from 128mm (5in) Flak guns to HEAT AT grenades lobbed from upper-floor windows.

Specifications	
Crew: 4	Speed: 37km/h (23mph)
Weight: 46 tonnes (45.27tons)	Range: 240km (149 miles)
Length: 9.9m (32ft 6in)	Radio: 10R
Width: 3.09m (10ft 2in)	Armament: 1 x 122mm (4.8in) D-25T gun, plus
Height: 2.73m (8ft 11in)	3 x 7.62mm (0.3in) DT MGs (1 coaxial, 1 fixed
Engine: 382.8kW (513hp) V-2 12-cylinder diesel	in bow, 1 ball-mounted in turret rear)

Specifications	
Crew: 4	Speed: 47km/h (29mph)
Weight: 29.2 tonnes (28.74 tons)	Range: (Road):400km (248.55 miles),
Length: 8.15m (26ft 9in)	(Terrain) 200km (124.27miles)
Width: 3m (9ft 10in)	Radio: 9R (When fitted)
Height: 2.45m (8ft)	Armament: 1 x 85mm (3.4in) D5-S gun
Engine: 372.5kW (500hp) V-2 diesel	

▲ SU-85 tank destroyer

3rd Ukrainian Front / VII Mechanised Corps

Most self-propelled guns developed for the Red Army during the war were intended to operate in both the anti-tank and close support roles. The SU-85 (and its successor, the SU-100) were exceptions to this rule, being deployed almost exclusively as tank destroyers.

Konev advances

In contrast to the bloody confusion at the Seelow Heights, Konev's attack, launched at almost the same time, made excellent progress – by 17 April, the 1st Ukrainian Front's forward units had broken through the main German defences and had crossed the River Spree. Konev seized the opportunity and obtained Stalin's permission to make straight for Berlin. With

Front	Army	Corps	Brigade/Regiment
ORDER OF BATTLE: THE ASSAULT ON BERLIN (APRIL 1945)			
2nd Byelorussian	Fifth Guards Tank	XXIX Tank	1st Tank & 4th Mech Bdes
1st Byelorussian	First Polish		4th Polish Heavy Tank, 13th Polish SP Assault Artillery
	Forty-Seventh		70th Guards Independent Tank Rgt
		IX Tank	23rd Tank, 95th Tank, 108th Tank
	Fifth Shock		11th Tank, 67th Guards Tank, 220th Tank, 92nd Independent Tank Rgt
	Eighth Guards		7th Guards Tank, 84th Guards Tank, 65th Independent Tank, 259th Independent Tank Rgts
	Sixty-Ninth		68th Tank, 12th SP Assault Artillery
	Thirty-Third		257th Independent Tank Rgt, 360th SP Assault Artillery, 361st SP Assault Artillery
	First Guards Tank	VIII Guards Mech	19th, 20th & 21st Guards Mechanized, 1st Guards Tank Bde, 48th Guards Tank, 353rd & 400th Guards SP Assault Artillery Rgts
		XI Guards Tank	40th, 44th & 45th Guards Tank, 27th Guards Mechanized, 362nd, 399th Guards, 1454 SP Assault Artillery Rgts
		XI Tank	20th, 36th & 65th Tank, 12th Motorized Rifle, 50th Guards Tank Rgt, 1461st & 1493rd SP Assault Artillery Rgts, 64th Guards Tank, 19th SP Assault Artillery, 11th Guards Independent Tank Rgt
	Second Guards Tank	I Mechanized	19th, 35th & 37th Mechanized, 219th Tank, 347th Guards, 75th & 1822nd SP Assault Artillery Rgts
		IX Guards tank	47th, 50th & 65th Guards Tank, 33rd Guards Mechanized, 341st, 369th & 386th Guards SP Assault Artillery Rgts
		XII Guards Tank	48th, 49th & 66th Guards Tank, 34th Guards Mechanized, 79th Guards Tank Rgt, 387th & 393rd Guards SP Assault Artillery Rgt, 6th Guards Independent Tank Rgt
	Third	XXXV, XL & XLI Rifle	1812th, 1888th & 1901st SP Assault Artillery Rgts
		II, III & VII Guards Cavalry	
		III & VIII Guards Tank	244th Independent Tank Rgts, 31st, 39th, 51st & 55th Independent Armoured Train

the Third Tank Army and Fourth Guards Tank Army in the lead, his forces charged along the autobahn towards the city.

On 19 April, Zhukov's forces finally broke through the last defences on the Seelow Heights and were also on their way to Berlin. The cost had been appalling – over 700 Soviet AFVs had been destroyed in the battle for the Heights and the Red Army had sustained at least 30,000 casualties (three times the German total).

Assault on Berlin

On 26 April, Soviet forces completed the encirclement of Berlin – the city had been under artillery bombardment since 20 April and attacks on the suburbs had begun on 24 April. (The initial attack was made by the First Guards Tank Army under cover of a barrage from 3000 guns and heavy mortars – 650 guns per kilometre of front) Stalin had finally decided that both Fronts should combine to assault the city, but that Zhukov would have the honour of taking the Reichstag, which Soviet propaganda portrayed as the symbol of Hitler's Reich.

The defenders of Berlin were a very 'mixed bag', ranging from hard-bitten veterans to hastily raised, virtually untrained *Volkssturm* militia, totalling possibly 60,000 men and 50–60 AFVs, supported by police and fanatical Hitler Youth units. The Soviet forces assembling for the attack on the city comprised five armies and four tank armies – 464,000 men, 12,700 guns and mortars, at least 2000 Katyushas and 1500 AFVs.

Between 24 April and 28 April, both Fronts slowly ground their way through the Berlin suburbs against

ORDER OF BATTLE: THE ASSAULT ON BERLIN (APRIL 1945) – continued			
Front	Army	Corps	Brigade/Regiment
1st Ukrainian	Third Guards	XXV Tank	87th Guards Independent Tank Rgt, 938th SP Assault Artillery Rgt
	Thirteenth		88th Independent Tank Rgt, 327th, 372nd Guards, 768th & 1228th SP Assault Artillery Rgts
	Fifth Guards	IV Guards Tank	
	Second Polish	I Polish Tank	16th Polish Tank Bde, 5th Polish Independent Tank Rgt, 28th Polish SP Assault Artillery Rgt
	Fifty-Second	VII Guards Mechanized	8th SP Assault Artilleryt, 124th Independent Tank, 1198th SP Assault Artillery Rgt
	Third Guards Tank	VI Guards Tank	51st, 52nd & 53rd Guards Tank, 22nd Guards Motorized Rifle, 385th Guards, 1893rd & 1894th SP Assault Artillery Rgt
		VII Guards Tank	54th, 55th & 56th Guards Tank, 23rd Guards Motorized Rifle Bdes, 384th Guards, 702nd & 1977th SP Assault Artillery Rgts
		IX Mechanized	69th, 70th & 71st Mechanized, 91st Tank Bdes, 383rd Guards, 1507th & 1978th SP Assault Artillery Rgts, 16th SP Assault Artillery Bde, 57th Guards & 90th Independent Tank Rgts
	Fourth Guards Tank	V & VI Guards Mech	
		X Guards Tank	68th Guards Tank, 70th Guards SP Assault Artillery, 13th & 119th Guards Independent Tank Rgts
	Thirty-First		152nd Tank Bde, 98th Independent Tank, 368th Guards, 416th & 1976th SP Assault Artillery Rgts

fierce resistance – the Third Shock Army took three days to advance 3km (1.8 miles). All Soviet units took heavy casualties, largely due to poor co-ordination between tanks, infantry and artillery. (General Chuikov's Eighth Guards Army initially sent unsupported columns of its tanks straight down main streets – *Panzerfausts* and AT guns trapped these columns by knocking out the lead and rear vehicles, before infantry AT teams moved in to destroy the remaining AFVs.)

As Chuikov ruefully remarked, 'A battle within a city is a battle of firepower.' Units quickly developed

▶ **Street fighting**
The mobility and power of the SU-76M light assault gun proved very useful in the infantry support role in the confined streets of Berlin.

▲ **T-34/85 medium tank**
1st Ukrainian Front / Third Guards Tank Army / IX Mechanized Corps
In addition to its improved armour-piercing performance compared to earlier 76.2mm weapons, the T-34/85's 85mm gun fired a far more effective 9.2kg (20.28lb) HE shell.

Specifications

Crew: 5

Weight: 32 tonnes (31.5 tons)

Length: 6m (19ft 7in)

Width: 3m (9ft 9in)

Height: 2.60m (8ft 6in)

Engine: 1 x V-2 V-12 cylinder 372 kW (493hp) diesel engine

Speed (road): 55km/h (33mph)

Range: 360km (223 miles)

Radio: 9R (When fitted)

Armament: 1 x 85mm (3.4in) ZiS-S-53 cannon; 2 x 7.62mm (0.3in) DT MGs (bow and coaxial)

▶ **GAZ-67 4x4 command car**
1st Byelorussian Front / HQ
The GAZ-67 was the result of a programme to develop a Soviet equivalent of the jeep. However, the total produced from 1943 to 1945 was barely more than 5500, compared to over 50,000 Lend-Lease jeeps received by the end of the war.

Specifications

Crew: 1 driver

Weight: 1.32 tonnes (1.3 tons)

Length: 3.35m (11ft)

Width: 1.685m (5ft 6in)

Height: 1.7m (5ft 7in)

Engine: 37.25kW (50hp) 4-cylinder petrol

Speed: 90km/h (56mph)

Range: 450km (280miles)

Radio: n/a

special assault teams comprising an infantry platoon or company, a tank platoon, a section of SP guns, a section of 'Katyushas' and a detachment of assault engineers.

The assault drills almost invariably involved artillery and 'Katyushas' smothering the objective with smoke and close-range direct fire before the infantry attacked. A Soviet war correspondent described how the gunners 'sometimes fired a thousand shells on to one small square, a group of houses, or even a tiny garden.' As the Red Army reached the city centre, the larger government buildings proved to have been turned into 'improvised fortresses', which were supported by fire from Berlin's three enormous flak towers. These were six storeys high, each with a thousand-strong garrison to man the tower's four twin 128mm (5in) and 12 quadruple 20mm (0.79in) guns. Dealing with

▼ 57th Guards Heavy Tank Regiment

The 21 JS-2s of a heavy tank regiment were a formidable striking force, but even these well-armoured vehicles proved to be vulnerable to well-handled *Panzerfausts* and *Panzershrecks*. In response to this threat, many JS-2s were fitted with thin sheet metal panels as 'stand-off armour' similar to those fitted to contemporary Panzer IVs.

1 x T-34/85 command tank and 21 x IS-2s

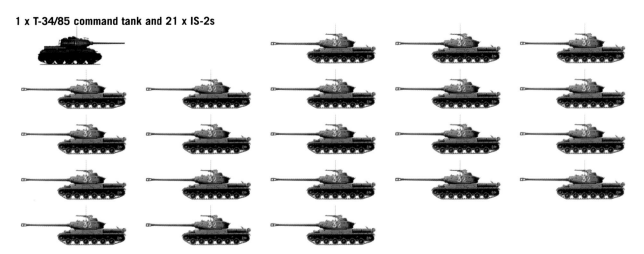

Third Guards Tank Army, AFVs	BM-13	T-34/76	T-34/85	IS-2	SU-57	SU-76	SU-85	ISU-122
VI Gds Tank Corps	8	–	207	–	–	21	21	21
VII Gds Tank Corps	8	–	207	–	–	21	21	21
IX Mechanized Corps	8	–	182	–	–	21	21	21
50th Motorcycle Rgt	–	–	10	–	–	–	–	–
1381st AA Rgt	–	–	–	–	–	–	–	–
1394th AA Rgt	–	–	–	–	–	–	–	–
91st Rocket Launcher Rgt	24	–	–	–	–	–	–	–
16th Assault Gun Bde	–	–	–	–	65	–	–	–
199th Light Artillery Bde	–	–	–	–	–	–	–	–
57th Guards Heavy Tank Rgt	–	–	1	21	–	–	–	–
90th Engineer Tank Rgt	–	18	4	–	–	–	–	–
19th Engineer Mine Bde	–	–	–	–	–	–	–	–
Army Troops	–	–	20	–	–	1	1	1

▶ **Streets of Berlin**
Accompanied by infantry, a T-34/85 advances down a leafy Berlin street, April 1945.

these demanded exceptional measures – at one stage, 500 Soviet guns were firing from a 1km (0.6-mile) section of the Unter den Linden.

Despite such massive firepower, Soviet losses continued to rise – at least 108 tanks were destroyed in the city centre by weapons ranging from 128mm (5in) AA guns to the ubiquitous *Panzerfaust*. As always, infantry casualties were the heaviest – between 19 and 30 April, one infantry company was reduced from 104 men to just 20 exhausted survivors after bitter street fighting.

Suicide and Surrender

By the time that the last German units surrendered on 2 May after Hitler's suicide and the capture of the battered shell of the Reichstag, the losses on both sides had been horrendous. Soviet casualties totalled over 352,000, including more than 78,000 dead – in addition, the First and Second Polish Armies lost almost 9000 men. The 'best estimate' of Soviet AFV losses is 2000 vehicles, while the two air armies supporting the offensive lost 527 aircraft – the majority to intensive AA fire.

The fall of Berlin effectively marked the end of the Red Army's war in Europe, but Stalin was already planning to unleash it against an old enemy half a world away – Japan.

Third Guards Tank Army, Personnel (1945)	Strength
VI Gds Tank Corps	12,010
VII Gds Tank Corps	12,010
IX Mechanized Corps	16,442
50th Motorcycle Rgt	–
1381st AA Rgt	396
1394th AA Rgt	396
91st Rocket Launcher Rgt	695
16th Assault Gun Bde	1112
199th Light Artillery Bde	–
57th Guards Heavy Tank Rgt	374
90th Engineer Tank Rgt	–
19th Engineer Mine Bde	–
Army Troops	–

▼ **British BSA M-20**

2nd Byelorussian Front / III Guards Tank Corps / HQ

Even by 1945, Soviet formations did not have the lavish scale of radio equipment of their Western counterparts, forcing them to rely more heavily on motorcycle dispatch riders than British or American forces.

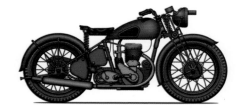

Specifications

Crew: 1

Weight: 0.185 tonnes (0.182 tons)

Length: 2.18m (7ft 2in)

Width: 0.73m (2ft 5in)

Height: 0.99m (3ft 3in)

Engine: 8.94kW (12hp), BSA 1-cylinder petrol

Speed: 104.6km/h (65mph)

Range: 280km (175miles)

Chapter 6

Victory in the East

After prolonged negotiations, the Soviet-Japanese
Neutrality Pact was signed in Moscow on 13 April 1941 to
formalize the uneasy peace that had lasted since the battle
of Khalkin Gol. Both sides recognized the existing frontiers
between Manchukuo, Mongolia and Siberia. Equally
importantly, they both agreed to remain neutral if either
should go to war with any other powers. Japan seriously
considered breaking the treaty to join Hitler's war on Soviet
Russia during the German run of victories in 1941/42,
but was too heavily committed to its own war in the
Pacific and Southeast Asia. As the tide of war turned
against Germany, Stalin began to plan an attack
on Japan to extend the Soviet empire
into the Far East.

◀ **Briefing**
The commander of a T-34/85 unit briefs his crews. Armoured units deployed to Manchuria included many
veterans of the European campaign, whose combat skills far outclassed those of the many raw recruits in
the Kwantung Army.

Operation *August Storm*
8 AUGUST – 1 SEPTEMBER 1945

Even in the darkest days of the war against Germany, the Soviet Union had retained substantial forces (averaging 40 divisions) to protect its borders with Manchuria, which had become the Japanese puppet state of Manchukuo, held by the 700,000-strong Kwantung Army.

THE NEUTRALITY PACT with Japan might theoretically guarantee Soviet security in the region, but after his experience with the Russo-German Non-Aggression Pact, Stalin was sceptical of the value of such treaties.

Stalin was determined to enter the war against Japan eventually to achieve long-standing strategic aims in the Far East. A key objective was to re-establish Russian dominance of Manchuria, which had been lost as a result of the humiliating defeat by Japan in 1905. Other aims included the consolidation of the Soviet hold on Mongolia and the

seizure of the entire Sakhalin peninsula and Kurile Islands from Japan. As the Pacific war dragged on, Britain and the United States were increasingly anxious for Soviet involvement in the war against Japan, especially as it seemed likely that it would take an invasion of the Japanese home islands to end the war, which could entail a horrifying 250,000 US casualties. (The actual American death toll for the entire war was 292,000.)

In April 1945, the Soviets abrogated the Neutrality Pact and began a massive redeployment effort that doubled the Soviet forces in the Far East to

▶ **T-26 Model 1935 light tank**

Trans-Baikal Front / Thirty-Sixth Army / 205th Tank Brigade

Although the T-26 was hopelessly outdated in terms of Western European armoured warfare by 1945, it was at least as good as the vast majority of Japanese AFVs.

Specifications	
Crew: 3	Speed: 28km/h (17mph)
Weight: 10.4 tonnes (10.3 tons)	Range: 200km (124 miles)
Length: 4.8m (15ft 8in)	Armament: 1 x 45mm (1.77in) AT gun;
Width: 2.39m (7ft 10in)	1 x 7.62mm (0.3in) DT MG; 2 x additional
Height: 2.33m (7ft 8in)	7.62mm (0.3in) DT MG ball-mounted into
Engine: 68kW (91hp) GAZ T-26 8-cylinder petrol	turret rear and turret hatch

▶ **T-26 Model 1940 light tank**

2nd Far Eastern Front / Second Red Banner Army / 73rd Tank Brigade

Well over 1200 operational T-26s had been held by Soviet units in the Far East throughout the war. Supplemented by more modern AFVs shipped from the European theatre, they played a useful role in Manchuria.

Specifications	
Crew: 3	Speed: 28km/h (17mph)
Weight: 10.4 tonnes (10.3 tons)	Range: 200km (124 miles)
Length: 4.8m (15ft 8in)	Radio: N/A
Width: 2.39m (7ft 10in)	Armament: 1 x 45mm (1.8in) AT gun;
Height: 2.33m (7ft 8in)	1 x 7.62mm (0.3in) DT MG
Engine: 68kW (91hp) GAZ T-26 8-cylinder petrol	

80 divisions. Between May and July 1945, at least 40 infantry, tank and mechanized divisions plus artillery and combat support units were transferred from Europe to the Far East. This massive undertaking stretched the capacity of the Trans-Siberian railway to the limit – 136,000 railway wagons were used for the transfer of men and equipment. As the movements peaked in June and July, 20–30 trains a day were despatched on the 9,000–12,000km (5500–7500-mile) journey to Mongolia.

Secret build-up

Surprise was an essential element of Red Army planning – after the abrogation of the Neutrality Pact, the Japanese were anticipating a Soviet attack, but Soviet security was so good that the offensive was expected either in the autumn, when the ground had dried out after the summer rains, or in the spring of 1946. The security measures themselves were simple but highly effective – whenever possible, units moved at night into assembly areas as far back from the frontier as possible, while senior officers travelled under assumed names, wearing the uniforms of junior officers. Some formations, such as the Sixth Guards Tank Army, left all their AFVs and heavy equipment behind in Europe and re-equipped with new tanks, assault guns and artillery straight off the production lines of the Urals armament factories.

A total of 11 combined-arms armies, one tank army and three air armies were assembled for the offensive, with a combined strength of some 1,577,725 men and 5556 AFVs, supported by

AFVS, FAR EAST, AUGUST 1945	Registered	Operable	Mid-life Repair	Thourough Repair	Discarded
BT-5	190	101	–	23	66
BT-7	1030	797	41	179	13
T-26	1461	1272	33	122	34
T-37	52	52	–	–	–
T-38	325	304	20	1	–
T-60/70	46	14	–	28	4
T-34	1899	1794	32	70	3
KV	77	47	5	23	2
IS	19	6	1	12	–
M4A2 Sherman	250	250	–	–	–
Mk III Valentine	81	78	3	–	–
M3 Stuart	1	–	1	–	–
M3 Lee	1	–	1	–	–
T-27	56	56	–	–	–
Tankettes	52	52	–	–	–
Other	5	5	–	–	–
Total Tanks	**5545**	**4828**	**137**	**458**	**122**
SU-76	952	944	9	–	–
SU-85	6	1	–	5	–
SU-100	262	261	1	–	–
SU-122	6	2	–	3	1
ISU-122	1	1	–	–	–
SU-152	11	–	–	11	–
ISU-152	197	188	1	8	–
Total SP Guns	**1435**	**1397**	**11**	**27**	**1**
Total	**6980**	**6225**	**148**	**485**	**123**

26,137 guns, mortars and rocket launchers. The air armies committed to the operation totalled 3800 aircraft while the Soviet Navy (the Pacific Fleet and Amur River Flotilla) had 600 warships and a further 1500 aircraft. Overall, the Soviet forces significantly outnumbered the Japanese – the ratios were a 2.2:1 advantage in men, 4.8:1 in artillery and tanks and a 2:1 advantage in aircraft.

Japanese weakness

Across the frontier in Manchukuo, the Kwantung Army was a shadow of its former self. In early 1941, it had numbered approximately 1,000,000 men and included some of the best units in the Imperial Japanese Army. In the opening stages of the Pacific War, it was regarded as a strategic reserve and kept up to strength to take advantage of any sudden Soviet collapse as a result of Operation *Barbarossa*. (It was considered equally important to maintain it as a strong garrison for the puppet state of Manchukuo, which had been built up as the primary industrial and agricultural centre of the Japanese Empire.)

However, as the Allies went over to the offensive in the Pacific war, Japanese Imperial General Headquarters began to withdraw elite divisions from the Kwantung Army to reinforce other theatres of war. By early 1943, Japanese strength in Manchukuo had been reduced to 600,000 men facing an estimated 750,000 Soviet troops deployed on its borders. Further units were withdrawn during 1944, and in March 1945 most of the remaining elite

formations, including the 1st Armoured Division, were transferred to the Japanese home islands.

The steady decline in the strength of the Kwangtung Army forced drastic changes in the contingency plans for the defence of Manchukuo. These had originally concentrated on the northern and eastern border areas, as it was believed that the western frontier was impassable for any major force due to the vast Mongolian desert and the natural barrier of the Grand Khingan mountains. In accordance with this assessment, the Japanese were busily constructing 17 fortified areas covering likely invasion routes along 1000km (621 miles) of the northern and eastern borders.

By May 1945, it was recognized that it was unrealistic to believe that a major Soviet offensive could be held at the frontier and a revised plan was adopted. This plan was based on fighting delaying actions on the borders before a phased retreat to a succession of defensive lines and finally to a fortified zone in south-eastern Manchuria approximately 650km (404 miles) from the northern and western borders. Despite the evidence of recent operations in Europe, Japanese planners believed that a combination of difficult terrain and the limitations of the Soviet transport system would force any major offensive to halt to resupply after 400km (249 miles) or so, giving defending forces the chance to regroup and counterattack. Based on these assumptions, only one-third of the Kwantung Army would remain in the border zones and the remainder would redeploy

Specifications	
Crew: 3	Engine: 103kW (138bhp) GMC diesel
Weight: 17.69 tonnes (19.5 tons)	Speed (road): 24km/h (15mph)
Length: 5.41m (17ft 9in)	Range: 145km (90 miles)
Width: 2.63m (8ft 7.5in)	Armament: 1 x 40mm (1.57in) gun;
Height: 2.27m (7ft 5.5in)	1 x 7.92mm (0.31in) Besa MG

▲ **Infantry Tank Mark III Valentine Mk II**

2nd Far Eastern Front / Second Red Banner Army / 73rd Tank Brigade

The Manchurian campaign marked the swansong of the Valentine, which had seen action in almost all theatres of war, from the Western Desert to the Pacific.

to man the defence lines in the interior. The unexpectedly early Soviet attack caught Japanese units in the midst of the redeployment programme and struck largely incomplete border fortifications.

To mask its fragility, the Kwangtung Army mobilized reservists and conscripts, forming new divisions and brigades to maintain the appearance of a capable fighting force. By early July 1945, it had expanded from 11 infantry divisions to over

24 divisions. However, a substantial proportion of its entire combat force (eight out of 24 divisions and seven out of nine brigades) was mobilized only 10 days before the Soviet attack. One of its two weak tank brigades was not formed until July 1945, and both brigades were stationed in south-central Manchukuo far away from the areas targeted by the Soviet offensive. Of the 24 divisions in the Kwangtung Army, the Japanese themselves

▲ **BT-5 Model 1935 fast tank**

Trans-Baikal Front / Sixth Guards Tank Army / VII Guards Mechanized Corps
The 'BT contingent' of the Sixth Guards Tank Army was itself a strange variety of types, including BT-5s.

Specifications

Crew: 3	Speed: 86km/h (53mph)
Weight: 14 tonnes (13.2 tons)	Range: 250km (155 miles)
Length: 5.66m (18ft 6in)	Radio: N/A
Width: 2.29m (7ft 6in)	Armament: 1 x 45mm (1.8in) Model 1932 gun;
Height: 2.42m (7ft 10in)	1 x 7.62mm (0.3in) coaxal DT MG
Engine: 373kW (500hp) Model M-17T	

Specifications

Crew: 5	Speed (road): 55km/h (33mph)
Weight: 32 tonnes (31.5 tons)	Range: 360km (223 miles)
Length: 6m (19ft 7in)	Radio: N/A
Width: 3m (9ft 9in)	Armament: 1 x 85mm (3.4in) ZiS-S-53 cannon;
Height: 2.60m (8ft 6in)	2 x 7.62mm (0.3in) DT MGs (bow and coaxial)
Engine: 1 x V-2 V-12 cylinder 372 kW (493hp)	
diesel engine	

▲ **T34/85**

Trans-Baikal Front / Sixth Guards Tank Army / IX Guards Mechanised Corps
The T-34/85 was largely immune to Japanese tank and AT guns deployed in Manchuria, while its 85mm (3.3in) gun could easily destroy any of the Kwantung Army's AFVs.

considered only seven or eight to be fully combat ready. The remaining formations were in terrible condition – eight of the infantry divisions were assessed as being only 15 per cent combat effective while all nine independent mixed brigades were rated at 15 per cent combat effectiveness or less.

These alarming ratings were largely due to hopelessly inadequate levels of equipment – the newly formed 149th Infantry Division did not have a single piece of artillery at the time of the Soviet invasion. Equally serious was the obsolescence of much of the equipment that had been issued. Japanese war industries had lacked both the resources and the management skills to mass-produce modern weapons, and as a result the Kwantung Army of 1945 was seriously deficient in heavy artillery, tanks and AT weapons. (It was rumoured that some units even lacked sufficient rifles and were reduced to arming their men with bamboo spears.) By August 1945, the Japanese strength in Manchukuo stood at 1155 tanks, 5360 guns and 1800 aircraft, most of which were obsolete. Apart from Japanese garrisons in South Sakhalin, Korea and the Kuriles, Soviet forces faced an inexperienced army totalling little more than 710,000 men.

Poor intelligence

Despite excellent security, the Soviet build-up of forces was detected by the Japanese, but its scale and pace were grossly under-estimated. The Kwantung Army's intelligence reports failed to note any concentrations on the western border of Manchukuo (where more than 650,000 men were massing) and estimated that there were only eight infantry and two tank divisions with 1000 supporting aircraft on the eastern border (where the Red Army attacked with 31 infantry divisions and 12 tank brigades). Even after greatly increased Soviet activity in July 1945, the Imperial General HQ's last situation report on 31 July 1945 was inaccurate: 'Russian relations with Japan will reach a crisis in the early autumn. Recent Russian war preparations against Japan have made unexpected progress. The Soviet Union will be ready to launch hostile action by the end of August. Because of military considerations, it is highly probable that she will enter war against Japan in the early autumn.'

Soviet plan

The Soviet operation was well-planned. The experience gained from the war in Europe was applied to solve the problems of staging an offensive across terrain that included mountains, forests, marshland, steppe and deserts. Specialized tasks were assigned to formations that had relevant experience – the Fifth Army, which had assaulted the German fortifications at Königsberg, was to break through the Japanese fortified zone in eastern Manchukuo, while the Sixth Guards Tank Army was to make use of mountain warfare skills gained in the Carpathians in

Specifications	
Crew: 2	Speed: 45km/h (28mph)
Weight: 5.8 tonnes (5.7 tons)	Range: 360km (224 miles)
Length: 4.29m (14ft 1in)	Radio: N/A
Width: 2.32m (7ft 7in)	Armament: 1 x 45mm (1.8in) Model 38 gun;
Height: 2.04m (6ft 7in)	1 x 7.62mm (0.3in) coaxial DT MG
Engine: 2 x GAZ-202 52+52kW (70+70hp)	

▲ **T-70 Light Tank**

Trans-Baikal Front / Thirty-Ninth Army / 735th Self-propelled Artillery Regiment

By 1945, surviving T-70s had mostly been assigned to SU-76M units as command vehicles.

crossing the Grand Khingan mountains. Even horsed cavalry had a role – 16,000 Mongolian cavalry formed part of Issa Pliev's Soviet-Mongolian KMG, which was to protect the right flank of the offensive by a massive raid, summarized in Pliev's briefing from Marshal Vasilevsky:

'You, Issa Aleksandrovich, will execute a raid in your favourite style across the Gobi Desert and the

Grand Khingan mountains. Your cavalry mechanized group will conduct a vigorous offensive on the axis Kalgan-Beijing, and will subsequently exploit success as far as the Gulf of Liadong. That is where our main forces will concentrate ... your mission – to secure the Front's forces against attack from the south.'

This was a strategic mission that would have been appreciated by Genghis Khan, using cavalry with

▲ M4A2 Sherman medium tank

1st Far Eastern Front / Fifth Army / 72nd Tank Brigade

This Sherman carries a pair of logs to act as 'unditching beams' – if the tank bogged down in soft ground, these were pushed under the tracks to give it the necessary grip to haul itself out.

Specifications	
Crew: 5	
Weight: 32.28 tonnes (35.58 tons)	
Length: 5.92m (19ft 5in)	
Width: 2.62m (8ft 7in)	
Height: 2.74m (9ft)	
Engine: 280kW (375hp) General Motors 6046 12-cylinder diesel	
Speed: 48km/h (30mph)	
Range: 240km (150miles)	
Armament: 1 x 75mm (2.9in) M3 L/40 gun; 1 x 12.7mm (0.5in)	
I Browning M2HB MG, 1 x turret mounted 12.7mm 0.50 cal MG	

▲ JS-3 Heavy Tank

Sixth Guards Tank Army / III Guards Mechanized Corps / 35th Guards Tank Bde

The JS-3 was the last Soviet heavy tank to enter production before the end of the war. The 122mm (4.8in) main armament was mounted in new hemispherical turret and it had a pointed bow, which gave rise to the nickname 'Shchuka' (Pike). As many as 350 JS-3s may have been produced in the first half of 1945, but it seems unlikely that any saw action before VE-Day. However, a detachment may have undergone combat trials in the Manchurian campaign.

Specifications	
Crew: 3	Speed: 40km/h (25mph)
Weight: 45.77 tonnes (45.05 tons)	Range: 185km (115 miles)
Length: 9.85m (32ft 4in)	Radio: 10R (when fitted)
Width: 3.09m (10ft 2in)	Armament: 1 x 122mm (4.8in) D-25T gun,
Height: 2.45m (8ft)	plus 1 x coaxial 7.62mm (0.3in) DT MG and
Engine: 447kW (600hp) V-2-JS V-12 diesel	1 x 12.7mm (0.5in) DShK HMG on AA mount

▲ SU-76M SP gun

Trans-Baikal Front / Thirty-Ninth Army / 735th Self-propelled Artillery Regiment

The lightweight SU-76M was well suited to operating on the poor roads and weak bridges encountered in Manchuria.

Specifications

Crew: 4	Engine: 2 x GAZ 6-cylinder petrol 52+52kW
Weight: 10.8 tonnes (11.9 tons)	(70+70hp)
Length: 4.88m (16ft)	Speed (road): 45km/h (28mph)
Width: 2.73m (8ft 11.5in)	Range: 450km (280miles)
Height: 2.17m (7ft 1.4in)	Armament: one 76mm (3in) gun and one
	7.62mm (0.3in) MG

▶ Harley-Davidson 42WLA, with M-72 sidecar and DP MG

Trans-Baikal Front / Sixth Guards Tank Army / 14th Guards Motorcycle Battalion

Motorcycle reconnaissance battalions covered vast distances during the brief Manchurian campaign.

Specifications

Crew: 2/3	Range: 201km (125 miles)
Engine: 17kW (23hp) V-2	Armament: 1 x 7.62mm (0.3in) DT MG
Speed: 105km/h (65.2mph)	

Specifications

Crew: 2	Engine: JXD 6 cylinder Hercules
Weight: 4.33 tons (9555lbs) (without fuel)	Speed: not known
Length: 6.55m (21ft 6in)	Range: not known
Width: 2.23m (7ft 4in)	Radio: none
Height: 2.76m (9ft 1in)	

▲ Studebaker US 6x6 U-5, 2½-ton fuel tanker

Trans-Baikal Front / Sixth Guards Tank Army / Supply Battalion

Formations tasked with seizing objectives deep inside Manchuria received the pick of logistical support, such as Studebaker 6x6 fuel tankers. Even so, the distances involved were such that air re-supply proved to be the only way to sustain the advance.

which he would have been familiar in conjunction with the latest tanks – the military technologies of the thirteenth and twentieth centuries working together.

The Last Battles

The Soviet plan was essentially simple – virtually all Manchukuo, a territory three times the size of France, would be seized in a gigantic pincer movement. The Trans-Baikal Front would attack eastwards across the Grand Khingan mountains and advance into central Manchukuo within 10–15 days. The 1st Far Eastern Front was to form the second arm of the pincer movement, attacking westwards from the area north of Vladivostock to link up with Trans-Baikal Front. The third major Soviet force, the 2nd Far Eastern Front, was to pin Japanese troops in northern Manchukuo, preventing them withdrawing southwards to reinforce other units.

On 9 August, the Trans-Baikal Front's attacks were launched. More than 654,000 men, 2400 AFVs and 49,000 other vehicles moved forward on a front of 2300km (1429 miles). The Sixth Guards Tank Army spearheaded the advance against very light opposition, as the Japanese considered the region impassable by major armoured formations. The tank army's planned rate of advance was 70km (43 miles) per day for its armoured units, but it reached its objectives after covering more than 350km (217 miles) on 12 August – a full 24 hours ahead of schedule. By this time, its supply lines were stretched to breaking point; its leading units were over 700km (435 miles) from their supply dumps. The tanks were virtually 'running on empty' and the advance had to be halted for 48 hours until 400 transport aircraft could fly in sufficient fuel to allow the resumption of operations.

On the Front's left flank, the Japanese put up fierce resistance around Hailar. Although assessed as only 15 per cent combat effective, the 80th Independent Mixed Brigade withstood repeated attacks by two Soviet divisions with heavy artillery support for several days before the surviving 3287 defenders surrendered on 18 August.

The 1st Far Eastern Front faced stronger opposition since it had to penetrate major Japanese defences and extensive areas of marshy terrain before linking up with the Trans-Baikal Front. Despite these obstacles, it advanced 150km (93 miles) in five days, fixing Japanese forces in eastern Manchukuo. The fortresses of the so-called 'concrete belt' were largely by-passed and pounded into surrender by supporting Soviet forces.

Away to the north, the 2nd Far Eastern Front's offensive had to cross two rivers – the Amur and the Ussuri – and their broad marshlands. In recognition of the problems posed by the terrain, the Front was relatively lightly equipped with only 1280 AFVs and barely 6000 guns and mortars. In compensation, it had the support of the Amur Red Banner Flotilla, a force of 200 naval craft that provided invaluable fire support in both river crossings. The Front had to fight its way through determined resistance, which slowed an advance already hampered by appalling terrain. Nonetheless, it was completely successful in preventing any major Japanese forces withdrawing into the interior.

The opening of the Soviet offensive coincided with the second atomic bomb strike against Nagasaki and reports of the collapse of Manchukuo probably hastened the Japanese surrender. Although the Kwantung Army formally surrendered on 17 August, Stalin ordered the advance to continue, exploiting the confusion caused by the difficulties of communicating the news to isolated Japanese units. This ensured Soviet control of key strategic objectives – the whole of the former Manchukuo, now once again Manchuria, North Korea, the Kurile Islands and southern Sakhalin. A planned invasion of the northern Japanese home island of Hokkaido was cancelled at the last minute for fear of antagonizing the United States.

Postscript

The last battles of the war were a strange mixture of old and new – horsed cavalry fought alongside modern tanks and armoured trains went into action for almost the last time. In another, more sinister way they were the shape of things to come. By the end of the war, the largely ineffective Japanese tanks and AT guns had forced the adoption of drastic, but sometimes highly effective, AT measures. In accordance with the spirit of *bushido* ('way of the warrior'), *kamikaze* ('divine wind') attacks were adopted – suicidal attacks by infantry using demolition charges, AT grenades and lunge mines. Soviet accounts of these attacks in the Manchurian campaign provide a chilling foretaste of the suicide bombers of the twenty-first century.

'Katyusha' salvo rocket launchers
1941–45

In June 1938, the Red Army's Main Artillery Directorate (GAU) ordered the Soviet Jet Propulsion Research Institute (RNII) to develop a multiple rocket launcher for the new 82mm (3.2in) RS-82 and 132mm (5.2in) RS-132 air-launched rockets.

INITIAL EFFORTS WERE concentrated on the RS-132 (RS: *Reaktivnyy Snaryad*, 'rocket-powered shell'), which was fitted with a larger warhead and redesignated M-13. A total of 233 prototype rockets were test-fired in late 1938 from ZiS-5 trucks and it was found that a salvo could straddle an area target at a range of 5500m (18,044ft). These test-firings were made from 24-rail launchers firing over the sides of ZiS-5 trucks, but this configuration was unstable and the problem was solved only when longitudinally mounted launch rails were adopted. The modified vehicles were completed in August 1939 as the BM-13 (BM: *Boyevaya Mashina*, 'combat vehicle' for M-13 rockets). Further trials took place throughout 1940 and the BM-13-16 with launch rails for 16 rockets was ordered into production, but only 40 vehicles were completed by the time of the German invasion in 1941.

Rocket Artillery Regiment, personnel	Strength
Regiment HQ	58
Battalion x 3	250
AA Platoon x 2	–
Rocket Battery x 2	–

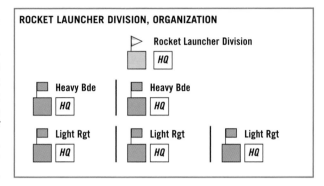

ROCKET LAUNCHER DIVISION, ORGANIZATION

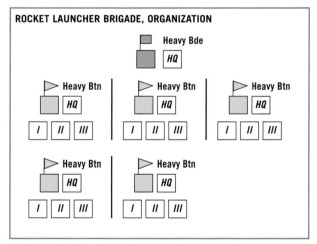

ROCKET LAUNCHER BRIGADE, ORGANIZATION

▶ **Willys MB Jeep with BM-8-8 82mm (3.2in) 'Katyusha' salvo rocket launcher**

3rd Ukrainian Front / IV Guards Mechanized Corps / 15th Guards Mech Bde
As the Soviet offensives approached the Carpathians, it became clear that the existing 'Katyusha' vehicles could not cope with such mountainous terrain. So the jeep was adapted to mount a light eight-rail launcher for 82mm (3.2in) rockets.

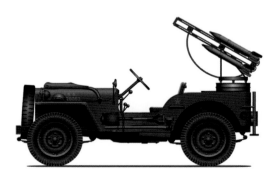

Specifications*

Crew: 1 driver

Weight: 1.04 tonnes (1.02 tons)

Length: 3.33m (10ft 11in)

Width: 1.58m (5ft 2in)

Height: 1.83m (6ft)

Engine: 44.7kW (70hp) 4-cylinder petrol

Speed: 88.5km/h (55mph)

Range: n/k

Armament: 8 x 82mm (3.2in) M8 rockets

(* For standard jeep)

The system consisted of an elevating frame that carried a bank of eight parallel rails on which the rockets were mounted (eight on top of the rails and a further eight hung beneath them). The 132mm (5.2in) diameter M-13 rocket of the BM-13 system had an overall length of 180cm (70in) and weighed 42kg (92lb). It was stabilized by pressed-steel cruciform fins and powered by a solid nitrocellulose-based propellant, venting through a single central nozzle at the base. Maximum range was just under 8500m (27,887ft), but the M-13-DD rocket, introduced in 1944, used two standard motors that

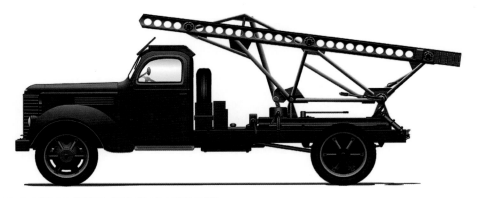

Specifications

Crew: 1 driver	Engine: 6 cylinder 75.3kW (101hp) engine
Weight: 3.9 tons (8700lb) (vehicle only)	Speed: not known
Length: 8m (26ft 3in)	Range: not known
Width: 2.21m (7ft 3in)	Armament: 16 x 132mm (5.2in) M13 rockets
Height: 2.4m (7ft 10in)	

▲ **International K7 ('Inter'), 2½-ton, 4x2 with BM-13-16 'Katyusha' salvo rocket launcher**

3rd Ukrainian Front / Fifth Shock Army

Although there is very little hard evidence, it seems highly likely that limited Lend-Lease deliveries of this vehicle were made and that some examples were adapted to carry the BM-13-16.

Specifications

Crew: 1 driver	Engine: 6 cylinder 82.77kW (111hp) engine
Weight: 5.1 tons (11,250lbs) (vehicle only)	Speed: not known
Length: 6.8m (22ft 6in)	Range: not known
Width: 2.22m (7ft 4in)	Armament: 16 x 132mm (5.2in) M13 rockets
Height: 2.33m (7ft 8in)	

▲ **International M-5-6-318 ('Inter'), 2½-ton, 6x6, with BM-13-16 'Katyusha' salvo rocket launcher**

1st Ukrainian Front / Fourth Tank Army

A total of 500 of these trucks were produced by International Harvester on a Quartermaster Corps foreign aid order from 1941, with most being sent to the Soviet Union. A number were fitted with the BM-13-16.

gave a maximum range of 11,800m (38,73ft). Most warheads were simple 22kg (48.4lb) impact-fused high-explosive (HE) fragmentation types, although there is a possibility that high-explosive anti-tank (HEAT) warheads may have been developed for use against tank concentrations. (Some reports indicate that illuminating and incendiary warheads were also used in small numbers.)

While the weapon was slow to reload and was less accurate than conventional artillery, it had immense firepower. In 7–10 seconds, a battery of four BM-13 launchers could fire a salvo delivering 4.4 tonnes (4.35 tons) of HE over a 4-hectare (10-acre) impact zone. Well-trained crews could then redeploy within minutes to avoid counter-battery fire.

The multiple rocket launchers were top secret at the beginning of the war and were operated under close NKVD supervision. They were assigned various code names such as 'Kostikov Guns', before being officially designated Guards Mortars. However, to the

troops they were 'Katyushas', the name coming from a popular song of the time and this was the title by which they would become world-famous.

On 7 July 1941, an experimental battery of seven launchers was first used in combat at Orsha – the

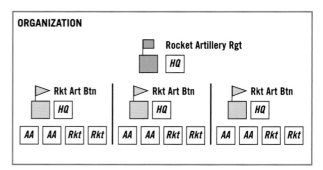

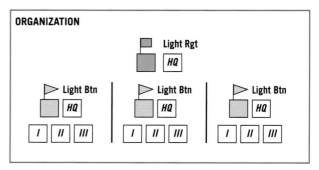

Mobile Rocket Launcher Production	1941	1942	1943	1944	1945
BM-8	400	900	400	500	200
BM-13	600	2400	2900	900	–
BM-31-12	–	–	–	1200	600

▲ **Fordson WOT8 30-cwt 4x4 with BM-13-16 'Katyusha' salvo rocket launcher**

South-Western Front / Sixth Army / 5th Guards Mortar Breakthrough Regiment

The WOT8, developed from the 3-ton WOT6, was the only British 30-cwt 4x4 wartime truck. Small numbers were included in the early deliveries to Russia in 1942, some of which were converted to carry the BM-13-16.

Specifications

Crew: 1 driver
Weight: 3.048 tons (3 tons) (vehicle only)
Length: 5.09m (16ft 8in)
Width: 2.28m (7ft 6in)
Height: 2.8m (9ft 2)

Engine: V8 cylinder 63.38kW (85hp) petrol
Speed: not known
Range: not known
Armament: 16 x 132mm (5.2in) M13 rockets

bombardment was spectacular, destroying the important railway junction together with German troop and supply trains. Following this success, the Red Army began priority production of the system and developed additional types of 'Katyusha'. In August 1941, the 82mm (3.2in) M-8 rocket entered service. Much smaller and lighter than the M-13, it could be fired from vehicles as small as a jeep, which could carry eight M-8s. Medium trucks mounted a bank of rails for no less than 48 rockets. The M-8's overall length was 66cm (26in), weight 8kg (17.6lb) (including a 5.4kg/11.8lb HE-fragmentation

Specifications

Crew: 1 driver	Engine: 8 cylinder 70.84kW (95hp) petrol
Weight: not known	Speed: not known
Wheelbase: 3.4m (11ft 2in)	Range: not known
Width: 2.13m (7ft)	Armament: 16 x 132mm (5.2in) M13 rockets
Height: 2.54m (8ft 4in)	

▲ **Ford/Marmon-Herrington ('Ford-Marmon') HH6-COE4 4x4 1½-ton with BM-13-16 'Katyusha' Salvo Rocket Launcher**

1st Ukrainian Front / Third Guards Tank Army / 115th Guards Mortar Breakthrough Regiment

Some of the 500 Ford/Marmon-Herrington 4x4 cab-over-engine (COE) conversions, delivered to Soviet Russia under Lend-Lease from late 1941 to 1942 were used to carry BM-13-16 rocket launchers, possibly the first foreign chassis used in this role.

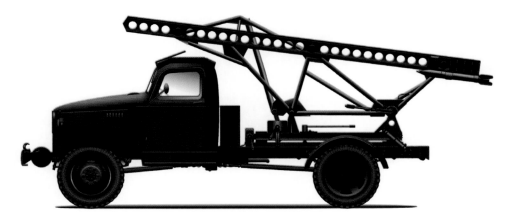

▲ **Chevrolet G-7117 4x4 1½-ton with BM-13-16 'Katyusha' salvo rocket launcher**

1st Belorussian Front / Forty-Seventh Army

Approximately 60,000 Chevrolet '1½-tonners' were supplied under Lend-Lease. While most were used as troop transporters and artillery prime movers, a number were converted to mount the BM-8-48 and BM-13-16.

Specifications

Crew: 1 driver	Engine: 6 cylinder 63.38kW (85hp) 4F1R petrol
Weight: not known	Speed: not known
Length: 5.69m (18ft 7in)	Range: not known
Width: 2.18m (7ft 2in)	Armament: 16 x 132mm (5.2in) M13 rockets
Height: 2m (6ft 6in)	

▲ **Studebaker US6 U3 2½-ton 6x6 with BM-8-48 'Katyusha' salvo rocket launcher**

4th Ukrainian Front / Second Guards Army / 133rd Guards Mortar Breakthrough Regiment

In mid-1943, the Red Army adopted the Studebaker 6x6 as the standard vehicle to mount the BM-8 and BM-13 salvo rocket launchers. With almost 105,000 such vehicles delivered to the Soviet Union by 1945, the Studebaker was available in quantity and gave the 'Katyusha' a high degree of cross-country mobility.

Specifications

Crew: 1 driver

Weight: 4.53 tonnes (10,000lbs) (vehicle only)

Length: 6.19m (20ft 4in)

Width: 2.23m (7ft 4in)

Height: 2.79m (9ft 2in)

Engine: 6 cylinder 64.8kW (87hp) petrol

Speed: not known

Range: not known

Armament: 48 x 82mm (3.2in) M8 rockets

Specifications

Crew: 1 driver

Weight: 4.53 tonnes (10,000lbs) (vehicle only)

Length: 6.19m (20ft 4in)

Width: 2.23m (7ft 4in)

Height: 2.79m (9ft 2in)

Engine: 6 cylinder 64.8kW (87hp) petrol

Speed: not known

Range: not known

Armament: 12 x 300mm (11.81in) M-31 rockets

▲ **Studebaker US 6x6 U3 2½-ton 6x6 with BM-31-12 'Katyusha' salvo rocket launcher**

1st Belorussian Front / Third Shock Army / IV Breakthrough Artillery Corps / 12th Breakthrough Artillery Division

The M-31 was a longer-ranged derivative of the M-30 heavy rocket. Initially both types were fired from static launchers, but in March 1944 a mobile version of the BM-31 entered service mounted on the Studebaker US6 chassis. The M-31's 28.9kg (63.5lb) warhead proved to be highly effective during the fierce street fighting in Budapest and Berlin.

warhead) and its maximum range was just over
5000m (1640ft). In 1944, an improved version of the
rocket came into service with a maximum range of
5500m (18,044ft).

These light and medium rockets were highly
effective, but there was a need for a heavier version,
which was initially met by the M-30. This used a
modified version of the M-13's rocket motor, which
was fitted with a bulbous 300mm (11.8in) HE
warhead containing 28.9kg (63.5lb) of explosive.
Maximum range was only 2800m (9186ft), but this
was considered acceptable in view of the warhead's
devastating blast effect. The M-30 was fired directly
from its packing case, four of which could be
mounted on a firing frame, referred to as a 'Rama'. In
late 1942, the improved M-31 was adopted. This was
very similar to its predecessor, but a new rocket
motor gave it a maximum range of 4300m
(14,107ft). (The later M-13-UK was modified to give
a degree of spin-stabilization, which greatly improved

▲ **Waiting to move out**
A brief rest halt for a BM-13-16 'Katyusha' battery. The rocket launchers are
mounted on US Studebaker truck chassis.

▲ **Load**
Loading the 42kg (92lb) M-13 rockets was a lengthy task, not to be undertaken while under counter-battery fire.

Aim
The launcher has been aligned on the target area and the crew take cover away from the vehicle prior to firing.

accuracy.) Initially the firing method was the same as that of the M-30, but in March 1944 a mobile version entered service consisting of launchers for 12 M-31s on a ZiS-6 6x6 truck.

Later production batches were mounted on Lend-Lease Studebaker US-6 6x6 trucks. These had such a good cross-country performance that in 1943 they were adopted as the standard mount for the BM-13 under the designation BM-13N (*Normalizovanniy*, 'standardize'), and more than 1800 of this type were produced by the end of the war.

Cheap, effective manufacture

All 'Katyushas' were simple, cheap weapons and could be manufactured in workshops and small factories that lacked the specialist machinery for producing conventional artillery or ammunition. This simplicity allowed fast construction – more than 3000 launchers of all types were produced during 1942. By the end of the year, 57 regiments were operational – together with the independent

battalions, they equated to 216 batteries: 21 per cent BM-8 light launchers, 56 per cent BM-13, and 23 per cent M-30 heavy launchers. While the majority of Katyushas were truck-mounted, a bewildering variety of other vehicles were also used in small numbers, including STZ-5 artillery tractors, plus the hulls of T-60 and KV-1 tanks. A few launchers were even fitted to armoured trains and river gunboats.

The Red Army's initial enthusiasm for the new weapon led to the creation of a large number of small units. The very first batteries had seven launchers each, but this was soon reduced at four per battery. On 8 August 1941, *Stavka* ordered the formation of eight rocket regiments, each of three battalions, with three four-vehicle batteries per battalion. (A total of 36 launchers per regiment.)

By the end of 1941, a total of 554 launchers were operational, equipping eight regiments, 35 independent battalions and two independent batteries. The increasing numbers of BM-13s allowed a battalion of eight launchers to be added to each tank corps from July 1942.

In June 1942, 20 independent battalions were formed to operate the new M-30 rockets, with each having 96 launchers in three batteries. These units were gradually concentrated into larger formations, finally leading to the establishment of seven full divisions in 1943, each of which had 864 launchers firing a total of 3456 rockets. (By 1944, these divisions were supplemented by motorized

Fire
Fire! A four-vehicle BM-13 battery unleashes its 64 rockets, carrying a total of over 300kg (660lb) of HE to a maximum range of 8500m (27,887ft).

164

heavy battalions, each of which were equipped with 48 BM-31 launchers.)

Close combat role

While 'Katyushas' were assembled *en masse* for carefully orchestrated preparatory bombardments for 'set-piece' battles, they were increasingly used in smaller numbers in the bitter street fighting of the last months of the war. Their employment in this role developed as the Red Army began to appreciate the problems posed by the heavily defended cities of central Europe.

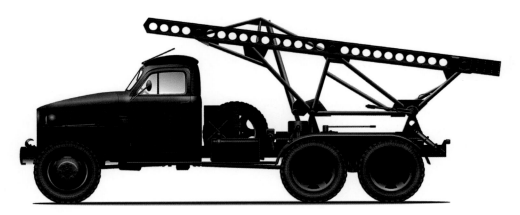

Specifications

Crew: 1 driver	Engine: 6 cylinder 64.8kW (87hp) petrol
Weight: 4.53 tonnes (10,000lbs) (vehicle only)	Speed: not known
Length: 6.19m (20ft 4in)	Range: not known
Width: 2.23m (7ft 4in)	Armament: 16 x 132mm (5.2in) M13 rockets
Height: 2.79m (9ft 2in)	

▲ **Studebaker US 6x6 U3 2½-ton with BM-13-16 'Katyusha' salvo rocket launcher**

1st Ukrainian Front / Third Guards Tank Army / 91st Guards Mortar Breakthrough Regiment

By 1945, 'Katyushas' were an essential part of the fire plan for every major Soviet artillery bombardment.

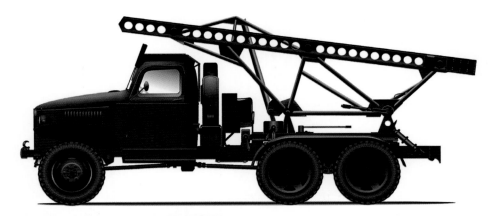

Specifications

Crew: 1 driver	Engine: 6 cylinder 77.55kW (104hp) petrol
Weight: 4.76 tonnes (10,500lbs) (vehicle only)	Speed: not known
Length: 5.86m (19ft 3in)	Range: not known
Width: 2.23m (7ft 4in)	Armament: 16 x 132mm (5.2in) M13 rockets
Height: 2.76m (9ft)	

▲ **GMC CCKW-352M-13 6x6 2½-ton with BM-13-16 'Katyusha' salvo rocket launcher**

2nd Belorussian Front / Forty-Eighth Army

Roughly 6700 Lend-Lease GMC trucks were shipped to the Red Army, a proportion of which were fitted with the BM-13-16.

Lend-Lease support vehicles

Lend-Lease came into existence on 11 March 1941 with the passage of the Lend-Lease Act, which permitted the President of the United States to 'sell, transfer title to, exchange, lease, lend, or otherwise dispose of, to any such government (whose defense the President deems vital to the defense of the United States) any defense article'.

ORIGINALLY DEVISED TO ALLOW the transfer of essential war supplies to Britain, it was extended to cover the Soviet Union in November 1941. It was a highly controversial plan that had been 'sold' to the American public by Franklin D Roosevelt's well-publicized explanation that his plan was comparable to one neighbour lending another a garden hose to put out a fire in his home.

'What do I do in such a crisis?' the president asked at a press conference. 'I don't say... "Neighbor, my garden hose cost me $15; you have to pay me $15 for it." ...I don't want $15 – I want my garden hose back after the fire is over.' By the end of June 1941, Stalin was bombarding Britain and the United States with increasingly urgent requests for war matériel – a typical early request listed 3000 fighters, 3000 bombers, 20,000 light AA guns, 3,000,000 pairs of boots and vast quantities of raw material. Although expressed as requests, there was always the implied threat that the Soviet Union could not continue the war if the supplies were not delivered. Gradually, the early extreme requests were moderated in recognition of what was actually available and, equally importantly, of what could be shipped to Russia.

British aid

Initially, Britain provided most of the matériel as the United States had only just begun the process of

US Vehicles	Lend-Lease exports	Total exports	Arrived	Lost en route	Diverted	En route Sept 1945
Trucks:						
¾-ton	25,240	25,240	24,564	78	598	–
1½-ton	153,415	159,494	148,664	6660	1826	2344
2½-ton	190,952	193,603	182,938	4300	1130	5235
2½-ton amphibious	589	589	586	3	–	–
5-ton and over	852	858	814	–	–	44
Special purpose	2792	2792	2784	8	–	–
Truck tractors w/o trailer	1941	1960	1938	6	–	16
Truck Subtotal	**375,781**	**384,536**	**362,288**	**11,055**	**3554**	**7639**
Jeeps:						
¼-ton 4x4	47,993	48,993	43,728	3657	1378	230
Amphibious	3510	3510	3510	–	–	–
Trucks & Jeeps Subtotal	**427,284**	**437,039**	**409,526**	**14,712**	**4932**	**230**
Ordnance Service Vehicles:						
Field repair trucks	1543	1543	1534	9	–	–
Tank recovery units	130	130	130	–	–	–
Tank transporters	655	655	629	26	–	–
Motor Vehicle Total	**429,612**	**439,367**	**411,819**	**14,747**	**4932**	**7869**
Motorcycles	35,170	35,170	32,200	1870	11	–
Track-laying tractors	8071	8074	7570	253	11	–

converting to a war economy and was straining to equip its own rapidly expanding forces. (A further factor was that until the Soviet Union was included in the coverage of the Lend-Lease Act in November 1941, all US-supplied items had to be paid for in gold.) The problems of actually 'delivering the goods' were, however, daunting. At first, the 'Arctic convoys'

were the only practical way and the first of these docked at Archangel in August 1941. At much the same time, British and Soviet forces jointly occupied Iran, opening up a land route to southern Russia from the Persian Gulf. A further option was to ship in supplies through Vladivostock for distribution via the Trans-Siberian railway, but Japan's entry into the

Specifications

Crew: 1	Engine: 53.7kW (72hp) Bedford 6-cylinder
Weight: 7 tonnes (6.89 tons)	petrol
Length: 5.99m (19ft 8in)	Speed: 61km/h (38mph)
Width: 2.26m (7ft 5in)	Range: 370 km (230 miles)
Height: 3m (9ft 10in)	

▲ Bedford QLD 4x4 3-ton general service
2nd Baltic Front / Twenty-Second Army / Supply Battalion

A total of 1100 Bedford trucks were delivered to Soviet Russia in 1942, including some batches of QLD General Service vehicles.

▲ Chevrolet C60L CMP 4x4 3-ton general service
1st Ukrainian Front / HQ Sixtieth Army / Supply Battalion

The Chevrolet C60L, built by General Motors Products of Canada from 1942 onwards, was a 'Canadian Military Pattern' (CMP) vehicle, a purpose-built military design. Although the total production ran to 209,000 vehicles, only a small number were taken into service with Soviet forces.

Specifications

Crew: 1 driver	Engine: 6 cylinder kW (85hp) petrol
Weight: not known	Speed: not known
Wheelbase: 4m (13ft 2in)	Range: not known
Width: 2.23m (7ft 4in)	Radio: none
Height: 3.04m (10ft)	

British and Canadian Vehicles	Shipped	Lost at Sea	Arrived
Lorries:			
Albion 3-ton	35	–	35
Austin 30-cwt	147	–	147
Austin 3-ton	333	–	333
Bedford 30-cwt	110	–	110
Bedford 3-ton	1662	275	1387
Dodge 30-cwt	157	–	157
Ford 30-cwt	868	137	731
Ford 3-ton	582	–	582
GMC	106	–	106
Total	**4000**	**412**	**3588**
Ambulances:			
Austin K-2	12	–	12
Motorcycles:			
BSA	685	–	685
Matchless	255	–	255
Norton	1	–	1
Velocette	225	–	225
Make unspecified	45	–	45
Total	**1223**	**–**	**1223**

(continued)	Shipped	Lost at Sea	Arrived
Machine Lorries:			
Albion 3-ton 4-wheel	42	5	37
Albion 3-ton, Ford 4-wheel	11	2	9
Other 3-ton	17	1	16
Leyland 3-ton 4-wheel	19	2	17
Albion 3-ton, Ford 4-wheel	11	–	11
Albion 3-ton 4-wheel	6	–	6
Albion 3-ton 4-wheel	1	–	1
Canadian 3-ton, Ford 4-whl	16	–	16
Ford 3-ton 4-wheel	3	–	3
Leyland 3-ton 6-wheel	2	–	2
Ford 3-ton 4-wheel	20	–	20
Ford 15-cwt 4-wheel	15	–	15
3-ton	2	–	2
Ford 3-ton 4-wheel	44	4	40
Albion 3-ton 4-wheel	5	–	5
Leyland 3-ton 6-wheel	7	–	7
Leyland 3-ton 4-wheel	9	–	9
Bedford 15-cwt Ford 4-whl	31	5	26
Ford 3-ton 4-wheel	2	–	–
Total	**263**	**19**	**242**

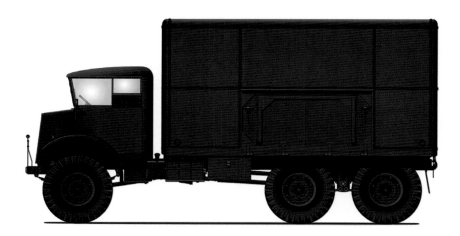

Specifications

Crew: 1

Weight: 8.7 tonnes (8.56 tons)

Length: 6.44m (21ft 1in)

Width: 2.28m (7ft 5in)

Height: 3.25m (10ft 8in)

Engine: 77.48kW (104hp) GMC 6-cylinder
petrol

Speed: 80.46km/h (50mph) (estimated)

▲ **General Motors C60X 6x6 3-ton mobile workshop**

HQ 2nd Ukrainian Front / Maintenance Battalion

The GM C60X, produced by General Motors Products of Canada from 1942 to 1944, was basically a lengthened version of the Chevrolet C60L. It was designed to carry various special body types, including the mobile workshop shown here. The Soviet Union received almost 1500 of the 2710 built from 1943 onwards, mainly through the Pacific route and the Persian Corridor.

▲ **GMC CCKW-352 6x6 2½-ton steel cargo body**

1st Byelorussian Front / HQ Sixty-Fifth Army / Supply Battalion

The GMC CCKW-352 and 353 were the standard medium trucks of the US Army throughout the war. More than half a million were produced from 1941 as the short 3.68m (145in) wheelbase (illustrated) and the long 4.2m (164in) wheelbase of the CCKW-353. The Red Army received only 6700 as Lend-Lease vehicles, almost all being the CCKW-352 type.

Specifications	
Crew: 1 driver	Engine: 6 cylinder 77.55kW (104hp) petrol
Weight: 4.76 tonnes (10,500lbs) (vehicle only)	Speed: not known
Length: 5.86m (19ft 3in)	Range: not known
Width: 2.23m (7ft 4in)	Radio: none
Height: 2.76m (9ft)	

war made this impractical until late 1942. (When it did come into operation, it became the route for roughly 50 per cent of all US Lend-Lease.) A final route for warplanes, transport aircraft, small high-value items and VIPs was the Alaska–Siberia Air Route, known as Alsib, which was used from October 1942.

Although initial Soviet requests were primarily for aircraft, tanks, AA and AT guns, the emphasis switched as Soviet war production revived in 1942. By this time, the factories evacuated to the Urals to escape the German invasion were supplying rapidly increasing numbers of tanks, artillery and aircraft. Resources were concentrated on the production of these top-priority weapons at the expense of support vehicles, which were in critically short supply following the massive losses sustained in the first year or so of the war. While the British vehicles supplied in 1941/42 were not well-suited to Russian conditions, they provided the Red Army with a critical degree of mobility that it would otherwise have lacked.

As US deliveries increased, the Soviets rapidly came to appreciate the sheer quality of the vehicles supplied. The vast majority of their own trucks were licence-built copies of antiquated US civilian designs of the late 1920s. These were of extremely rugged construction and were well-suited to coping with the appalling Russian roads.

Their engines were also designed to run efficiently in the depths of Russian winters and to tolerate very low octane fuel, which was all that was available for most road vehicles. These qualities could not disguise the fact that such vehicles were at best obsolescent compared to the US-supplied vehicles, which were modern military designs.

A further bonus was that many of these American trucks had all-wheel drive, which gave a useful degree of cross-country mobility. These advantages were partially off-set by a number of drawbacks. Vehicles such as the Studebaker demanded more careful servicing and better fuel than their Soviet counterparts, and performance was often reduced due to constant overloading, insufficient maintenance and the use of low octane fuels.

By 1944–45, nearly two-thirds of the truck strength of the Red Army was US-built. Without these vehicles, the great offensives of the period, such as the advance from the Vistula to the Oder would have been impossible. During this offensive, four tank armies were routinely operating up to 90km (56 miles) ahead of the remaining Soviet forces – each army used 600–750 tonnes (591–738 tons) of fuel per day, which required 270–300 trucks to carry it.

Despite the huge numbers of trucks supplied, there were never enough – only three of the four tank armies could be assigned special motor transport units, each with almost 600 trucks.

Amphibious units

Whilst the 586 DUKWs supplied represented only a small percentage of the total Lend-Lease shipments, they were highly valued. All were concentrated in nine 'independent special-purpose motorized battalions' (see organizational table, right), which were part of the Red Army's armour branch. Each battalion had approximately 60 DUKWs and these units were extensively used in the many river crossings undertaken during 1944/45, notably by the 2nd Byelorussian Front in its assault crossing of the Oder. (One battalion was assigned to the 2nd Far Eastern Front for the Manchurian Campaign, taking part in the crossings of the Amur and Ussuri rivers.) The Ford GPA 'amphibious jeep' was

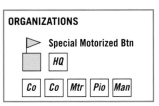

ORGANIZATIONS

▷ Special Motorized Btn

☐ HQ

Co | Co | Mtr | Pio | Man

Specifications

Crew: 1	Height: 1.75m (5ft 9in)
Weight: 1.63 tonnes (1.6 tons)	Engine: 44.7kW (60hp) 4-cylinder petrol
Length: 4.62m (15ft 2in)	Speed: 104.6km/h (65mph)
Width: 1.63m (5ft 4in)	

▲ **Ford GPA 4x4 ¼-ton amphibian**

3rd Ukrainian Front / Thirty-Seventh Army / LCVI Rifle Corps / Reconnaissance Company

3500 of the 12,000 GPAs produced between 1942 and 1943 were sent to the USSR under Lend-Lease. The Red Army found them so useful that a close copy of the design was manufactured in Soviet Russia in the immediate post-war period.

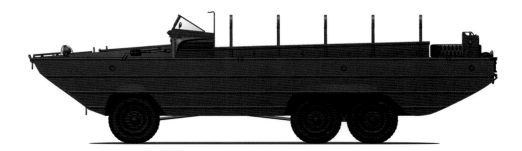

▲ **GMC DUKW-353 6x6 2½-ton amphibious truck**

3rd Ukrainian Front / HQ Fifth Shock Army / Supply Battalion

A total of 586 Lend-Lease DUKWs were supplied to the Red Army in 1943/45 and a copy of the design was put into production in the Soviet Union after the war.

Specifications

Crew: 1	Height: 2.69m (8ft 10in)
Weight: 6.75 tonnes (6.64 tons)	Engine: 62.8kW (91.5hp) GMC Model 270
Length: 9.75m (32ft)	Speed: 80km/h (50mph)
Width: 2.51m (8ft 3in)	

supplied in larger numbers (roughly 3500 vehicles) and was primarily used by reconnaissance units, although some may well have equipped the independent special-purpose motorized battalions.

US Lend-Lease support vehicles had considerable influence on post-war Soviet designs and were supplied in such vast numbers that they became a common sight throughout Soviet Russia and eastern Europe. (In Russia, the popular belief grew up that the stencilled 'USA' prefixed serial numbers which were left on most vehicles stood for 'Ubiyat Sukinsyna Adolfa' – Kill that Son-of-a-Bitch Adolf.)

Lend-Lease supplies to the Soviet Union continued to be sent until 12 May 1945, but, under the 'Milepost' agreement, deliveries continued for the duration of the war with Japan. (The scheme formally terminated on 20 September, but it is probable that the last shipments were made at the end of the month.) Total Lend-Lease aid exceeded $50 billion, of which the USSR received over $11 billion.

The scale of the Lease-Lend programme is vividly illustrated by the lists of war matériel shipped to the Soviet Union between November 1941 and 30 September 1945.

▲ **Austin K2/Y 4x2 2-ton ambulance**

Voronezh Front / Fortieth Army / Medical Battalion

It is likely that a small number of these ambulances were included in British deliveries to Russia in 1941/42.

Specifications

Crew 2	Height: 2.79m (9ft 2in)
Weight: not known	Engine: 44.7kW (60hp) Austin 6-cylinder petrol
Length: 5.49m (18ft)	Speed: 80km/h (50mph)
Width: 2.21m (7ft 3in)	

▶ **Dodge WC51 4x4 weapons carrier**

2nd Byelorussian Front / HQ Seventeenth Army / Supply Battalion

Almost 25,000 WC series vehicles were supplied to the Red Army between 1943 and 1945.

Specifications

Crew: 1	Engine: 68.54kW (92hp) Dodge T214 6-
Weight: 3.3 tonnes (3.25 tons)	cylinder petrol
Length: 4.47m (14ft 8in)	Speed: not known
Width: 2.1m (6ft 11in)	Range: 384km (240 miles)
Height: 2.15m (7ft 1in)	

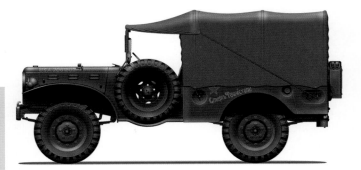

Lend-Lease production figures

The total of Lend-Lease AFVs supplied to the Red Army equalled approximately 16 per cent of Soviet wartime tank production and 12 per cent of SP gun production.

THE FIRST SOVIET UNITS equipped with Valentines and Matilda went into action in December 1941. By 1943, units solely equipped with Lend-Lease vehicles accounted for as much as 17 per cent of the total Red Army tank force. Large-scale deliveries of the M4A2 Sherman in 1944/45 led to entire tank and mechanized corps being equipped with the type, including I Guards Mechanized Corps.

Official Soviet sources heavily criticized the quality of Lend-Lease tanks, often comparing them unfavourably to the T-34 and KV-1. While this was undoubtedly true of many types such as the

Valentine and Matilda, they were all that British factories could supply at the time and were far superior to the T-60 and T-70 that were in volume production at the time.

PORT OF DELIVERY, %						
Year	1941	1942	1943	1944	1945	Total
Northern	0.4	17.0	8.3	33.6	12.8	72.1
Iran	0	10.1	58.9	92.6	19.4	181.0
Far East	0	5.4	27.9	13.4	12.8	59.5
Total	0.4	32.5	95.1	139.6	45.0	312.6

BRITISH & CANADIAN AFVS, LEND-LEASE (1941–45)	Sent	Lost	Arrived
Brit Inf Tk Mk II Matilda	1184	–	–
Matilda Mk III	113	–	113
Matilda Mk IV	915	221	694
Matilda Mk IV CS	156	31	126
Brit Inf Tk Mk III Valentine	2394	–	–
Valentine Mk II	161	25	136
Valentine Mk III	346	–	346
Valentine Mk IV	520	71	559
Valentine Mk V	340	113	227
Valentine Mk IX	836	18	818
Valentine Mk X	74	8	66
Valentine Bridgelayer	25	–	25
Brit Inf Tk Mk IV Churchill	301	–	–
Churchill Mk II	45	19	26
Churchill Mk III	151	24	127
Churchill Mk IV	105	–	105
Cromwell	6	–	6
Tetrarch	20	–	20
Universal Carriers	1212	–	–
Canadian Valentine Mk VII	1388	180	1208
Canadian Universal Carriers	1348	–	–
Total Valentine	**3782**	**320**	**3462**
Total Universal Carrier	**2560**	**224**	**2336**

AMERICAN AFVS, LEND-LEASE (1942–45)	Sent	Lost	Arrived
M3/M3A1 Stuart	1676	–	–
M5 Stuart	5	–	–
M24 Chaffee	2	–	–
Total Light Tanks	**1682**	**443**	**1239**
M3 Lee medium tank	1386	–	–
M4A2 Sherman (75mm/2.9in)	2007	–	–
M4A2 Sherman (76mm/3in)	2095	–	–
Total Medium Tanks	**5374**	**417**	**4957**
M26	1	–	–
M31B2 ARV	115	–	–
M15A1 MGMC SP AA	100	–	–
M17 MGMC SPG AA	1000	–	–
T48 SPG (SU-57)	650	–	–
M18 tank destroyer	5	–	–
M10 3in GMC TD	52	–	–
M2 halftrack	342	–	–
M3 halftrack	2	–	–
M5 halftrack	421	–	–
M9 halftrack	413	–	–
Total Halftracks	**1158**	**54**	**1104**
Universal Carrier T16	96	–	–

SOFT VEHICLES, LEND-LEASE	1941	1942	1943	1944	1945	Total
Towing Vehicles						
Studebaker	–	3800	34,800	56,400	19,200	114,200
GM	–	1400	4900	400	–	6700
International	–	900	1800	100	300	3100
Chevrolet	–	2700	13,100	25,100	6800	47,700
Ford	–	400	500	–	100	1000
Dodge 3/4	–	–	4300	10,700	4600	19,600
Trucks						
Ford-6	–	7600	18,600	29,000	5800	61,000
Dodge 11/2 ton	–	8000	1500	100	–	9600
Dodge 3 ton	–	–	1400	300	–	1700
Bedford	–	1100	–	–	–	1100
Ford Marmon	200	300	–	–	–	500
Austin	200	300	–	–	–	500
Light Vehicles						
Willys	–	5400	13,900	14,300	6200	39,800
Bantam	–	500	100	–	–	600
Chevrolet	–	–	–	–	200	200
Special Auto						
Dodge Staff Car	–	–	–	100	100	200
Ford Amphibian	–	–	–	1900	300	2200
GM Amphibian	–	–	–	–	300	300
Trailer	–	–	–	600	200	800
Mack Diesel	–	–	–	–	900	900
Other	–	–	200	300	–	500
Total	**400**	**32,400**	**95,100**	**139,300**	**45,000**	**312,200**

▶ **Studebaker 'Katyushas'**

With their launch rails protected by canvas covers, US-supplied Studebaker 2.5-ton trucks of the 4th Ukrainian Front carry their M13 salvo rocket launchers through a town in Czech Moravia, March 1945.

Tractors and towing vehicles

While not as 'glamorous' as the tank arm, the Red Army's tractors and artillery played a vital role in supporting armoured operations throughout the war.

THE MOTLEY COLLECTION of home-produced and Lend-Lease tractors gave mobility to increasingly powerful artillery formations, whose firepower paved the way for the tank armies to spearhead the spectacular advances of 1944/45.

As the twentieth century began, the problems of moving increasingly heavy artillery were becoming acute. Horse teams could not draw guns weighing much in excess of 4.5 tonnes (4.4 tons), while traction engines and early trucks lacked cross-country mobility. The most promising solution, a prototype tracked artillery tractor, was produced by Hornsby, an engineering firm based in Grantham, UK. It was first tested by the British Army as early as 1909, but required further development. The disillusioned developers sold the

▶ **Industrial might**
The principal Soviet tank factories, mostly built under the two Five-Year Plans that laid the foundations of Soviet war industry. The Kharkov and Izhorskiy complexes were lost in 1941, and the sieges of Leningrad and Stalingrad severely disrupted production in these cities.

patent for their caterpillar tracks to a US company, Holt Tractors (which later became the Caterpillar Tractor Company).

Agricultural use

Holt developed the tracks for a series of agricultural tractors, some of which were bought by the British Army in 1915 as artillery tractors. By 1918, some 2100 Holts were in British service and others had been sold to the Soviet Union.

▶ **T-26T**

First Army Group / VI Tank Brigade, Khalkin-Gol, 1939

The T-26T was a fully armoured variant of the T-26T2, which was issued to a handful of artillery units in 1933. Small numbers of both types remained in service until 1945, with a few even participating in the Manchurian Campaign.

Specifications

Crew: 2	Height: 1.83m (6ft) (Estimated)
Weight: 8.5 tonnes (8.36 tons) (Estimated)	Engine: 66.2kW (90hp) 4-cylinder petrol
Length: 4.8m (15ft 9in)	Speed: 30km/h (18.6mph)
Width: 3.41m (11ft 2in)	Range: 175km (108.75 miles)

▶ **Heavy Tractor *Stalinez* – ChTZ S-60**

Bryansk Front / Fiftieth Army / 151st Corps Artillery Regiment

The *Stalinez* S-60 was a close copy of the US Caterpillar 60, designed for industrial and agricultural use. It was issued to Red Army artillery units during the mid 1930s as a prime mover for medium and heavy artillery.

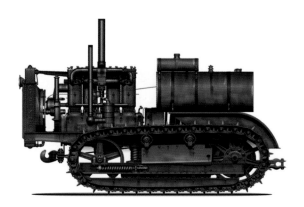

Specifications

Crew: 1	Height: not known
Weight: 9.5 tonnes (9.35 tons)	Engine: 44.7kW (60hp) 4-cylinder petrol
Length: not known	Speed: 7km/h (4.35mph)
Width: not known	Range: 80km (49.71 miles)

SOVIET VEHICLE FACTORIES

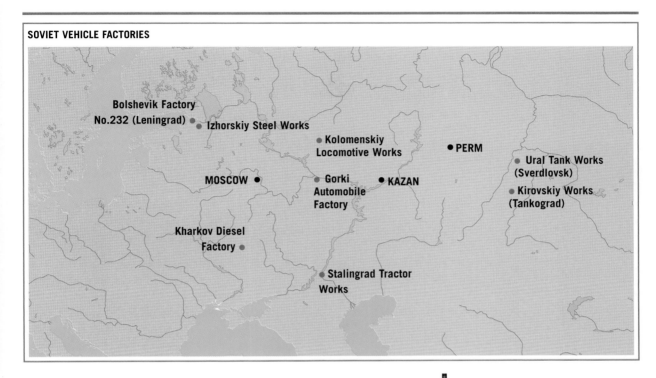

▶ **Heavy Tractor *Stalinez* – ChTZ S-65**

Western Front / Nineteenth Army / 596th Corps Artillery Regiment

The S-65 was another derivative of the Caterpillar 60 design. Although initially intended as a civilian vehicle, many of the 37,626 S-65s built from 1937 to 1941 were brought into service as artillery tractors.

Specifications

Crew: 1	Height: 2.151m (7ft 1in)
Weight: 11.2 tonnes (11.02 tons)	Engine: 55.87kW (75hp) diesel
Length: 4.086m (13ft 5in)	Speed 7km/h (4.35mph)
Width: 2.416m (7ft 11in)	Range: 90km (55.82 miles)

▶ **Heavy Tractor *Stalinez* – ChTZ S-65 with cab**

Western Front / Twenty-Second Army / 56th Corps Artillery Regiment

A high proportion of S-65 artillery tractors were fitted with a variety of cabs to allow them to operate efficiently in the extremes of the Russian climate.

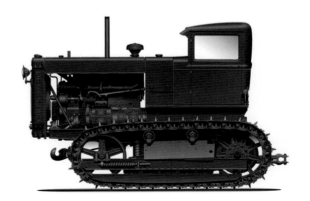

Specifications

Crew: 1	Height: not known
Weight: 11.2 tonnes (11.02 tons)	Engine: 55.87kW (75hp) diesel
Length: 4.086m (13ft 5in)	Speed: 7km/h (4.35mph)
Width: 2.416m (7ft 11in)	Range: 90km (55.82 miles)

Track-laying Tractors, Lend-Lease program	Strength
Heavy, M1, Prime Mover, Class 2:	
Allis-Chalmers HD10W	413
Caterpillar D7	243
International TD18	494
Others	1082
Subtotal	2232
Medium Heavy, Prime Mover, Class 3:	
Allis-Chalmers HD7W	2106
Caterpillar D6	296
International TD14	246
Others	2393
Subtotal	5041
Others:	
Tractor, Crawler type, Class 2	836
Tractor, Crawler type, Class 3	10
Tractor, Crawler type, Class 4	157
Tractor, Elec. Light Duty, 2000 & 2500lbs	115
Subtotal	1118
Cranes and Shovels:	
Crawler type, Class I	17
Crawler type, Class II	27
Crawler type, Class III	405
Crawler type, Class IV	62
Crawler type, Class V	43
Crawler type, Class VI	6
Subtotal	560
Total	8951

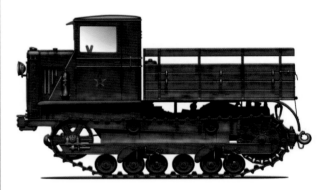

▲ **High-Speed Tractor** *Stalinez – S-2 skorostnoy*
Southern Front / Eighteenth Army / LV Rifle Corps / 437th Corps Artillery Regiment
A total of 1263 S-2s were produced between 1939 and 1942. Unlike most earlier types, the S-2 was a purpose-built artillery tractor, although its 'S' (*skorostnoy* – fast) designation was something of a misnomer since its maximum towing speed was no more than 16km/h (10mph) on roads.

Specifications
Crew: 1
Weight: 11.7 tonnes (11.51 tons)
Length: not known
Width: not known
Engine: not known
Speed: 24km/h (14.91mph)
Range: 180km (111.85 miles)

▶ **Medium Tractor M1 – Allis-Chalmers HD-7W**
1st Byelorussian Front / First Polish Army / 5th Heavy Artillery Brigade
A total of 2100 HD-7W Lend-Lease artillery tractors were supplied to the Red Army and the Polish formations on the Eastern Front, where they were extensively used as tractors for the 152mm (5.9in) ML-20 howitzer.

Specifications
Crew: 1
Weight: 6.35 tonnes (6.25 tons)
Length: 3.25m (10ft 8in)
Width: 2.05m (6ft 8in)
Height: 1.75m (5ft 9in)
Engine: 33.6kW (45hp) General Motors 3-cylinder diesel
Speed: not known
Range: not known

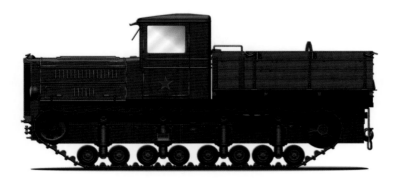

Specifications

Crew: 1

Weight: 10.5 tonnes (10.33 tons)

Length: 5.767m (18ft 11in)

Width: 2.21m (7ft 3in)

Height: 2.54m (8ft 4in)

Engine: 96.85kW (130hp) 4-cylinder diesel

Speed: 30km/h (18.64mph)

Range: 170km (105.6 miles)

▲ Heavy Tractor *Komintern*

Southern Front / Twelfth Army / XIII Rifle Corps / 468th Heavy Howitzer Regiment

The *Komintern* used the suspension of the T-24 medium tank and it proved capable of towing even the 18.3-tonne (18-ton) B-4 203mm (8in) howitzer. Roughly 2000 vehicles were produced between 1935 and 1941.

Specifications

Crew: 1

Weight: 15.5 tonnes (15.25 tons)

Length: 6.22m (20ft 5in)

Width: 2.35m (7ft 8in)

Height: 2.74m (9ft)

Engine: 260.75kW (350hp) diesel

Speed: 36km/h (22.37mph)

Range: 270km (167.77 miles)

▲ Heavy Tractor *Voroshilovyets*

Kalinin Front / Third Shock Army / 429th Howitzer Regiment

The *Voroshilovyets* was intended to supersede the *Komintern* artillery tractor. As many as 450 may have been produced between 1939 and 1942.

▶ Heavy Tractor M1 – Allis-Chalmers HD-10W

3rd Ukrainian Front / Fourth Guards Army / 41st Guards Rifle Division

Over 400 HD-10W tractors were issued to Red Army heavy artillery units.

Specifications

Crew: 1

Weight: 9.731 tonnes (9.58 tons)

Length: 3.81m (12ft 6in)

Width: 2.38m (7ft 9in)

Height: 1.98m (6ft 6in)

Engine: 48.5kW (65hp) General Motors 4-cylinder diesel

Speed: not known

Range: not known

Specifications

Crew: 1	Height: not known
Weight: 6.55 tonnes (6.45 tons)	Engine: GM 4-71 diesel
Length: not known	Speed: 38km/h (23.61mph)
Width: not known	Range: 290km (180 miles)

▲ High-Speed Artillery Tractor Ya-12

1st Ukrainian Front / Third Guards Tank Army / 199th Light Artillery Brigade

The YA-12 was the first of a new generation of artillery tractors, combining the suspension of the T-60 light tank and the Lend-Lease GM4-71 diesel engine. A total of over 1600 vehicles were completed between 1943 and 1945.

▶ Heavy Tractor M1 – International TD-18

4th Ukrainian Front / Second Guards Army / LV Rifle Corps / 2nd Guards Breakthrough Artillery Division.

Almost 500 Lend-Lease TD-18s were shipped to the Soviet Union, primarily for use as heavy artillery prime movers.

Specifications

Crew: 1	Engine: 78.97kW (106hp) International
Weight: 9.75 tonnes (9.6 tons)	Harvester 6-cylinder diesel
Length: 4.21m (13ft 10in)	Speed: not known
Width: 2.41m (7ft 11in)	Range: not known
Height: 2.69m (8ft 10in)	

▶ Heavy Tractor M1 – Caterpillar D-7

4th Ukrainian Front / Fifty-First Army / 26th Artillery Division

The 7500 Lend-Lease tractors supplied to the Red Army by 1945 included roughly 240 D-7s.

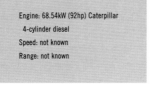

Specifications

Crew: 1	Engine: 68.54kW (92hp) Caterpillar
Weight: 14.34 tonnes (14.11 tons)	4-cylinder diesel
Length: 4.1m (13ft 5in)	Speed: not known
Width: 2.5m (8ft 2in)	Range: not known
Height: 2.44m (8ft)	

In 1918, 2000 Bolshevik tractors were ordered for the Red Army. These were copies of the World War I vintage Holts supplied to the Tsar's army. The chaos of the Russian Civil War meant that only eight had been produced by 1922, when production switched to an improved type, the Nr. 75, which was also based on a Holt design. This type remained in production throughout the 1920s and was primarily used by AA units.

Between 1922 and 1930, roughly 3500 tracked artillery tractors based on the German Hanomag WD-50 were produced as the *Kommunar* series. The rapid expansion of Soviet industry and the obsession with production targets led to an ill-trained workforce turning out appallingly bad vehicles – an American engineer who visited the factory in the late 1920s commented, 'If they run at all, their life is limited to a few hours.'

Licensed production

In 1932, the ChTZ factory began licence production of the US Caterpillar 60 design as the S-60, completing almost 69,000 in five years. Production was then switched to a diesel-powered derivative, the S-65, over 37,000 of which were completed before the German invasion. From 1937, these were supplemented by the first Soviet-designed tractor, the STZ-3, which like the earlier types was essentially a

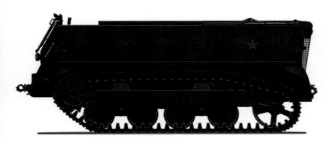

▲ **High-Speed Tractor M5**

1st Ukrainian Front / Thirteenth Army / 17th Artillery Division

The M5 was a purpose-built artillery tractor, capable of road speeds of up to 56km/h (35mph) while towing medium artillery. Almost 200 Lend-Lease vehicles were sent to the Soviet Union in 1944.

Specifications

Crew: 1	Engine: 154kW (207hp) Continental R6572 6-cylinder petrol
Weight: 13.8 tonnes (13.58 tons)	
Length: 5.03m (16ft 6in)	Speed: 48km/h (30 mph)
Width: 2.54m (8ft 4in)	Range: 290km (180 miles)
Height: 2.69m (8ft 10in)	

Specifications

Crew: 1	Height: 3.1m (10ft 2in)
Weight: 7.189 tonnes (7.07 tons)	Engine: 70.8kW (95hp) AEC 6-cylinder diesel
Length: 6.32m (20ft 9in)	Speed: 58km/h (36mph)
Width: 2.4m (7ft 10.5in)	Range: 579km (360 miles)

▲ **AEC Matador 0853 4x4 medium artillery tractor**

1st Byelorussian Front / 4th Artillery Corps

Small numbers of Matadors were included in the early consignments of British vehicles sent to Russia on the Arctic convoys.

slow agricultural vehicle with a maximum speed of 6–7km/h (3.7–4.3mph). Despite the obvious drawbacks of such low speeds, all these models were issued to the Red Army as well as civilian industries and state farms.

The STZ-3 was considered to be a marked improvement on earlier tractors – 4000 were issued for military use by 1941 and a militarized version was produced as the STZ-5. This had the cab repositioned at the front of tractor to create space for a rear-mounted cargo compartment and was a far more effective artillery tractor than the earlier types, especially as it had a top speed of 20km/h (12.4mph). However, production fell well short of the Red Army's needs and it received only 7000 vehicles before the German invasion.

Military tractors

As early as 1930, it had been recognized that civilian-based tractor designs were far from ideal for army use and the first exclusively military type, the *Komintern*, went into production shortly thereafter, based on the suspension of the T-12 medium tank. Only 50 or so vehicles were completed before production switched to an improved version using T-24 suspension in 1935. Approximately 2000 were issued to the Red Army, primarily to medium artillery regiments. By

the late 1930s, it was becoming apparent that a more modern design of heavy artillery tractor was needed and the *Voroshilovyets* was developed with an improved suspension and a 261kW (350hp) diesel engine that gave it a road speed of 36km/h (22.4mph). In service, it met all expectations, proving to be a capable towing vehicle for the massive 203mm (8in) B-4 howitzer.

In the era of military modernization and experimentation between 1931 and 1937, considerable efforts were made to produce a family of fully tracked and at least partially armoured support vehicles, many based on the hull of the T-26. Prototypes of APCs, ammunition transporters and command vehicles were all tested, but the only versions to enter limited production were the fully armoured T-26T artillery tractor and the very similar, but only partially armoured, T-26T2. Only very small numbers of both types were built, in contrast to the final pre-war artillery tractor, the *Komsomolyets*. This was primarily intended as a towing vehicle for 45mm (1.8in) AT guns and had a fully enclosed two-man armoured cab with a hull-mounted MG, plus six open seats for the gun crew. Over 4400 were built between 1937 and 1941.

Huge numbers of all these pre-war tractors were lost in the opening stages of Operation *Barbarossa*

▲ Scammell Pioneer SV2S 6x4 heavy breakdown tractor
Voronezh Front / HQ Sixtieth Army / Maintenance Battalion
The Scammell Pioneer was another British vehicle supplied to the Red Army in small quantities early in the war. With its relatively powerful diesel engine and the ability to convert it to halftrack configuration by fitting tracks over the rear wheels, it was well suited to Russian conditions.

Specifications

Crew: 3	Height: 2.87m (9ft 5in)
Weight: 9.74 tonnes (9.58 tons)	Engine: 80kW (102hp) Gardner diesel
Length: 6.17m (20ft 3in)	Speed: not known
Width: 2.64m (8ft 8in)	Range: 690km (430 miles)

and many civilian vehicles had to be hastily impressed for use by artillery units, tank recovery teams and a wide range of other military duties. The supply of a wide variety of (mainly) US Lend-Lease tractors from late 1941 eased the situation, but there were never enough to go round until 1943–44.

By that time, the pressure on Soviet war industries had eased to the extent that resources were available to start work on a new artillery tractor design, which went into production as the Ya-12 in late 1943. This used the suspension of the now obsolete T-60 light tank and the Lend-Lease GM 4-71 diesel engine, and over 1600 were completed by the end of the war in May 1945.

While many of the older vehicles were scrapped or turned over to civilian use after the war, production of the newer models (notably re-engined variants of the YA-12) continued until at least the late 1940s.

▲ **Reo 28XS 6x4 truck tractor**

1st Ukrainian Front / Third Guards Tank Army / Maintenance Battalion

The Red Army's need for tank transporters was partially met by 190 Reo 28XS vehicles during 1943–44. However, the type's usefulness was limited by its 18-tonne (20-US ton) semi-trailer, which restricted it to carrying lighter AFVs.

Specifications

Crew: 1 driver	Engine: Hercules HXD 6 cylinder 134.2kW
Weight: 8.6 tons (18,960lbs) (without load)	(180hp)
Length: 7.18m (23ft 7in)	Speed: not known
Width: 2.43m (8ft)	Range: not known
Height: 2.64m (8ft 7in)	Radio: none

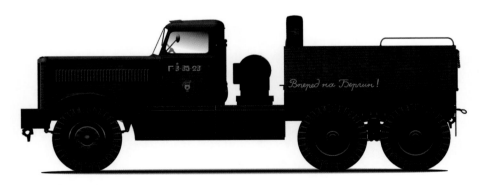

Specifications

Crew: 1	Engine: 149.75kW (201hp) Hercules
Weight: 20.4 tonnes (20.07 tons)	DFXE diesel
Length: 7.1m (23ft 3in)	Speed: not known
Width: 2.6m (8ft 6in)	Range: 250km (156 miles)
Height: 2.97m (9ft 9in)	

▲ **Diamond T-980 6x4 truck tractor**

1st Ukrainian Front / Third Guards Tank Army / 6th Guards Tank Corps

After the limitations of the Reo became apparent, 295 Diamond Ts and 40.8-tonne (45-US ton) M9 trailers were supplied to the Red Army to transport the heavier AFVs coming into service in the last year of the war.

Tank divisions, 1941

In June 1941, the vast majority of the Red Army's armoured divisions were well below strength. Many of their tanks were unserviceable or poorly maintained, largely due to abysmal levels of crew training. Unsurprisingly, these formations were massacred by the veteran panzer divisions in the summer of 1941. The reconstruction of Soviet armoured forces was going to be a long, hard struggle.

SOVIET TANK DIVISIONS (JUNE 1941)					
Division	Commander	Tank Regiment	Assigned	Destruction	Site
1 TD	Maj-Gen V.I. Baranov	1, 2	Independent	24 April 42	–
2 TD	Maj-Gen E.N. Solyankin	3, 4	III Mech Corps	12 July 41	Minsk
3 TD	Col K.Yu. Andreev	5, 6	I Mech Corps	7 Dec 41	–
4 TD	Maj-Gen A.G. Potaturchev	7, 8	VI Mech Corps	4 July 41	Bialystok
5 TD	Col F.F. Fedorov	9, 10	III Mech Corps	27 June 41	Olita
6 TD	Col V.M. Alekseev	11, 12	XXVIII Mech Corps	24 July 41	–
7 TD	Maj-Gen S.V. Borzilov	13, 14	VI Mech Corps	17 July 41	Disna
8 TD	Col P.S. Fotchenkov	15, 16	IV Mech Corps	24 Sept 41	–
9 TD	Col V.G. Burkov	17, 18	XXVII Mech Corps	–	–
10 TD	Maj-Gen S.Ya. Ogurtsov	19, 20	XV Mech Corps	23 Sept 41	–
11 TD	Col G.I. Kuzmin	21, 22	II Mech Corps	8 Sept 41	South Russia
12 TD	Maj-Gen T.A. Mishanin	23, 24	VIII Mech Corps	13 Sept 41	Dneipropyetrovsk
13 TD	Col F.U. Grachev	25, 26	V Mech Corps	4 Aug 41	Smolensk
14 TD	Col I.D. Vasil'ev	27, 28	VII Mech Corps	5 Oct 41	–
15 TD	Col V.I. Polozkov	29, 30	XVI Mech Corps	8 Aug 41	Uman
16 TD	Col M.I. Mindro	31, 149	II Mech Corps	8 Aug 41	Uman
17 TD	Col I.P. Korchagin	33, 34	V Mech Corps	4 Aug 41	Smolensk
18 TD	Maj-Gen F.T. Remizov	35, 36	VII Mech Corps	20 Oct 41	Viazma
19 TD	Maj-Gen K.A. Semenchenko	37, 38	XXII Mech Corps	24 Sept 41	Kiev
20 TD	Col M.E. Katukov	39, 40	IX Mech Corps	29 Sept 41	Kiev
21 TD	Col L.V. Bunin	41, 42	X Mech Corps	4 April 42	–
22 TD	Maj-Gen V.P. Puganov	43, 44	XIV Mech Corps	5 July 41	Slutsk
23 TD	Col T.S. Orlenko	45, 144	XII Mech Corps	28 Sept 41	–
24 TD	Col M.I. Chesnokov	48, 49	X Mech Corps	9 Sept 41	Luga
25 TD	Col N.M. Nikiforov	50, 113	XIII Mech Corps	28 June 41	Bialystok
26 TD	Maj-Gen V.T. Obukhov	51, 52	XX Mech Corps	14 July 41	–
27 TD	Col A.O. Akhmanov	54, 140	XVII Mech Corps	–	–
28 TD	Col I.D. Chernyakhovskiy	55, 56	XII Mech Corps	3 Jan 42	–
29 TD	Col N.P. Studnev	57, 59	XI Mech Corps	6 July 41	Minsk
30 TD	Col S.I. Bogdanov	60, 61	XIV Mech Corps	3 July 41	–
31 TD	Col S.A. Kalikhovich	46, 148	XIII Mech Corps	5 July 41	Bialystok
32 TD	Col E.G. Pushkin	63, 64	IV Mech Corps	17 July 41	Volodorka

SOVIET TANK DIVISIONS (JUNE 1941)					
Division	Commander	Tank Regiment	Assigned	Destruction	Site
33 TD	Col M.F. Panov	65, 66	XI Mech Corps	–	–
34 TD	Col I.V. Vasil'ev	67, 68	VIII Mech Corps	30 June 41	Dubno
35 TD	Maj-Gen N.A. Novikov	69, 70	IX Mech Corps	24 Sept 41	Kiev
36 TD	Col S.Z. Miroshnikov	71, 72	XVII Mech Corps	–	–
37 TD	Col F.G. Anikushkin	73, 74	XV Mech Corps	17 July 41	–
38 TD	Col S.I. Kapustin	75, 76	XX Mech Corps	15 July 41	–
39 TD	Col N.V. Starkov	77, 78	XVI Mech Corps	6 Aug 41	–
40 TD	Col M.V. Shirobokov	79, 80	XIX Mech Corps	29 Sept 41	Kiev
41 TD	Col P.P. Pavlov	82, 81	XXII Mech Corps	24 Sept 41	Kiev
42 TD	Col N.I. Voeikov	83, 84	XXI Mech Corps	18 Aug 41	–
43 TD	Col I.G. Tsibin	85, 86	XIX Mech Corps	29 Sept 41	Kiev
44 TD	Col V.P. Krimov	87, 88	XVIII Mech Corps	–	–
45 TD	Col M.D. Solomatin	89, 90	XXIV Mech Corps	8 Aug 41	Uman
46 TD	Col V.A. Koptsov	91, 92	XXI Mech Corps	2 Aug 41	Chola
47 TD	Col G.S. Rodin	93, 94	XVIII Mech Corps	24 Sept 41	Kiev
48 TD	Col D.Ya. Yakovlev	95, 96	XXIII Mech Corps	26 Aug 41	Velikiye Luki
49 TD	Col K.F. Shvetsov	97, 98	XXIV Mech Corps	8 Aug 41	Uman
50 TD	Col B.S. Bakhorov	99, 100	XXV Mech Corps	7 Sept 41	–
51 TD	Col P.G. Chernov	101, 102	XXIII Mech Corps	13 Aug 41	–
52 TD	Col G.M. Mikhailov	104, 105	XXVI Mech Corps	–	–
53 TD	Col A.S.Beloglazov	106, 107	XXVII Mech Corps	–	–
54 TD	Col M.D.Sinenko	108, 109	XXVIII Mech Corps	–	–
55 TD	Col V.M. Badanov	110, 111	XXV Mech Corps	29 July 41	–
56 TD	Col I.D. Illarionov	112, 113	XXVI Mech Corps	–	–
57 TD	Col V.A. Mishulin	114, 115	Independent	4 Aug 41	–
58 TD	Maj-Gen(?) A.A. Kotlyarov	116, 117	XXX Mech Corps	2 Dec 41	–
59 TD	Col S.P.Chernoba	118, 119	Independent	–	–
60 TD	Maj-Gen(?) A.F. Popov	120, 121	XXX Mech Corps	10 Feb 42	–
61 TD	Col B.M. Skvortsov	141, 142	Independent	1946	disbanded, Far East
69 TD	–	–	–	20 Oct 41	Viazma
101 TD	–	202	–	20 Oct 41	Viazma
102 TD	–	204	–	20 Oct 41	Viazma
104 TD	–	208, 209	–	16 Aug 41	disbanded
105 TD	–	210, 211	–	4 Sept 41	disbanded
107 TD	–	–	–	20 Oct 41	Viazma
108 TD	–	216, 217	–	29 Nov 41	disbanded
109 TD	–	218, 219	–	1 Sept 41	disbanded
110 TD	–	220, 221	–	12 Sept 41	North Russia
111 TD	–	–	–	1946	disbanded, Far East
112 TD	–	–	–	6 Nov 42	–

Soviet tank strengths

Stavka analysts frequently 'fine-tuned' the official organization of armoured units, but the reality was often very different from the neat tables prepared by staff officers. Mechanical breakdowns and combat losses could quickly reduce a unit to a fraction of its authorized strength.

IN 1941–42, many formations had a bizarre appearance, as they were equipped with a strange collection of whatever tanks were available. As an example, in October 1941, the 24th Tank Brigade's strength stood at:

- 4 x KV-1
- 22 x T-34
- 1 x BT
- 9 x T-26
- 22 x T-40

Captured vehicles were also used in some numbers, notably StuG III assault guns and Panther tanks, which were available in sufficient quantities to equip whole units by the final year of the war.

▲ **Fighting the propaganda war**
A column of KV-1 heavy tanks from the 6th Soviet Tank Regiment pose for a propoganda photograph.

Causes of T-34 Tank Losses (as percentage)

T-34 Tank Losses	20mm (0.78in)	37mm (1.5in)	short 50mm (2in)	long 50mm (2in)	75mm (2.9in)	88mm (3.5in)	105mm (4.1in)	128mm (5in)	AT rocket	Unknown
Up to September 42	4.7	10.0	7.5	54.3	10.1	3.4	2.9	–	–	7.1
Stalingrad operation	–	–	25.6	26.5	12.1	7.8	–	–	–	28.0
Central Front, Operation 1943	–	–	10.5	23.0	40.5	26.0	–	–	–	–
1st Byelorussian Front Jun–Sep 44	–	–	–	–	39.0	38.0	–	–	9.0	14.0
1st Byelorussian Front Jan–Mar 45	–	–	–	–	29.0	64.0	–	1.0	5.5	0.5
1st Ukrainian Front Jan–Mar 45	–	–	–	0.5	19.0	71.0	0.6	–	8.9	–
4th Ukrainian Front Jan–Mar 45	–	–	–	–	25.3	51.5	0.9	–	9.0	13.5
1st Byelorussian Front Oder–Berlin 1945	–	–	–	1.4	69.2	16.7	–	–	10.5	2.2
2nd Guards Tank Army, Berlin 1945	–	5.4	–	–	36.0	29.0	6.6	–	22.8	–

Soviet and German AFV Strength on the Eastern Front

AFVs: Eastern Front	Jun 41	Mar 42	May 42	Nov 42	Mar 43	Aug 43	Jun 44	Sep 44	Oct 44	Nov 44	Dec 44	Jan 45
Soviet	28,800	4690	6190	4940	7200	6200	11,600	11,200	11,900	14,000	15,000	14,200
German	3671	1503	3981	3133	2374	2555	4470	4186	4917	5202	4785	4881

These figures include tanks and all kinds of SP guns, but the number of serviceable vehicles on both sides was less than the figures shown. The Soviet figures do not include the permanent armoured force held on the Manchurian Front.

Eastern Front: Tank Balance	1941	1942	1943	1944	1945	Total
Soviet tank production	6274	24,639	19,959	16,975	4384	72,231
German tank production	3256	4278	5966	9161	1098	23,759
Production ratio (German:Soviet)	1:2	1:5.6	1:3.3	1:1.85	1:4	1:3
Soviet tank losses	20,500	15,000	22,400	16,900	8700	83,500
German tank losses	2758	2648	6362	6434	7382	25,584
Tank exchange ratio* (German:Soviet)	1:7	1:6	1:4	1:4	1:1.2	1:4.4

* German tank losses here include all fronts; the tank exchange ratio shown is an estimate of the Soviet-German loss ratio.

Soviet and German AFV Strength at the Beginning of Seleted Major Offensives

AFVs: Major Offensives	Date	Formation		Strength	
Sector		German	Soviet	German	Soviet
Leningrad	14 Jan 44	18 Army	Leningrad Fr; Volkov Fr	200	1200
Krivoi Rog/Nikopol	30 Jan 44	6 Army	3 Ukrainian Fr; 4 Ukrainian Fr	250	1400
R. Pripet/Nikolaev	4 Mar 44	1 Pz Army; 4 Pz Army; 6 Army; 8 Army	1 Ukrainian Fr; 2 Ukrainian Fr; 3 Ukrainian Fr	1300	6400
Uman/Kirovrad	5 Mar 44	8 Army	2 Ukrainian Fr	310	2400
Crimea	8 Apr 44	17 Army	4 Ukrainian Fr; Ind Cst Army	70	900
Vitebsk/R. Pripet	22 Jun 44	Army Group Centre	1 Baltic Fr; 1 Byelo Fr; 2 Byelo Fr; 3 Byelo Fr	800	4100
Kovel/Tamopol	12 Jul 44	A Group N Ukraine	1 Ukrainian Fr	700	2040
Chelm/Rava Russkaya	18 Jul 44	4 Pz Army	3 Gds Army; 13 Army; 1 Gds Tk Army	174	550
Mariampol/Daugavpils	19 Jul 44	3 Pz Army	1 Baltic Fr; 3 Byelo Fr (parts)	95	1100
Bendory/Chemovitsy	20 Aug 44	A Group S Ukraine	2 Ukrainian Fr; 3 Ukrainian Fr	400	1880
Narva	14 Sep 44	Army Group North	Leningrad Fr; 1 Baltc Fr; 2 Baltic Fr; 3 Baltic Fr	400	3000
Warsaw/Tarnow	12 Jan 45	Army Group A	1 Byelo Fr; 1 Ukrainian Fr	770	6460
E. Prussia	13 Jan 45	Army Group Centre	2 Byelo Fr; 3 Byelo Fr	750	3300
Pomerania	1 Mar 45	3 Pz Army	1 Byelo Fr (parts)	70	1600
Oder/Neisse confluence to Stettin	16 Apr 45	A Group Vistula	1 Byelo Fr; 2 Byelo Fr	750	4100
R. Neisse	16 Apr 45	4 Pz Army	1 Ukrainian Fr	200	2150

Soviet tank production

Improved Soviet war production was achieved at the expense of civilian living standards – the most thorough application of the principle of total war – and with the help of Lend-Lease supplies. Germany's advantages in good-quality engineering and skilled labour were offset by greater Soviet efficiency in using their often limited resources. Soviet factories were ordered to concentrate on the production of low-cost, low-maintenance AFVs in contrast to German attempts to gain decisive qualitative superiority by producing sophisticated, costly designs such as the Panther. All major Soviet types were incrementally upgraded while simplified and refined manufacturing processes increased production.

TANK PRODUCTION BY TYPE AND YEAR	1941	1942	1943	1944	1945	Total
Light Tanks						
T-40	41	181	–	–	–	222
T-50	48	15	–	–	–	63
T-60	1818	4474	–	–	–	6292
T-70	–	4883	3343	–	–	8226
T-80	–	–	120	–	–	120
Sub-total	**1907**	**9553**	**3463**	**–**	**–**	**14,923**
Medium Tanks						
T-34	3014	12,553	15,529	2995	–	34,091
T-34/85	–	–	283	11,778	7230	19,291
T-44	–	–	–	–	200	200
Sub-total	**3014**	**12,553**	**15,812**	**14,773**	**7430**	**53,582**
Heavy Tanks						
KV-1	1121	1,753	–	–	–	2874
KV-2	232	–	–	–	–	232
KV-1S	–	780	452	–	–	1232
KV-85	–	–	130	–	–	130
IS-2	–	–	102	2252	1500	3854
Sub-total	**1353**	**2533**	**684**	**2252**	**1500**	**8322**
Total Tanks	**6274**	**24,639**	**19,959**	**17,025**	**8930**	**76,827**
Assault Guns						
SU-76	–	26	1928	7155	3562	12,671
SU-122	–	25	630	493	–	1148
SU-85	–	–	750	1300	–	2050
SU-100	–	–	–	500	1175	1675
SU-152	–	–	704	–	–	704
ISU-122/ISU-152	–	–	35	2510	1530	4075
Sub-total	**–**	**51**	**4047**	**11,958**	**6267**	**22,323**
Total AFVs	**6274**	**24,690**	**24,006**	**28,983**	**15,197**	**99,150**

Soviet AFV production history – all theatres

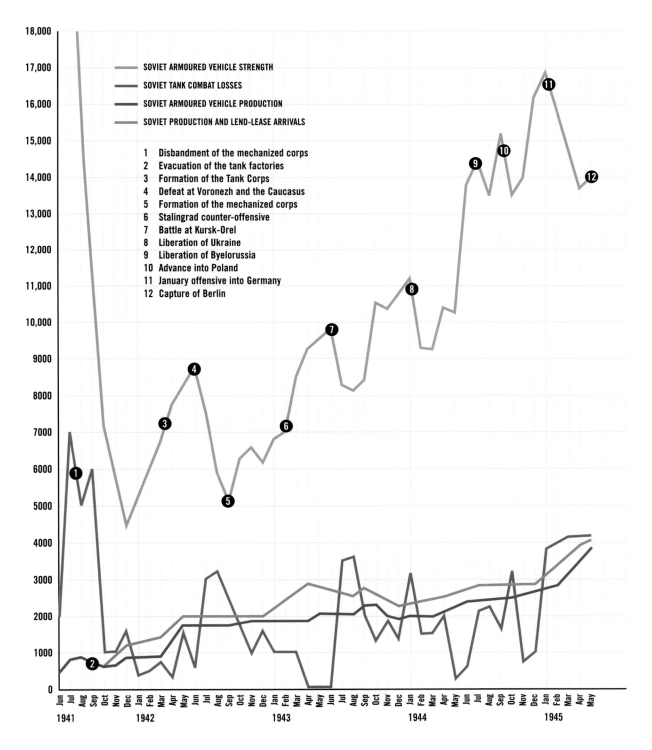

SOVIET ARMOURED VEHICLE STRENGTH
SOVIET TANK COMBAT LOSSES
SOVIET ARMOURED VEHICLE PRODUCTION
SOVIET PRODUCTION AND LEND-LEASE ARRIVALS

1   Disbandment of the mechanized corps
2   Evacuation of the tank factories
3   Formation of the Tank Corps
4   Defeat at Voronezh and the Caucasus
5   Formation of the mechanized corps
6   Stalingrad counter-offensive
7   Battle at Kursk-Orel
8   Liberation of Ukraine
9   Liberation of Byelorussia
10 Advance into Poland
11 January offensive into Germany
12 Capture of Berlin

Bibliography

Perret, Bryan. *Iron Fist, Classic Armoured Warfare Case Studies*. Brockhampton Press, 1999.

Porter, David 'Armour in Battle' articles in *Miniature Wargames* Magazine. Issues 186 (November 1998) and 201 (February 2000).

Zaloga, Steven J. & Grandsen, James. *Soviet Tanks and Combat Vehicles of World War Two*. Arms and Armour Press, 1984.

Zaloga, Steven J. & Grandsen, James. *The Eastern Front, Armour, Camouflage and Markings, 1941 to 1945*. Arms and Armour Press, 1989.

Zaloga, Steven J. & Ness, Leland S. *Red Army Handbook 1939–1945*. Sutton Publishing Ltd, 1998.

Websites

http://www.o5m6.de/ – Oliver Missing's excellent website 'Engines of the Red Army in WW2', which contains superb illustrations of an ever-increasing range of Soviet and Lend-Lease AFVs. (Our thanks to Oliver for providing so many of the colour profiles for this book.)

http://rkkaww2.armchairgeneral.com/index.htm – 'RKKA in World War II'. Another extremely useful website covering the equipment and operations of the Red Army during World War II.

http://www.winterwar.com/mainpage.htm – 'The Battles of the Winter War'. This website provides fascinating details of all aspects of Finland's 'Winter War' against the Red Army.

Index

Page numbers in *italics* refer to illustrations, photographs and tables.